DIPLOMACY IN PEACE AND WAR

Recollections and Reflections

T.N. KAUL

1979

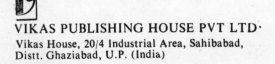

VIKAS PUBLISHING HOUSE PVT LTD·
Vikas House, 20/4 Industrial Area, Sahibabad,
Distt. Ghaziabad, U.P. (India)

VIKAS PUBLISHING HOUSE PVT LTD
Vikas House, 20/4 Industrial Area, Sahibabad
Distt. Ghaziabad, U.P. (India)
Branches : Savoy Chambers 5 Wallace Street, Bombay/10 First
Main Road, Gandhi Nagar, Bangalore/8/1-B Chowringhee
Lane, Calcutta/80 Canning Road, Kanpur

ISBN 0 7069 0749 3

1V02K3901

First Impression, 1979

Second Impression, 1979

Printed at Nu Tech Photolithographers, Jhilmil Tahirpur
Industrial Area, Shahdara, Delhi-110032

Dedicated to Gandhi, Nehru, Tagore
and
To the Youth of India and the World

Preface

A number of books have been written in the past two years about the recent events in India. An attempt has been made in this book to look at India since independence as a connected whole, mainly in relation to our immediate neighbours and the super powers, and look ahead rather than backward. The temptation to write or re-write history, or to make a detailed documented analysis has been resisted. An attempt has been made merely to recapitulate and recollect some important events and offer a few reflections on them. It is not the purpose of this book to pass judgment on pre or post emergency internal developments, except in so far as they are relevant to India's foreign relations.

The basic principles and milestones of India's foreign policy since independence—non-alignment, the Panchsheel Agreement of 1954, the Tashkent Declaration of 1966, the Indo-Soviet Treaty of 1971, the Simla Agreement and Indo-Bangladesh Treaty of 1972 and the Indo-US Agreement of 1974—have been highlighted.

The opinions and assessments are entirely my own and do not represent the views of the past or the present Government. I have gained much through discussion with friends and colleagues—too numerous to be thanked and mentioned by name. I always received valuable help and cooperation from colleagues in the Foreign Office and in the Missions abroad. I am deeply grateful to them and to my old friend and colleague Om Sharan, without whose help my handwritten "hieroglyphics" could not have seen the light of day.

My thanks are also due to my son Pradeep Kaul, my daughter Preeti Sahgal and my friend Rashpal Malhotra who went through the manuscript and made many useful suggestions, though I could not incorporate them all.

I have deliberately not consulted or sent my manuscript to the External Affairs Ministry as I do not wish to embarrass them by soliciting their direct or indirect approval. I believe it is in the national interest that there be as much open discussion as possible, especially on external affairs which seem often to be shrouded in mystery. Too much secrecy and too little sharing of information with the public are apt to lead to distortion of policies in a democracy and tend to create dictatorial tendencies in the ruling class and wild speculation in the media.

This book is mainly a record of impressions and observations which are capable of differing interpretations. No secret official records or documents have been consulted. This survey is based entirely on my own recollections. I do not claim infallibility, but I do believe that an eye-witness account, howsoever subjective, may be of some use in the pursuit of truth, for truth is many-faceted and multi-dimensional—subjective and objective, present as well as future oriented. No single person or government has the monopoly of truth.

My assessments and observations will, I hope, provoke and stimulate interest among serious students and scholars to dig deeper into the archives and documents of this period—1947-1979—and bring out the close relation and interaction between our external and internal policies, in the context of fast changing trends and of dynamics of development in the modern world.

In ancient and medieval times, when communications were poor, some countries were tempted to embark on imperialistic and expansionist policies in their respective regions, depending on their military and economic strength and the personality of their rulers. Thus arose Imperial China, the Indian Empire in the Maurya, Gupta and Mughal periods, the Pharaohs of Egypt, the Roman and Greek Empires, the Iranian, Byzantine, Mongol and Ottoman Empires.

With the growth of sea power, the Spanish, the Portuguese, the British, the French, the Dutch and later the Germans came on the scene and founded their respective empires overseas. Czarist Russia also expanded its empire, but mainly across the land mass. Like China and India, it was a continental empire—they were able to integrate the various ethnic groups and survived, by and large, as viable entities. The "overseas" empires shrunk to their original size after a relatively brief interlude of a few centuries, as they could not integrate peoples or assimilate territories separated by thousands of miles of oceans.

The survival of nations, in the long run, depends basically on their spiritual strength and national character and not merely on their size or military might. In the broad sweep of history, it is countries like India, China, Russia, Great Britain, France and Japan that have absorbed the onslaught of foreign cultures and internal revolutions and survived territorially, culturally and politically. There are others too but they are comparatively younger, like the USA, and have not yet stood the test of history. There are yet others in Asia, Africa and Latin America, that are coming through the throes of developing into viable, stable and enduring states and some of them may indeed have a great future.

These facts of history have to be emphasized, not from any chauvinistic or ideological point of view, but to indicate that some nations are inherently stable and strong, with some enduring qualities and have, therefore, survived the vicissitudes of history; others acquire strength—military and economic—but lose it because it is based on colonial or imperialist domination over others and is not inherent in themselves; there are yet others, especially in the developing world, which are capable of acquiring strength and stability and likely to survive in spite of their present weakness.

The world, instead of developing towards the concept of One World, is breaking up into many worlds—economically, ideologically and militarily. This state of affairs cannot endure either between, or within, various countries and regions. Gandhi and Nehru pointed the way towards One World. The older generation in India and the other countries has failed to work towards this goal. However, there is hope that the youth in various countries—communist, capitalist, non-aligned, developed, developing and poor—will be able to make the world a better place to live in than we of the older generation have been able to do.

I should therefore like to dedicate this effort to the memory of Gandhi, Nehru and Tagore, who inspired us to look upon India's struggle for freedom as part of the world struggle, and to the youth of India and all countries of the world who, I hope, will be able to achieve what we failed to—One World of Tagore's, Gandhi's and Nehru's dreams; where nations, and individuals within nations, will have equality of opportunity, equal rights as well as obligations, One World that is not regimented or uniform in its way of life, but rich in its cultural diversity, where there is no exploitation of one country or individual by another; where each contributes its best to the common good of all. Tagore painted a beautiful picture of this One World:

Where the mind is without fear and the head is held high;
*   Where knowledge is free;*
Where the world has not been broken into fragments by narrow
*   domestic walls;*
Where words come out of the depth of truth;
*   Where tireless striving stretches its arms towards perfection;*
Where the clear stream of reason has not lost its way into the
*   dreary desert sand of dead habit;*
Where the mind is led forward by thee into ever-widening thought
*   and action—*
Into that heaven of freedom, my Father, let my country awake.

"HERMITAGE"   T.N. KAUL
Village Neri-Kotli
Via Rajgarh-Solan,
Himachal Pradesh

Contents

1   Legacy of Gandhi

Gandhi, according to John Gunther, reminded one of Jesus Christ and one's grand-father. For most people, he was the apostle of peace and non-violence—peace not of the graveyard, and non-violence, not of the weak. Indians called him *Bapu*, or "father of the nation."

How far did Gandhi's philosophy influence India's foreign policy and her relations with the world? How far is Gandhi relevant today?

Gandhi left most of the drafting of the resolutions of the Indian National Congress to Nehru, but he exercised a subtle and yet deep influence on Nehru's mind. Nehru's acquiescence in the calling off by Gandhi of the civil disobedience movement when it was at its peak, because a dozen policemen had been burnt to death by some villagers at Chari Chaura, is an instance in point. Nehru was flabbergasted at his Guru's decision but obeyed because he accepted Gandhi's "inner voice" in the larger perspective of India's history. It was a unique (mutual and not one-sided) relationship between the agnostic and rationalist Nehru and the saintly and spiritualist Gandhi. When Gandhi found that Nehru and his colleagues in the Indian National Congress wanted independence even at the cost of the unity of the sub-continent, he let them have their way even though he was not in agreement with them.

Gandhi, perhaps, foresaw the shape of things to come and nominated Nehru as his "political heir" in preference to others who were more "Gandhian" than Nehru. Gandhi exercised a softening and sobering influence on Nehru, the leader of independent India. Although they did not see eye to eye on certain things, particularly in the field of economic theory, there was very little difference in their attitude to foreign policy. They agreed on the basic policy of peace, equality of individuals as well as nations, the right of all colonial countries and peoples to independence, opposition to all forms of discrimination against and exploitation of one country or individual by another, on grounds of race, colour, creed, sex or wealth.

Nehru formulated the foreign policy of India in consonance with these basic principles. Non-alignment and peaceful coexistence, opposition to racist policies in Africa and elsewhere and anti-colonialism—the pillars of India's foreign policy in Nehru's time—were the application of Gandhi's thought to the concrete conditions prevailing in India and the world. Disarmament, general and total, the non-use of force or threat of force in the resolution of international disputes, were a further development by Nehru of Gandhi's doctrine of *Ahimsa* (non-violence).

When India became free her's was an almost lone voice in international forums. But as more and more countries achieved independence, in Asia and Africa, these principles of foreign policy and international conduct, gained greater strength. This led to a world-wide movement of non-alignment, which cut across regional, racial, geographical and geo-political barriers. It brought together developing and newly independent countries throughout the world, in spite of their different social, economic and political systems. It softened the impact of the cold war on them and contributed to the lessening of tensions in the world.

In spite of bitter and strained feelings between India and Pakistan, owing to large-scale mutual killings and partition of the sub-continent, Gandhi persuaded the Government of independent India to give a sum of Rs 550 million to the newly formed Government of Pakistan. Gandhi called the British Government of India "satanic" and yet he had no bitterness against the people of Britain. This was perhaps one of the reasons why Nehru did not take India out of the Commonwealth even when India proclaimed herself a Republic on 26 January 1950.

Gandhi's India was economically poor and militarily weak and yet it was able to exercise a healthy, peaceful and sobering influence on the war-like trends developing after World War II. This was because Nehru insisted, as Gandhi had done, on the use of right means to achieve right ends. Right ends could not justify the use of wrong means. Peace could not be maintained through war and domination. Nehru raised his voice against threats to peace and the sovereign equality of nations in consonance with the philosophy of Gandhi.

A country's foreign policy cannot be divorced from its national interests and internal policies. Nor can it ignore the legitimate interests and aspirations of other countries. The art of diplomacy lies in reconciling idealism with self-interest and the legitimate rights and interests of other countries and peoples with one's own. In the field of foreign affairs one has to deal with sovereign countries which have different policies and interests from one's own. No country, however powerful economically or strong militarily, can impose its will or policies on others for long. But, in order to stand up to such pulls and pressures it must not be dependent on others. This is but an extension of Gandhi's doctrine of self-reliance in domestic affairs to foreign policy.

International cooperation is necessary in the world of today and no country can live in isolation, splendid or otherwise. But cooperation must be based on the sovereign equality of nations and a spirit of partnership rather than domination. The sooner India achieves self-reliance, the greater will be her ability to play her due role in national as well as international affairs. As long as India goes round with a begging bowl seeking so-called "aid" from the more developed countries, her voice in international affairs will not be very effective.

What is the relevance of Gandhi's ideas in India and the world of today? With the possibility of a nuclear holocaust threatening to destroy humanity, the importance of Gandhi's philosophy of non-violence is even greater today than ever before. But Gandhi's non-violence would not tolerate injustice to or domination of one country by another. When Bhagat Singh and B.K. Dutt dropped a bomb in the Central Legislative Assembly in 1929, Gandhi said "violence is bad but slavery is worse." True to the philosophy of the Geeta, he blessed the despatch of India's armed forces in October 1947, to defend the people of Kashmir against Pakistani invaders. Whatever Gandhian experts may say, and however they interpret his philosophy, Gandhi was a practical idealist. His ideals were capable of application to concrete and complex situations, as he proved during India's successful non-violent struggle against the British rule in the country.

Gandhi's was a unique philosophy combining the best of christianity, communism, humanism and universal brotherhood. His concept of a "classless" society embraced not only the material but also the spiritual and the ethical. He did not believe in capitalism or the so-called concept of a free market economy based on competition and the profit motive; nor did he believe in the Marxist doctrine of the inevitability of violent class conflict. Thus emerged the concept of a "mixed economy" in India. His influence on Nehru in particular, and others in general, was so deep that it left an indelible mark on India's internal policies and external relations.

Gandhi is not alive today, but he lives in the hearts and minds of the mass of the Indian people. His ideals will always inspire India, but his ideas will have to be applied to each concrete situation in the context of the changing scene in India and the world. Gandhism is not a doctrinaire or dogmatic creed, as some have tried to portrary, but a dynamic philosophy that can be applied to complex and concrete problems, as Nehru tried to do.

The legacy left by Gandhi to India was many sided and multi-dimensional. It embraced the individual and his relationship with his family, society, country and the world. It also covered the sort of relations that could and should develop between various sections of the society and between countries and the world in general. It penetrated the deep layers of thousands of years of tradition, culture and religion and produced an awakening that is still strengthening the roots of India's internal and external policies.

The seeds of the struggle against racialism were sown by Gandhi in South Africa in the first two decades of this century. The method of civil disobedience and non-cooperation—the most effective weapon an unarmed people can use against a mighty empire—was evolved by Gandhi in South Africa and further developed in India's struggle for independence. It symbolised the urge for independence and freedom of all nations suffering under colonial and imperialist rule. Gandhi's emphasis on peace and peaceful struggle are more relevant today. India's emphasis on disarmament in general, and nuclear disarmament in particular, is but a natural corollary of Gandhi's concept of Peace.

When India did not have nuclear capability, India's unilateral declaration that she would not use nuclear technology except for peaceful purposes might have sounded hollow or, at best, making a virtue of necessity. But when India demonstrated her nuclear capability in May 1974, and still declared her determination to use it exclusively for peaceful purposes, it should have carried greater weight and credibility with the nuclear weapon powers. But, some of them, instead of appreciating this and making a similar declaration themselves, started to pressurise India to sign the discriminatory nuclear non-proliferation treaty (NPT) and accept controls which they themselves were not prepared to accept. Why should India give up her sovereign right to use nuclear technology, including underground explosions, for peaceful purposes, or accept controls unless the nuclear weapon powers are prepared to do the same? No one has the right to mortgage the present or future interests of India for their private or personal beliefs or to please new-found friends. This is a mis-application of Gandhism.

Another example of the distortion of Gandhism is the new-fangled notion of "genuine" non-alignment. Non-alignment is not a catch word or mere slogan to play with. It has been evolved and developed through the long struggle of India and other countries against colonial and imperialist domination. It arose out of Gandhi's emphasis on peace—in a world which was divided into two hostile military blocrs at the end of World War II. It gained greater relevance for the newly independent developing countries during the period of the cold war which still grips the world, though in a more subtle and sinister form. As more and more countries emerged into independence from colonial rule in Asia, Africa, the Caribbean and other parts of the world, it was the only policy that could keep them from being sucked into the battle ground of the Great Power military, political and ideological rivalry. The new developing countries wanted to safeguard their hardwon political independence and needed peace for economic development. There was no other way to achieve this but to keep out of the Great Power military and political blocs.

Today, when colonialism and imperialism are manifesting themselves in new and more dangerous forms, like economic domination, military and political intervention, non-alignment is all the more relevant and necessary for developing countries.

Non-alignment is not the same as neutrality. Neutrality is a static concept which declares that a country would not take sides in a conflict irrespective of which side is right and which is wrong. Non-alignment, on the contrary, reserves the right of a country to judge each issue on its merits, as it affects its own national

interests and those of world peace. As Nehru said in his address
to the US Congress in 1949: "When freedom is threatened or
justice denied, India cannot and shall not be neutral." Non-
alignment does not mean sitting on the fence. It is a positive,
dynamic concept capable of being applied to each situation on its
merits. No doctrine or philosophy, no policy or principle, can
survive in this fast changing world if it becomes static or dogmatic—neither capitalism nor communism nor non-alignment.

The essence of non-alignment is the independence to judge
each issue on its merits, irrespective of pulls and pressures from
one side or the other. The word "genuine" gives it a touch of
"equidistance" from and "neutrality" between the great powers.
Why should a non-aligned country ignore its own interests and
be equally friendly with two great powers—one of whom is
friendly and the other hostile to her? Non-alignment believes in
friendship with all, but on the basis of sovereign equality and
reciprocity. We should be friendly to a country to the extent a
country is friendly to us, but if it is hostile, we should still try to
blunt its hostility and win its friendship without diluting our
friendship with others. We must not cringe before some or be
afraid to become more friendly with others who have stood and
continue to stand by us.

The doctrine of "genuine" non-alignment seems to insinuate
that India was more friendly to the USSR than to the USA previously and the new doctrinaires would now seem to want to
"redress the imbalance." They are either naive or do not believe
in non-alignment. The sooner they give up this facade, the better
for India and the non-aligned world. The criteria for non-alignment were laid down at Belgrade in 1961 and reaffirmed at Cairo
in 1964 and Lusaka in 1969. They unite countries with different
political, social and economic systems and cut across regional,
political and geographical boundaries. The imperialists are out to
divide the non-aligned. Let not the practitioners of the so-called
"genuine" non-alignment fall into their trap.

Indo-Soviet friendship has stood the test of time. Article IV
of the Indo-Soviet Treaty of 1971 expresses respect for India's
policy of non-alignment. Let others who wish to do so, enter
into a similar treaty with us. Why do they fight shy? Why should
we stray from our fundamental beliefs and jeopardise our own
interests to please them? Non-alignment, like Gandhi's non-vio-

lence, is not a concept born of weakness, but of moral strength, conviction and sheer necessity for survival. Let us keep the legacy of Gandhi and Nehru in tact and not dilute it by misinterpreting our basic principles to please others or delude ourselves. Concepts like non-alignment which have been tested by time should not be weakened to gain temporary political advantages. This was not the way Gandhi or Nehru would have acted.

We have to see how far Gandhi's philosophy and Nehru's policies are relevant to India in the world of today, how and how far the India of today can implement them. It is against this background that an attempt has been made to assess India's relations with her immediate neighbours and the super powers since independence—from Jawaharlal Nehru to Lal Bahadur Shastri and Indira Gandhi to Morarji Desai.

Can India resolve her border dispute with China peacefully? Is it possible for India, Pakistan and Bangladesh to work out a policy of friendship and cooperation and extend it to the whole of South Asia and thus create an area of peace and a bridge of understanding between South-East and South-West Asia? Is India's friendship with the Soviet Union an impediment to the development of friendly relations with the USA and/or China? What is the relevance of non-alignment in a world divided into hostile blocks on political, ideological, economic, social, regional and military grounds? What are the prospects for peace and disarmament, detente and international cooperation? Are we going away from the concept of "one world" to "many worlds" under the influence of the super powers? What role can India play in the dynamic and fast-changing world of today? What are the various facets of India's policy in the sub-continental, sub-regional, regional, inter-regional and global fields?

These are some of the questions that will be touched upon briefly in succeeding chapters in the context of our developing relations with our immediate neighbours and the super powers, and on the basis of our experiences in this field since independence.

2 Stalin's Russia

Delhi in July 1947, presented a picture of hope and enthusiasm, but also one of impending upheavals. The *de facto* partition was to become a *de jure* division of the sub-continent on 14 August. Communal massacres and refugee movements had already started. There was apprehension about the future. Gandhi's efforts succeeded in toning down tension to some extent, but only temporarily. Worse was yet to come.

Meanwhile Nehru had decided to open diplomatic relations with the USA, the USSR and the UK. Krishna Menon became the High Commissioner in the UK, Asaf Ali Ambassador to the USA and Vijaya Lakshmi Pandit was selected for Moscow. This showed the importance Nehru attached to these three countries at that time.

There was no trained diplomatic service in existence. Volunteers were invited from the existing services and outside. I was holding an interesting post of Secretary of the Indian Council for Agricultural Research in Delhi. The wanderlust in me was still strong. On my return overland from London to India in 1937, I had not been allowed by the Viceroy's Government to visit the USSR although I was within sight of it from the Iranian side. The Soviet Union had always seemed like a distant dream since my student days. I had read Lenin, Marx and the two volumes by Sydney and Beatrice Webb. I offered to go to Moscow, was selected as First Secretary and set off on 15 July 1947, with a small party to open the Indian Embassy there.

In London, Krishna Menon introduced me to the Soviet Ambassador there and warned me not to mention that I was related to Nehru. I protested that I had no relationship with Nehru at all (non-Kashmiris thought—and some surprisingly still do—that all Kashmiris are related to Nehru or one another). We flew from London to Berlin and stayed the night at the Indian Military Mission.

Our hosts invited their Soviet counterpart to meet us. I had my first experience of Russian drinking and breaking of glasses after each drink and was a little surprised at this. Vodka for Russians seemed like tea or milk in India, probably because of the cold climate. But, why break glasses?

We flew from East Berlin to Moscow in a Soviet Dakota and were met at the airport by a representative of the Soviet Protocol Department and a First Secretary of the British Embassy. Nehru had warned me not to give the impression that we were still tied to the apron-strings of Britain. I was polite with the British First Secretary, thanked him for having come to receive us but declined his offer to drive us to town for dinner. We availed ourselves of the transport provided by the Soviet protocol (we were given a fat bill for it later) and were lodged in Hotel Metropole. A more gloomy and old fashioned hotel I have not yet seen. It still is, more or less, the same. It was the haunt of most foreign correspondents and diplomats. There was acute housing shortage after World War II and apartments were not readily available, let alone houses.

The Soviet Union had suffered more damage than most other countries and lost 20 million people in the war—almost one from each family. Relics of war were still visible in the vicinity of Moscow. I admired the courage and endurance of the Russians who had faced death and starvation and yet stood firm to win the war. The 900-day-long siege of Leningrad is inspiring an example.

Life in Moscow was austere, drab and difficult. Fresh fruit and vegetables were seldom available, and sometimes when they were flown from Georgia, they cost a fortune. When I bought a bouquet of 12 roses for Mrs Pandit's arrival in early August, it cost the equivalent of Rs 10 for each rose. Meat, butter, sugar, woollens, leather goods were available only at exorbitant rates and beyond the reach of an average Russian. Diplomats got their supplies from Helsinki or Stockholm, but the average Russian had a hard time making both ends meet. Their staple diet was black bread, potatoes, onions and carrots, with a few slices of meat once a week or so. And yet, they were tough, hardy and well buit, especially the women. You could see them do all the hard chores, like sweeping the snow on the streets. They wore a white woollen scarf round their head, thick felt boots and a padded patched up coat over their old dress.

Children were, however, a delightful sight and well cared for. Tiny tots tied on wooden planks, well padded and warmly clad, were carried by their mothers and appeared cheerful and calm, almost typical of the stoic Russian temperament. The best milk went to the children and there were creches and nurseries for the small children of working women.

It was to this Moscow that Vijaya Lakshmi Pandit, sister of Nehru, came as the first Ambassador of India. She came with high hopes and expectations of making an impression on the Soviet leaders. She soon discovered that this was not such an easy task. Stalin was ruling the Soviet Union with an iron hand. Diplomats in particular and foreigners in general, were looked upon with suspicion as potential spies. Contact with the Soviet citizens was almost impossible except with officials and a few selected ones who were allowed to attend National Day receptions. Movement of all foreigners including diplomats was forbidden beyond a 25 miles radius of Moscow. Permission was, however, given to visit a few selected places like Tolstoy's tomb at Yasnopolyana and Leningrad. Diplomats, were also allowed to hire "Datchas" or small cottages in the Moscow suburbs where they went for weekends. Mrs Pandit had also rented one and we all ate the delicious *Baz Bhatta* (vegetable Pulao) cooked by her every Sunday.

After staying in Hotel Metropole for a week, Mrs Pandit was shown a special favour by being given a small house at No. 8 Glazovsky Peryulok (Eye Lane) for her residence as well as office. The rest of us—A.V. Pai, Prem Krishen, Prem Bhatia, myself, Dr H. Goshal (our Russian language expert) and the non-diplomatic staff—stayed on at good old Metropole.

It was not an easy life. Little problems of housekeeping consumed a lot of time. Even maids and chauffeurs could not be hired directly but were planted by Burobin—the bureau for "service" of foreigners. House repairs, plumbing, electricity, petrol, etc. were a daily headache. Mrs Pandit one day asked me to tell the Chief of Protocol that she did not like to wake up and see first thing in the morning, two old and ugly maids and wanted to change them. I conveyed it, word for word, to Molotchkov (Chief of Protocol) who smiled and said: "Are you sure this is your Ambassador's request." I told him to go and ask her. He dared not do that and sent, the next day, two English-speaking young maids. A week later Mrs Pandit asked me to look for a letter from the Prime Minister, which was missing. I asked the English-speaking maid. She smiled and said, "Oh, yes I have seen it in Madam's writing desk," and sure enough it was there! After that we took special precautions to lock up all papers in a safer place.

This was Stalin's Russia, full of fear and suspicion, against foreigners as well as the Soviet citizens. The militiaman was everywhere. There was a current joke. Whenever there was silence at the dinner table, people would say "A militiaman is born."

Mrs Pandit was given an ovation in the Bolshoi Theatre for her message on the 800th anniversary of the founding of Moscow. This perked us all up a little and we thought perhaps the Soviet Government would appreciate the gesture Nehru had made to them by sending a renowned personality and his own sister as ambassador. But, strange were the ways of the Soviet bureaucracy in those days. They would not let her visit the Soviet Asian Republics and not even Georgia. The excuse was that there was no "suitable" hotel accommodation available. The most astounding thing was the failure of the Soviet Government to even send a message of condolence on Gandhi's assassination. They did not care to send anyone to sign the condolence book in the embassy. I went to the Head of the South-Asia Division in the Soviet Foreign Office and told him informally that this was a serious lapse and would create a very bad impression in India. He replied non-chalantly: "Gandhi said the Soviet Union is an enigma to him. Well, he is an enigma to us." I was shocked and left him in no doubt about my feelings. A day later, I learnt the Soviet Ambassador in Delhi went to condole—three days after the tragedy.

This incident shook my belief in the efficiency or intelligence of Stalin's Soviet system. They were out of touch with Indian realities and looked at India through their coloured dogmatic glasses. For them India was not yet independent, but only an appendage of Britain. Mrs Pandit's eldest daughter, Chandralekha and I discussed this with Vijayalakshmi and suggested that we get out of the Commonwealth. In our youthful enthusiasm we drafted a telegram from her to the Prime Minister giving various reasons for our recommendation. Mrs Pandit approved and sent it off. But Nehru had to keep wider considerations in mind than the mere reaction of the Soviet Government and rejected the recommendation.

The Soviet press was openly critical and contemptuous of India and called it a "lackey and running dog of British imperialism." Gandhi and Nehru were described as bourgeois reformists—a term of contempt in Communist parlance, in the Great Soviet Encyclopaedia. Vyshinsky once told Vijayalakshmi, through his Hindi interpreter *"Paradhinta ke Bojh Dhire Dhire hee Utarte Hain."* (The burdens of slavery take time to be shaken off).

Mrs Pandit was disappointed. She had come with all goodwill to set Indo-Soviet relations on a sound footing, but she got little response from the Soviet side. She made no secret of her feelings and told the western press correspondents who used to meet her once a fortnight or so. The Soviet pressmen did not dare enter a foreign mission. They must have been told about it by their foreign colleagues and in turn, must have reported it to their bosses. That was perhaps what Mrs Pandit intended. The strain was too much for her nerves. She would be in a nasty temper every morning. One day she smiled and I ventured to ask: "Are you feeling well today?" She replied "Yes, why do you ask?" I replied "because you have not scolded anyone this morning." She had a sense of humour and laughed at her own expense.

She made a few worth-while contacts. The most interesting one was with Mme. Kollantai, the first woman envoy in the world. Lenin had sent her as his first Envoy Extraordinary and Minister Plenipotentiary to Sweden. We visited her in an apartment where she proudly exhibited a photograph of her with Lenin with an inscription in Lenin's own hand. Stalin's portrait was conspicuous by its absence. She was too well known a personality to be afraid and Stalin had no reason to believe she was a threat to his position. Probably at her suggestion, the Soviet Government arranged an Indo-Soviet "Vecher" (evening) in cooperation with the embassy. We were allowed to invite selected Soviet writers and artists. It was a modest success but hardly 50 Soviet citizens were allowed to attend. Mrs Pandit naturally felt disappointed and said she did not want to be fed on such crumbs of cultural contact.

We were taken to a collective farm but were not impressed by it. The Soviet economy had not yet recovered from the war damage. Then there was demonetisation of the Rouble to one-tenth its previous value. We were not affected by it but many Soviet citizens who had managed to save huge bundles of Roubles suffered. We were not allowed to visit any factories and could not, therefore, judge how accurate the claims of the Soviet experts were. In any case, they only gave the percentage increases and not actual figures, not even a base figure. It was like a jigsaw puzzle and one had to solve the mystery by complicated mathematical calculations.

We did manage a visit to Leningrad—the city of Peter the Great and the cradle of the Great October Socialist Revolution. It was heavenly compared to Moscow. People talked a little more freely. The scenery was not drab like that of Moscow. Architecture was beautiful. The "Hermitage" was a world of art in itself. The Neva, unlike the Mockva was a real expanse of water and a glorious sight at sunrise and sunset. The Summer Palace, the Winter Palace, the Admirality, were worth seeing and veritable treasures of art and architecture.

Moscow too had its own charm. Leningrad was typically European. Moscow was typically Russian—a hybrid mixture of European, Byzantine, Tartar, Muslim and Turkish influences on art and architecture. It represented a cross section of the Soviet society and one came across Uzbeks, Tadjiks, Azerbaijanis, Byelorussians, Ukrainians, Georgians, Armenians and others. Moscow had the Bolshoi and the MXAT (Moscow Art Theatre), the Puppet Theatre, a gypsy theatre and even a Jewish theatre. One could forget the difficulties and drabness of outside life watching Ulanova dance in Gizelle, Romeo and Juliet or Swan Lake at the Bolshoi. One could see Shakespearean comedies, Sheridon's "School for Scandal" and Oscar Wilde's "Importance of Being Earnest" at the MXAT. There were also numerous art galleries and museums. We tried to see as much as we could but after sometime it all became monotonous.

Soon after came Zhdanov's Decrees in 1948 which were ruthlessly enforced. Jews were looked upon with suspicion and called Bezrodni Kosmopolit (rootless cosmopolitans). All foreigners, even those from communist countries, were considered spies. What little contact with the Soviet citizens was possible before was forbidden at one stroke. Even Anna Louise

Strong, an American, a devout communist and friend of Russia, was put in prison on suspicion of being spy.

One day at an official party I asked a senior Soviet official why they treated all foreigners—friends and foes—with equal suspicion. He had no hesitation in telling me, in all sincerity and seriousness, "During World War II, many posed as our friends but some of them turned out to be our enemies. We do not want to take any risks. We would rather lose 100 friends than incur the risk of having one enemy among them."

We were followed everywhere. Our telephones were tapped, Russian staff interrogated and our lodgings in hotels were searched in our absence. There was no privacy. People looked grim and went their way, quietly with their heads bowed. If ever there was a drunk lying on the road or in a park, people were afraid to help him up until the militia came and took him to prison, if he was still alive in the freezing snow.

Moscow was a grim city in 1947, pervaded by an atmosphere of terror, mistrust and neglect of human rights and dignity. In spite of Stalin's great contribution to the solving of the linguistic and cultural problems of the minorities, and welding together of the Soviet people in the war against fascism and nazism, he paid little attention and showed less respect for the elementary rights of individual human beings. Writers, artists, professors and intellectuals in general were treated like mere cogs in a machine that ground everything and everyone ruthlessly. The lot of the common people was even worse because they did not have the bare material necessities of life. The emphasis was on large multi-storeyed buildings, typical of Stalin's grandiose schemes, than on cheap apartments for ordinary folk. Those who dared openly differ or criticise the government were either prosecuted secretly and convicted without trial, or liquidated by life-long exile to Siberia. Some who survived became mental or physical wrecks for life.

In foreign affairs little consideration was shown towards newly independent countries like India. We were lumped together with the British, as if we were not independent. In spite of their claim to be part Asian, the Soviet leaders did not understand Asia. It is true they had suffered terribly during World War II and one could not expect the same facilities and creature comforts in the Moscow of 1947 as in Washington D.C. One could understand

and appreciate this, but what was intolerable was the atmosphere of suspicion, suffocation, hostility and isolation. The diplomatic crowd had to depend on one another and there was no contact with the people. The people were afraid to meet foreigners or talk freely even among themselves. There was an all pervading atmosphere of fear. Even the militiaman turned stiff and tense, whenever Stalin passed by in his black limousine, which had dark bullet-proof windows.

Mrs Pandit never asked for a meeting with Stalin—not even when she was about to leave Moscow in April 1949. I suggested to her that she might ask for a farewell meeting with Stalin, but she replied: "Why should I? He can send for me if he wants to." When we reached Bombay she told the Press bluntly "I did not meet Stalin even once!" She never tried.

Indo-Soviet relations were at a low ebb from 1947 to 1949. It was not for any lack of desire or initiative on our part, but mainly due to the failure of the Soviet leaders to understand the new India, their preoccupation with Europe and America, the low priority they gave to India at that period and the tremendous internal problems they were facing after World War II. They were perhaps hoping that China would fall in line with them and India would follow in due course. "The road from Moscow to Calcutta lay through Peking." This was the period of dogmatic Stalinism in the Soviet post-war history. The cold war was at its coldest. We were glad to be back home in April 1949, and breathe the fresh air of free and non-aligned India.

3 Truman's America

President Truman was a simple man, with a strong common sense and perhaps more typical of the average American than any US President before or after him. Ford was perhaps the nearest to him and put up Truman's portrait, along with Lincoln's, at the White House. Truman was not haughty or pretentious and mixed with the common people freely. He was human and fatherly. There were no "Presidential airs" about him. Even as the President he would often walk in the neighbourhood of the White House, without the usual paraphernalia of security staff etc. I remember him standing in a corner in the reception room of our embassy when Nehru gave a party in his honour. Nehru noticed him and immediately ordered me to go and talk to him, as he and Mrs Pandit were busy receiving guests.

Truman had a will of steel and when the occasion demanded he could be tough. The dismissal of General Douglas McArthur was an instance in point. It needed courage to dismiss such a popular war hero, but Truman would not tolerate disobedience of Presidential orders.

He was also a very "human" President, loyal to his family and friends. When a well know columnist wrote a nasty and unfair piece about his daughter, Margaret's piano-playing skill, Truman had no hesitation in publicly calling the columnist "SOB." This would have been the reaction of any father to an unfair comment about his daughter and Truman was typically American in this. Even though no US President had used such language publicly, few criticised Truman. Infact, everyone sympathised with him.

Vijayalakshmi Pandit was appointed India's Ambassador to the USA in 1949. She should have been sent there in 1947 rather than to Moscow. She was in her elements there—a charming hostess, gracious, popular, great conversationalist, very much in demand as a guest speaker. She could be blunt when necessary. For example when asked on Chicago Round Table, "What do you think of President Truman's Point Four Programme?" she replied: "It is ridiculous." Next day at the State Department when I was asked what she meant, I replied she was only trying to help the US administration with the Congress to get more funds in order to make any impression in the underdeveloped world. What was $4 million spread among a dozen countries or more? They smiled and said nothing, half believing, half doubting. When I related this to Mrs Pandit, she said, "Well done, you will be an ambassador before I can say Jack Robinson." She had a sense of humour and relied on her junior colleagues, in fact expected them, to smoothen any feathers she might have ruffled.

Sometimes Mrs Pandit could be stubborn and get herself into trouble, over little things. I recall an instance when she was leading the UN Delegation in 1947. The telephone rang, she picked it up and said without batting an eyelid, "Mrs Pandit's secretary speaking. I am afraid Mrs Pandit is out of station." When the caller protested that she could recognise the voice, she replied without a moment's hesitation, "Oh, I am her daughter and work for her when the secretary is out. Our voices are very similar." I was standing by and laughed. Mrs Pandit said with a triumphant smile, "You should learn how to deal with these busy bodies in America, or they will pester you to death." I tried to imitate my secretary's voice, but failed to convince even myself. This is an art only gifted people have. Even Mrs Pandit was found out several times but forgiven because of the sweet voice and charming way in which she could put off visitors. She was a great lady and could get away with a lot of minor lapses.

She had a ready wit and could send an audience into peels of laughter. When asked by a young mother in the question hour, after her address to a women's gathering in San Francisco, "Mrs Pandit, do you believe in breast-feeding?" She replied, "Yes, I do. I have three daughters who have been breast fed by me and are healthier than the American girls of their age." Whether this was true or not is another matter, but she had the reply ready without having to think for a moment. One day I asked her in New York, "Do you really mean everything you say in public." She looked me straight in the eye and said, "If you want to get along with me discount 90 per cent of what I say to others."

She was popular and a favourite speaker at the NAACP (National Association for the Advancement of Coloured People). They looked upon her as a champion of their cause because she was Nehru's sister. She was also in demand at women's meetings. But her relations with the State Department were not too cordial. They were polite, but cold and aloof. She had, however, the compensation of being fussed over by non-officials. She could travel widely in the country without any hindrance.

Mrs Pandit entertained well and was fond of playing hostess to politicians, film stars, bankers, writers and journalists. She chose her guests so that they could mix well together. She would not be satisfied with the second best and engaged a French chef even though he proved financially ruinous. Once the French Ambassador's wife praised the pie made by the French chef for dessert (it resembled the hat she wore that evening) and the next day Mrs Pandit had one sent to her which she auctioned at a women's fete.

Occasionally Mrs Pandit gave a luncheon for two or three. I was present at one in early 1950 when the only guest was John Foster Dulles. I still remember his feeling ill-at-ease and pulling at the two ends of his napkin throughout the meal. He could not succeed in convincing Mrs Pandit that non-alignment was a wrong policy. He poured venom against communist China and Russia and pointed out the danger of international communism. He wanted India to line up with America on Korea and in her ideological conflict with China and Russia. Mrs Pandit gave him her sweet smile, listened patiently but did not commit herself and said she would report to the Prime Minister. It was almost a monologue and Dulles was talking like a man possessed, a fanatic who believed passionately in what he said and considered all others wrong. After this luncheon there were hardly any repeat performances.

Dean Acheson was quite the opposite of Dulles in some ways. He looked more British than American in his dress, manners and mannerisms. With a meticulously clipped moustache, a black homburg on his head and an umbrella in his hand, he looked the picture of a British Foreign Secretary. He was suave, polished, polite. Even when provoked once by Mrs Pandit in a meeting at the State Department, he kept his temper calm and cool and merely said, "I do not understand ambassador. Perphaps time will show." It was Acheson who drew an arc— a sort of *cordon sanitaire*—embracing the whole of South-East Asia, Japan and Taiwan within the American sphere of influence as vital to the US security. His attitude towards China and the USSR and international communism was as tough as that of Dulles.

Suddenly one day in September 1949, came the news of a successful atomic explosion by the USSR. It was a world shaking event for it broke the monopoly of atomic power of the USA. America would have to come to terms with Russia to avoid an atomic war. There was obvious disappointment in the USA and fear of atomic war crept in the minds of the people. There was talk of large-scale movement from urban to rural areas and the prices of urban property started falling. Instead of compelling both super powers (they qualified for this title after the atomic explosions) to come to a disarmament agreement, it only started a nuclear arms race and wars by proxy to test their conventional weapons, on other nations' territories.

It was at this time that Nehru, a man of vision and far sighted, sent a message simultaneously to Truman, Stalin and Attlee imploring them to remove the impending threat of war. I was a mere First Secretary in Washington. However, I had the confidence of Mrs Pandit and she showed me the Prime Minister's message. I respected her confidence but it was not easy to keep secrets in the USA. The next day James Reston, head of New York Times Bureau in Washington D.C., came to see me in the chancery and asked me point blank whether I would confirm or deny that our Prime Minister had sent a message to Truman, Stalin and Attlee. I said it was not fair of him to ask me—why didn't he ask the State Department? Thereupon he showed me a copy of the text of the message but would not reveal the source and asked, "Now would you confirm or deny Sir?" I asked him to wait a minute, walked into Mrs Pandit's room and told her about the situation. She said, "Use your discretion—if you trust the man, tell him in confidence, if not, say 'no comment'." I came back to my room and asked Reston, "If I give you an answer, will you promise that you will not reveal the source?" He agreed and I confirmed that the message was authentic. It was no use denying it or saying "no comment" when Reston already had a copy and would soon find out. He respected my confidence and did not reveal the source of confirmation as Indian Embassy. One has to have a certain amount of trust and confidence in others—especially journalists.

Col. Unni Nair, my colleague in the embassy, was First Secretary, Public Relations, and I have not come across a more efficient, knowledgeable, patriotic and courageous man. He could make friends with all sorts of people and call them by first names within five minutes of meeting them. He won their respect, trust and friendship because of his charming ways and transparent honesty and frankness. I often went to the National Press Club in Washington D.C. with him and met the inimitable press crowd there.

Unni Nair volunteered for service with our Mission in Korea. Mrs Pandit would not let him go. He sought my advice as a friend and said he must go to Korea. It was important for him. He did not like static situations and would be able to do a much better job there. He was doing an excellent job in the USA. I sympathised and respected his itch to move on to dynamic situations and persuaded Mrs Pandit to let him go. When she agreed and cabled New Delhi, they were surprised but jumped at Unni's voluntary offer. A few weeks later came the shocking news that Unni's jeep had been blown up by a mine and he along with three other journalists (two British and one American) had died on the spot. I was heart broken for he was my best friend and I had been instrumental in his going to Korea.

It is a pity that Unni is no more. He would have done great things in life with his dynamism, courage, honesty and efficiency. When he died there were over a hundred editorials in the US newspapers praising him. I know of no other public relations man who had earned such enconimus.

Talking of Unni Nair my memory goes back to a great writer and columnist—Walter Lippmann. I met him first at a small luncheon in the embassy. He was not only a great writer and a famous columnist, but a man of principles which he scrupulously observed in his columns. He was in a class by himself and I have not yet met or read any columnist of his calibre and stature. He gave his own assessment of events and in most cases it was an ethical, philosophical, objective and novel assessment, based on facts and not on their distortion. For him facts were sacred while views were free unlike many reporters and commentators today who regard facts as free and their own views as sacred.

Another well known but highly controversial man was Henry Luce. I met him in his office in New York with Mrs Pandit in 1949. He spoke fast, almost in jerks, and appeared always in a hurry to finish what he had to say. He was anti-Peking, anti-communist and very much pro-America. Right or wrong he believed in his pet causes and fought for them with courage and conviction. His *Time* magazine wielded considerable influence on the US public opinion and he was mainly responsible for its technical excellence. A first rate publisher, Henry Luce was ultra-conservative in his views. His wife, Clare Booth Luce, was quite the opposite—charming, liberal, suave and beautiful, made friends easily and did not rub people on the wrong side. She became an ambassador later.

Mrs Pandit succeeded in persuading her brother, the Prime Minister, to visit the USA in October 1949. Nehru took an instinctive dislike to the crude and vulgar attempts by the US big business, under the inspiration of the US Government, to make all kinds of loan, credit, grant and collaboration offers. I was a small fry and got a knock on the head from Nehru for suggesting to him that if we were short of foodgrains, we could get wheat from America at concessional rates. Nehru literally flared up and said, "What do you think India is, a beggar? We must become self-sufficient in foodgrains in a year or two." He added, "I am sitting on the top of a volcano. If we don't tackle the base of the problem, it will burst and overwhelm us all."

He sincerely believed that by 1952 India would be self-sufficient in foodgrains. Alas, his party's and government's failure to introduce and implement land reforms speedily did not let this happen. Instead we took 17 million tons of foodgrains from the USA under PL-480 in the sixties and delayed our self-sufficiency programme by more than two decades. I am not blaming the US Government for this but only ourselves. Even though we have been more or less self-sufficient in foodgrains for the last three or four years, this happy state cannot last

long, in view of our increasing population and the vagaries of
the weather, unless we give land to the tiller.

One wonders why Nehru's first visit to the USA in 1949, was
a failure. Was it due to any fault of Nehru, or of the State
Department or were there deeper underlying causes? Nehru was
an admirer of America's dynamism and the spirit of adventure of
its people, their faith in democracy and equality of opportunity. He read American poets and writers with great interest.
He began to acquire a liking for American musicals after he saw
"South Pacific" with Mary Martin and Enzo Pinza acting in it.
But, he disliked intensely the American belief that they could
win everything and everybody with money.

One evening in New York as he was listening to the radio, in
his hotel suite, he smiled to himself. I ventured to ask, "Sir,
what is amusing you?" He laughed and said, "Didn't you hear
this radio advertisement by an undertaker's firm—why live if a
decent funeral costs only $50? These Americans are crazy
people."

The State Department was wooden and lacking in imagination. They either could not or deliberately did not pay due
regard to Nehru's sensibilities. For instance, instead of calling
a joint session of the Senate and the House of Representatives,
they insisted on Nehru reading out the same address in both
chambers separately. I do not understand why we agreed to this.
Nehru read his address in the House with confidence and
dignity, although he hated reading his speeches. But when he
went straight from the House to the Senate, he rushed through
the same written speech in half the time. He was obviously
bored with it.

In his talks with the US Government not much headway was
made because the two sides were talking at different wave
lengths—Nehru represented an ancient but resurgent young India,
full of enthusiasm and idealism, talking in the larger perspective
of history and looking forward to the future of mankind, pro-
pagating his passion for peace and cooperation rather than war
and confrontation, his policy of non-alignment and anti-
colonialism. The US side talked a different language in those
days—danger from Russia and China, the need to save freedom
and peace through NATO and more military alliances, dangling
the carrot of the US aid in return for towing their line, wanting

her big business tycoons to penetrate the trade, industry and economy of other countries. Nehru was the representative of a sensitive and proud people. He loathed this gauche and "commercial" approach of the US and was more disgusted than impressed by it.

The main reason for the failure to reach any agreement was the lack of mutual respect and understanding and perhaps too many expectations of each side from the other—expectations based on wrong premises. The US still looked on India through British eyes and regarded her as a weak, backward, under-developed country in dire need of financial resources, while India looked upon America as a champion of democracy and freedom, the supporter of the underdog and a believer in independence of all nations and peoples. America expected India to fall in line with her policies while India expected America to respect India's policy of non-alignment, if not agree with it. The gulf in the two viewpoints was too wide to be bridged by one visit. It would take decades of patience and perseverance from both sides to understand and respect each other.

There was a positive side to Nehru's visit also. He loved meeting Einstein, Eisenhower who invited him to address Columbia University (of which he was the President at that time), various artists, writers and last but not the least the common man. The greatest compliment I heard paid to Nehru during this visit was by a New York taxi driver who said, "Nehru is a regular guy." Another section who were deeply impressed by Nehru were the Black Americans and some of the intellectuals, but they were neither in power nor had the riches and pull to influence the US policy.

I had on occasion to meet some interesting personalities with Mrs Pandit. We visited Paul Robeson in New York. I can never forget that tall, smiling, strong man with a deep resonant and beautiful voice. He was born in the wrong country at the wrong time. He did not receive the rich rewards he deserved. His political views were not liked. A great American was neglected to die in relative obscurity and poverty. But, his name will live forever in human history, as a great singer and a great human being.

We also met some film-stars in Hollywood—Glen Ford, Walter Pidgeon, Gregory Peck, Jane Russel, Ava Gardner and

others. I was a little disappointed to see that they were not
really half as glamorous as they looked on the screen. They
lived in a world of their own, in an atmosphere that was
artificial and far removed from reality. They had the talent and
were intelligent, but most of them lived on edge. I guess film
stars in most countries are like that. They have to pay a price
for the high publicity and adulation they receive.

Los Angeles, even in those days, was a city of crime. Unni
Nair and I were invited to a "joint" on Sunset Boulvard one
evening. Fortunately we left early, just before midnight. Next
morning we heard, that the place had witnessed some shooting,
killing and a raid by the police.

San Francisco was as beautiful as Los Angeles was ugly. Its
beauty was not at that time marred by high-rise buildings and
sky-scrapers. Little trams went up and down the hill leading
to Mark Hopkins Hotel. The sea and the suburbs are still there
and as lovely as before. The Golden Gate Bridge is a wonder-
ful sight. Many frustrated people still jump from it to join
whatever God they believe in. Every year witnesses over 100
suicide jumps from this beautiful bridge. Chicago, New York,
Philadelphia were the other cities we often visited. They were
not as big and crowded then as they are today, but they were
big enough. New York city is, in many ways, the unofficial
capital of the world—in banking, trade, fashions and last but
not the least, in having the UN Headquarters. At that time the
UN was located in a modest place in Fulshing Meadows, Long
Island. In some ways it was a better place than the present 38-
storey building on First Avenue. Perhaps it would be better to
locate UN Headquarters in a neutral country like Switzerland,
Austria, Sweden or elsewhere. New York has its advantages but
also many flaws.

America was big, great, modern and full of life. It had its
dark spots but on the whole it still represented the new world
of science and technology, of trade and banking. It had a lot
to learn about the rest of the world and vice versa. Nehru made
an honest and sincere attempt to come to a closer understanding with America but failed. Where he failed would others
succeed? I wondered then and still do.

After almost a year-and-a-half I felt somewhat jaded and

disillusioned with Truman's America. The newspapers and magazines took so much time even to glance through. After reading them one felt like having eaten a lot of nuts and rich snacks at a cocktail party. The people were nice, open, frank and friendly. But, there was transparent racial discrimination against blacks, too much respect and power given to money, a craze for night life in the cities, but comparative peace and quiet in the rural and suburban areas. America was great in science and technology but there was a feeling of an inferiority complex vis-a-vis Britain, in particular, and western Europe in general. All this was only to be expected but what disappointed one was the absence of any revolutionary ideals in politics, an attempt to line up various countries on the basis of anti-communism, the arrogance of economic and military power and an urge to interfere in the internal affairs of other countries and to dominate them economically and politically and if they did not give in, then create military situations against them. This was, by and large, the methodology of Stalin's Russia also except that there was no open and blatant racialism there; on the contrary, they gave full support to the anti-apartheid resolutions in the UNO, unlike Truman's America.

When I saw at first hand the horse-trading going on between the USA and the USSR at the UN from 1947 to 1950, my youthful idealism and faith in the UNO were badly shaken. The resolution on the creation of Israel, for instance, was an example of collusion between the two at the expense of other countries and sowed the seeds of an indefinite period of tension and war in the region. Why did the USA and the USSR and their allies oppose the much more sensible and far-sighted proposal made by India, Yugoslavia and Iran for the creation of a federation of Israel and the Arab States? Of course, it was partly due to the adamant attitude of the Arabs and Israelis themselves, but if the USA and the USSR had supported the Indo-Yugoslav-Iran proposal, it would have gone through. Could it be that both the USA and the USSR thought that Israel would be in its own sphere of influence and a convenient tool to keep the Arab states under control? Or was it, perhaps, a deliberate plan to create tension in the region and test their weapons on one side against the other? One would like to give the benefit of doubt to both and attribute their joint move to a genuine desire to seek a temporary solution of a complicated problem which did not affect them directly.

I had been in the USA for a year-and-a-half and had all the creature comforts there, but something was lacking. In spite of America's advance in science and technology what seemed to be lacking was the old American revolutionary spirit. Perhaps, I had expected too much from America—the bastion of freedom and democracy, the first colony of Britain to revolt against the mother country and become independent. It had been an inspiration to other colonies in their freedom struggle. It was, as it were, the first war of independence and successful anti-colonial struggle in recent history. Washington, Lincoln and Jefferson were household names in India even though the British rulers did not encourage the teaching of American history in Indian schools. American missionaries, by and large, had done good work, especially in the medical and educational fields in rural India. American leaders like Franklin Roosevelt had given moral and even some political support to India's right to independence, much to the annoyance of the British rulers.

What had happened to this great America after World War II? Why was it supporting apartheid in South Africa, backing feudal dictators and corrupt regimes in Asia, Africa and Latin America, opposing and refusing to recognise the People's Republic of China? Why was it not giving equal rights and opportunities to its own black population? Why had revolutionary America become conservative? Was it, perhaps, because it had not seen World War II on its own territory, or because it had become an affluent society, or because it had suddenly woken up after the end of World War II as a leader and super-power with a monopoly of atomic weapons? Whatever the reason, I was as disappointed with Truman's America as I was disillusioned with Stalin's Russia. Asia—India and China, in particular—seemed far more revolutionary and forward looking, under the leadership of such great minds as Gandhi, Nehru and Mao, than the power seeking leaders of America or Russia.

I expressed my feelings to Mrs Pandit one day. She smiled and thought I perhaps wanted promotion as counsellor, which was due, and promised to get it for me. I felt a little hurt at this and sent her a brief note saying "China beckons to me." She was also a little hurt and asked if she had not treated me well.

I thanked her for her many kindnesses and told her the truth—that my heart was in India and China and I would like to go back home, or failing that to China. There appeared to be a vacancy in our embassy in Peking and I was posted as counsellor, as no one else of my seniority was perhaps keen to go there. Some friends thought I was silly in leaving Washington for Peking. But, I had no doubt that I was doing the right thing. I would have preferred a posting in India where so much was happening. I had been to two important countries in our newly formed diplomatic service. I felt a little disappointed with my experience there, as with the short stint at the UNO, as Deputy Secretary General of our delegation. Not having succeeded in getting a posting to India, I was happy to go to Peking where also much was happening.

4　China Calling

I flew from New York to Delhi in September 1950, for a briefing, before proceeding to Peking. Sir Girja Shankar Bajpai was the Secretary-General in the External Affairs Ministry. When I called on him he was frank and told me that one reason for sending me to Peking was "to keep an eye on our Ambassador —Sardar Panikkar—who is inclined to take too pro-Chinese a view." I was somewhat surprised to hear this but kept it to myself and merely said that I would keep my mind, eyes and ears open. Whether it satisfied Sir Girja or not I do not know. I began to entertain admiration and respect for Panikkar after reading some of his brilliant despatches in the Foreign Office. I knew his previous background as an adviser to various Princes and the Chamber of Princes before Independence, but I also knew that he was an intellectual, had the open mind of an intellectual, and was a patriot with a keen sense of history. He had written some learned and scholarly books already. But I did not know him well personally.

Nehru called me to breakfast at his house. No one else was present. I thought he would dismiss me after a brief chat but he went on for about an hour. It was scintillating to listen to his analysis of India's and China's past, the recent, present and the possibilities in future. This in brief is what he said:

India and China are two great and ancient countries. Both have re-emerged after a period of foreign domination—India as a peaceful, non-aligned country and China as a militant, communist one. The Chinese leaders are suspicious of America's intentions because the USA has refused to recognise the exist-ence of mainland China. Because of this they are suspicious even of friendly countries along their borders, like India, which they believe is still dominated by the West. However, we should try to correct this wrong impression. Their suspicion is mainly due to their isolation from the outside world—physical, mental, political, economic and cultural.

In the past when both India and China were great, their respective cultures, trade and commerce, spread to various parts of Asia, but never came into direct conflict. There was almost a sort of demarcation line between the two in Indo-China, as the very name implies.

Between a strong, united, militant, communist China and a democratic, united, non-aligned India one is not sure whether there will be cooperation or conflict. Both need peace to reconstruct their economies. The peace of Asia and, indeed of the world, can be affected one way or the other by the sort of relations that develop between new India and new China. If we can be friends and cooperate with each other, that will stabilise peace and prevent great power domination of Asia. It should, therefore, be our attempt to remove suspicion from the minds of the Chinese leaders and make Sino-Indian relations an example—of two countries with different social, political and economic systems cooperating with each other on the basis of equality, mutual benefit and respect for each other's sovereignty and integrity.

Here were the seeds of Panch Sheel germinating in the great and far-seeing mind of Nehru, but he was not sure how new China would respond. I asked him about Tibet. He thought for a while and then said that India did not want to follow Britain's imperialist policy and claim extra-territorial rights in Tibet. It should be our endeavour to make the Sino-Indian border an area of peace. Tibet had cultural, religious and commercial links with India. These should be maintained. Even the British had recognised China's suzerainty over Tibet. When there was a strong government in Peking it effectively exercised this suzerainty and when it was weak, Tibet asserted her independence. Now that there was a strong government in Peking, if they could assure Lhasa that they did not wish to interfere with their religious and cultural life and would give them local autonomy, it might be possible to find a peaceful solution of the problem. India was not in a position to give any military assistance to Tibet as we were involved with Pakistan. It would not, in any case, make much difference but only bring greater domination and less autonomy for Tibet. At the same time, India should have no illusions and be prepared for all eventualities. China had been expansionist in the past, when she was not communist and may become expansionist again. India must become economically strong, politically united and stable and try to defuse tension and create a climate of peace in this region instead of conflict and confrontation. It is possible that if India and China cooperate with each other, it will soften, to some extent, the present cold war between the West and the East.

Nehru went on in this vein for almost an hour. He was, perhaps, thinking aloud and had not fully formulated a definite policy. It depended on the response of China and her attitude towards India and other non-communist neighbours in Asia. Much depended also on China's developing relations with the Soviet Union and America's attitude to new China.

The success of any country's foreign policy depends largely on its internal strength and stability and its history, culture, traditions, goals and interests. Even so, it cannot be a one-sided affair. You have to deal with countries that are sovereign, have their own national interests to safeguard. Much depends on their attitude, ambitions and response to the gestures of other countries. Could India and China, following different political and social systems, with different cultures and traditions, see far enough into the future, and safeguard their respective national interests and those of peace in Asia, through cooperation with each other, and prevent Asia becoming a playground for imperialist games?

This was the question. It was almost a test case. The cold war was at its height. The two super powers were trying to suck within their respective orbits as many countries as they could without directly going to war themselves. Wars were being fought between them by proxy.

The Korean conflict was getting hotter. America took shelter under the UN resolution and sent its troops and those of its allies to South Korea under the UN cover. India had voted for the first resolution, but was absent from the second and refused to send any troops under the so-called UN Command to Korea. The resolution had been adopted by the UN Security Council in the absence (deliberate perhaps) of the USSR. Flushed by their initial success, the so-called UN Command, under General Douglas McArthur, wanted to push across the 38th Parallel and on to the Yalu river on the Sino-North Korean border. Chou En-lai had sent a warning through

our ambassador in Peking that if the 38th Parallel was crossed,
China would have to send its "volunteer" troops across to Korea
and drive the invaders out as they would pose a threat to China's
own security. The Americans did not take this warning seriously
and called Sardar Panikkar "Mr Panicky." I was given a letter
by Nehru for Panikkar conveying the American reaction to call
the Chinese "bluff." While at Calcutta on my way to Peking via
Hongkong, I got a telephonic message from K.P.S. Menon,
Foreign Secretary, to destroy the letter Nehru had given me. It
was because the American troops had just then crossed the 38th
Parallel and the Chinese had kept their promise and sent wave
after wave of their volunteer troops across to help their North
Korean allies. Panikkar's assessment had been proved right and
Chou En-lai's warning was not mere bluff.

Soon the tide turned against America and its allied troops.
McArthur wanted to use the atom bomb and cross the Yalu
river to wipe out the Chinese bases across the border, but he was
overruled by President Truman and relieved of his command.
The quite little Truman had shown his mettle and thus prevented the Korean conflict from developing into world war.

It is significant that Chou En-lai had chosen to convey the
warning to the Americans through the Indian Ambassador in
Peking. He perhaps thought that India's assessment would carry
greater conviction with the US Government or perhaps he
wanted to gather support among the non-aligned countries for
China, or both. But, what is clear is that had India voted for the
resolution in the Security Council branding China as aggressor
(the Soviet delegate attended this meeting and vetoed the resolution) India would have weakened her non-aligned position and
international stature. She would then have been considered a
mere satellite of the USA. India's stand in the Security Council
and the correctness of her assessment of Chou En-lai's warning
raised India's stature and increased her ability to exercise a
sobering influence on the cold war. Her lone voice (at that time)
began to receive a little more attention in international forums
and world chancelleries. But, it also created resentment against
her in the West and the USA and jealousy among some other
countries, especially Pakistan.

5 En-route to Peking

Flying from Calcutta, we made a brief halt at Hong Kong to buy various things for the winter in Peking. I did not call on the British, American or any other missions in Honkong deliberately because I knew their prejudice against the Peking Government. I wanted to go with an open mind to find things for myself.

Hongkong, a small island, looked like a booming British colony, full of luxury goods and antique shops with smuggled jade and jewellery, silks and brocades from the mainland. It was an artificially built city that seemed in a hurry to make good while the sun of the British Empire still shone over it. The vast majority of the Chinese population (barring a few rich merchants and compradores) lived in hovels and Sampans. One felt suffocated by this spectacle of the two cities in one. It was connected by a ferry service to Kowloon on the mainland in what was called the "New Territories" which were under the British control and extended up to the Chinese border across a hilly road. Kowloon at that time (October 1950) was less built than Hongkong and more Chinese than British. I decided to stay in one of the hotels there rather than on the island which was more expensive, over-crowded and colonial. Somehow one felt closer to China in Kowloon than in Hongkong, not only geographically but even socially and culturally.

Hongkong was like a British cantonment in pre-independence India and bound to be sucked into the mainland one day. In any case, the lease under which it was given to Britain was to expire in 1997, and Peking seemed in no undue hurry to liberate it. It depended entirely on the mainland for its water supply, fuel, vegetables and for its very survival. The Chinese could take it whenever they wished. They had bigger problems to tackle first —both internally and externally. Besides, they needed Hongkong as a clearing house for commerce, especially for their import and export trade.

The Peking Government, though communist in its goals and ideals, appeared at that time to be more pragmatic than dogmatic. They had their own list of priorities—internal consolidation, land reforms, liquidation of KMT (Kuo Min Tang) elements, law and order problems, training of cadres, safeguarding their far-flung borders against spies, saboteurs and infiltrators, extending their one-party military control and civilian administration to the war-torn and faction-ridden provinces. China faced tremendous social, economic and political problems, as great as India's, if not greater. Besides, she had the threat from South Korea and Taiwan (Formosa), both backed by America's military might and economic power.

But, China was in a better position in 1950 than Russia had been in 1919. She was not alone. She had an ally in the Soviet Union (Sino-Soviet differences had not surfaced yet). She had a well-knit party, with trained cadres, who had been tested in a continuous civil war with the KMT. She had a large PLA (People's Liberation Army) and a military-cum-political leadership which had stood together through the difficult days of the Long March and thereafter. She had a man of vision in Mao Tse-tung and an able administrator-cum-diplomat in Chou En-lai, besides a host of dedicated leaders like Chu Teh, Liu Shao-chi and others. Inner-party differences and personal jealousies had not had time to simmer and boil. The leaders were busy with tremendous internal and external problems, and worked as a team under the outstanding leadership of Mao.

China, like India, was too big and nationalist to become the client state of any other country. While new India was non-communist and believed in parliamentary democracy and the multi-party system, new China was communist and followed the one-party system. India and China both needed peace to reconstruct their social and economic structure. But China was militant and expansionist, while India was not. China was isolated by the West in general and America in particular, at that time, while India had contacts both with the capitalist and the socialist camps. Could or would these two great countries of Asia develop friendly and cooperative relations and safeguard their respective national interests and peace in

Asia, and avoid coming into conflict?

These were some of the questions that had been in my mind after my meeting with Nehru in Delhi. After my disappointing experience in Stalin's Russia and Truman's America, I came to China with the hope of finding some common bonds and interests between India and China. Part of it was perhaps due to the "Asian" sentiment against the "western domination of Asia," as Panikkar called it. The main reason was, however, a quest for peace, a search for some form of cooperation between two great countries that had both suffered in the past through internal strife and dissension and external exploitation, and yet, managed to survive and re-emerge as sovereign independent nations.

With these thoughts in my mind, I took a slow British boat of 8,000 tons, run by Jardine and Matheson, from Kowloon to Taku Bar near Tientsin.

The British are good traders and, unlike the Americans, do not usually mix ideology with their trade. The English captain of the boat and his Scottish engineer were decent and pleasant but avoided talking politics. They did not lose their nerve nor did they swear when the Chinese border troops fired a warning shell across their bow. They stopped and let the Chinese officer and his men board the ship and were civil to them. I suppose they had to be, for there was no alternative. They offered cigarettes, tea and drinks to the Chinese who politely declined. The Chinese navigated the boat to Taku Bar, the harbour channel for Tientsin.

The sea was rough, and the little boat rocked and rolled. The voyage was short (only three days). We heaved a sigh of relief on disembarking at Taku Bar and boarded a slow moving train to Peking via Tientsin. From the train, Tientsin looked like a poor imitation of a western industrial town like many in India. The journey to Peking was brief and uneventful. But the sight of the Tartar wall around the inner city, the many watch towers on it and gates leading through it, the houses with tiled roofs and eaves curved upwards, gave one an impression of a typical Chinese city. It was a bitterly cold November evening with some snow on the ground and chilly winds blowing in from the Gobi desert. The embassy had rented for me a western-type house inside a Chinese-style compound in one of the *hutungs* or lanes. It was cosy and comfortable but did not go with the Chinese architecture all round it. It looked out of place there, and I decided to move into a typical Chinese house as soon as possible.

My first impression of Peking was that of an ancient, drab and dilapidated city until I saw its beautiful parks and drove past the Forbidden City the next morning to meet my ambassador.

My first meeting with Panikkar cleared some of my doubts. I tried to probe his mind and he mine. I found him not only interesting to talk to but also stimulating, deliberately provocative, dramatic at times, but with a sense of history which enabled him to see far ahead and adjust his mind accordingly. No wonder he had been as popular with the KMT Government in Nanking as he was with the new set up in Peking. But, as Nehru had told me Panikkar had a streak of the dramatic and he some times thought events would occur with lightening rapidity. My first impression of Panikkar was that of an intellectual with a brilliant mind and a negotiator *par excellence.* He did not put you off by a show of his superior mind but won your confidence and admiration by his skilful probing, encouraging you to express your opinions and keeping his options open. He was not dogmatic but pragmatic. I found his knowledge and assessment of the West deep and penetrating, but he seemed to have a prejudice against the USSR, which he balanced by his admiration for new China so as not to appear anti-communist.

Panikkar worked like a student preparing for a competitive examination, and wrote his notes for his book, "Asia and Western Dominance," every morning. When he had finished a chapter, he would drop in at the chancery for an hour or so. I tried to persuade him to spend a little more time in the office, by furnishing his room as lavishly as possible in those days, but he stuck to his habit of not spending more than an hour there daily, and left office matters entirely to me.

The diplomatic corps in Peking at that time was rather small —half a dozen Socialist embassies, a few Scandinavians and the Swiss Ambassador plus the Burmese, Indonesian, Pakistani and Indian embassies. There were a few care-taker Charges from western Europe, like the Dutch, Belgian and French. The British had a Charge too, Sir Lionel Lamb, with a fairly large China section. The Soviets had the largest set-up. American interests were being looked after by the Dutch. Panikkar found most of the diplomatic representatives rather dull, and his main contacts were with the British and the Swiss, I kept in touch with the Soviets, Burmese, Indonesians, Finns and others.

Panikkar would call me almost every afternoon or evening for a chat over a cup of tea or a drink, and exchange his impressions and ideas with me. We talked about the cold war, America, the USSR, India and China mainly. He would tell me with a twinkle in his eyes, how he had hood-winked some of the Western representatives. They used to flock to him every time he met Chou En-lai or other Chinese leaders to get some crumbs of information to send to their Foreign Offices. Panikkar took an almost mischievous delight in sending them off the trail. Some of them tried to double-check with me and, when I told them the truth, they would naturally believe my ambassador rather than me. I told him about it and suggested that he should not mislead them. He laughed and said that they were a bunch of fools, and he had utter contempt for them. The result was that they thought that I was a communist and Panikkar a liberal, and reported this to their governments, as I came to know later. When this reached Prime Minister Nehru via some channels, he said, "Kaul is not a communist, but even if he was one, I would trust him." This was mentioned to me, among others, by the late H.V.R. Ienger who was then Principal Private Secretary to the Prime Minister.

My main contacts were with the Chinese Government at the lower level, and they helped us to confirm what had been said at the Ambassador's level. He and I worked as a team and kept no secrets from each other. However, we sometimes differed in our theoretical and academic analysis of the Soviet and the Chinese brands of communism. Panikkar, like the professor he was, would ask me to quote chapter and verse. When I did so, he would laugh and say, "I was only trying to find out if you had read the history of the CPSU(B)." It was delightful, stimulating and most interesting to work with a man like Panikkar.

We often exchanged ideas about the situation in India and the various personalities involved. We shared our admiration for and conviction in Nehru's policies. His knowledge of the scene was much deeper and more intimate than mine. He delighted in running down people whom he called "Somnathists" or revivalists who wanted to rebuild old temples desecrated by some of the Muslim invaders. He was vehemently secular in his outlook and non-religious with a vengeance. He told me with some pride that he had started a "Beef and Pork" club in Delhi many years ago. When I told him that I had once taken beef by mistake and did not like its taste, he said, "Ah, then you should try frog's legs, monkey's brain, python's heart—they are real delicacies." I thought he was pulling my leg but, a few days later, I found him eating these "delicacies" with relish. I could not emulate his example; not because of any religious scruples, but purely for aesthetic and gastronomical reasons. So that was Sardar Panik-kar, a mixture of interesting opposites—with Lenin's big head and a short Ho Chi-minh beard, sharp penetrating eyes, a gourmet, a brilliant conversationalist, deliberately provocative, always interesting and stimulating. He had the capacity to adjust himself to all situations—an ideal diplomat with a scholarly background and analytical mind—in other words "a man for all seasons."

6 Mao's China

The US Government and media insisted on calling the capital city Peiping (not Peking) which, in Chinese, means northern "province" and not "capital." The ordinary American or any person, who did not know Chinese, would not notice this deliberate distortion, but the Chinese did and resented it. However, ostrich-like, the US Government refused to see reality until it was forced to, as in the case of recognition of the USSR.

Peking is the real capital of China—historically, politically, geo-politically and culturally. It was founded by that great Mongol ruler of China, Kublai Khan, in 1267. It is not on the coast, but not too far from it either. Peking is the centre that holds the balance between north and south China as well as north-east and south-west China. It has been the capital of the Chinese Empire except for brief periods. A few hours by rail or road from the Great Wall and the Ming Tombs, it also has within its heart such marvels of architecture as the Temple of Heaven, the Nine Dragon Pagoda, the inimitable Forbidden City and now the Gate of Heavenly Peace or Tien An-men, which foreign correspondents call the Chinese Red Square. The Summer Palace and Winter Palace are popular places for picnics with many temples and pagodas in their vicinity. For diplomats, there is a sea resort, Peita Ho, where they can hire a cottage.

I discovered all these and other places soon after my arrival, and found them enchanting. For the gourmet, there were many famous restaurants which gave excellent food at moderate prices, e.g., the Peking Duck and the Mongolian restaurants. For the lover of art, there were many museums where one could spend hours every week. For the collector of antiques, there were scores of shops and hundreds of pedlars selling faked "Tang" horses or "ancient" scrolls, Ming porcelain, silks and brocades. It was fun haggling with them over the price of various articles.

These were the early days of the Chinese revolution when petty trade and private shops were still allowed. But one could see signs of the revolution engulfing all fields of activity and all sections of the society.

The Chinese word for "liberation"—*chefang*—has been interpreted by some foreign scholars to mean "liberation from poverty, disease and corruption." I am not a sentimentalist but, at that time, this interpretation of Chinese "liberation" was, by and large correct, especially when compared to the KMT days. There was no more fear of the landlord's oppression or the policeman's exactions. You could leave doors unlocked, and not a thing would be stolen. There was no fear of molestation by hired hooligans or desperados as in the days of the warlords and the KMT. What struck me most was the genuine enthusiasm of the common man, the youth in particular, about the new regime. There was almost an evengelical atmosphere everywhere and complete faith in Mao's leadership. He was like a god who appeared twice a year—on 1st October and 1st May—on the podium in Tien An·men, flanked by the lesser gods and disciples, the members of the politbureau. But his portraits hung everywhere, and his name was glorified even in the national anthem "The East is Red."

All this reminded me sometimes of Stalin's Russia and Gandhi's India. But there were differences. Mao was not feared as Stalin was. Mao was loved and worshipped as Gandhi was, but unlike Gandhi, Mao was not easily accessible. Although the militia were present everywhere, as in Moscow, they were not rude or domineering but polite and helpful. Everyone was called "comrade" as in Russia, but the Chinese word for "comrade"—*thungchir*—has a slightly different nuance. It means "he who has the same mind or thought." (I recall hailing a Chinese policeman in Hongkong as "thungchir" and getting a cold stare in return.) The Chinese revolution was in full swing and still retained the earlier evangelical fervour of the great October revolution under Lenin. The Stalinist dogmatism of the Russian Revolution had not yet polluted its pristine purity.

There was another significant difference. Whereas the Chinese communist leaders had brought about the revolution first in the rural areas, and then formulated their doctrines in the caves of Yenan, the Russian Revolution radiated from cities like

Leningrad and Moscow to the rural areas. China was mainly
an agricultural country, while Russia was more industrialized.
Stalin's Russia used the police and militia to force recalcitrants
to confess or sent them to Siberia or the Karaganda mines. The
Chinese communists used the much more powerful and effective
weapon of social, public and group opinion to convert people.
It was strange for a democratic bourgeois Indian to see Chinese
denounce their colleagues, children expose their parents and
neighbours report against each other. The "ideological remoulding movement" in China was physically less cruel than in
Stalin's Russia, but phychologically and emotionally more
ruthless and effective. There was no individual privacy and
everyone was a member of a group and led a group life. The
"San Fan" and "Wu Fan" movements (or Three Antis and Five
Antis aimed mainly against corruption and bureaucratism) were
launched nationwide with ruthless efficiency. Landlords were
denounced, tried and punished by the people's courts—spat at,
flogged, beaten and executed. No mercy was shown to the
"enemies of the people," KMT or other spies. All foreigners
were suspect, and contact with them was forbidden. Those
who still maintained some contact with diplomats—like some
professors—were criticized in group meetings by their students.
Officials reported against and criticized their superiors.

Then came the "Oppose America, Defend Korea and Save
the Fatherland" campaign on a nationwide scale. Even children
in kindergarten schools were taught to shoot at dummy American soldiers. The campaign was something to be seen to be believed. Fanatic zeal pervaded all spheres of national life. Parks were
beautified, canals dug, dams built and roads constructed with
mass revolutionary effort by high party officials, bureaucrats
and the common people. The "sleeping tiger" of Asia had at last
woken up and his voice reverberated throughout Asia. Where
was all this going to lead to? Could it go on at this high pitch
for long? Would it lead to excesses and inner-party conflict and
struggle for power as had happened in Stalin's Russia?

No one could predict with certainty at that time. But one
thing was clear. In spite of China's alliance with and reference
to the Soviet Union as "the head of the socialist camp" and
the "citadel of communism," the Chinese nation was on the
march and would not be subservient to any other power,

however great and strong. Whether Chinese communism took a dogmatic turn or remained pragmatic, it had succeeded in uniting the country and welding the people into one nation for the first time in its long history. In the process, many elements like landlords, campradores, businessmen, traders, warlords, etc., had been "liquidated"—the estimate varied from 10-20 million—but the country had been made safe for the remaining 590 million Chinese. It was, as Liu Shao-chi explained, the "dictatorship of the proletariat," that is, "dictatorship of the people against the enemies of the people." Liu Shao-chi was considered, at that time, second to Mao and the interpreter of his Thought. Chou En-lai and Chu Teh came next. Lin Piao and the others had not yet emerged in the first rank of the party.

It was a fascinating picture—a nation on the march, a permanent revolution in the making. They had set their sights high like all revolutionaries do. Time would show how far they succeed. It was a new experiment, unprecedented in human history, of creating a new man, a new kind of human relationship, a new sense of values. It was fascinating but also frightening in its potentialities and possibilities. Its ability to do good was immense, but its capacity to cause harm was equal, if not greater. A united nation of 600 million, with one ideology and unbounded enthusiasm, strong will and determination, could be a weapon not only to save peace and defend China but a weapon, even more powerful than the atom bomb, which might destroy other nations in its fanatical fervour, to spread its ideology and expand its frontiers. The future would show which way China would go. In alliance with the USSR, it could not only meet any challenge from the rest of the world but even dominate it. Even all alone it could create a sphere of influence around itself. Its friendship with the USA or the West was inconceivable at that time. However, friendship with India was possible, and if China and India could work together in peace and friendship, they would set an example to the rest of the world as to how two proud nations could live in peaceful and cooperative coexistence in spite of different social, political and economic systems. Was this worth pursuing? As Nehru had told me in Delhi, it would be wothwhile to make an endeavour towards achieving it, however long and difficult the path. But China was, at that time, condemning India as a stooge of Anglo-

American imperialism, especially regarding Tibet. How could friendship and understanding be developed in this atmosphere?

Diplomacy in peace time is sometimes more difficult than in war time, but it is even more so when there is no peace and no war. Such was the situation between India and China in the late fifties, and such seems to be the situation in the world today.

7 Tibet

It was early November 1950. The Chinese troops were advancing towards Lhasa from Chamdo. The Tibetan delegation had drawn a blank in the US State Department and the British Foreign Office, but had probably received promise of some arms from the USA. India did not wish to make any false promises and advised them to enter into peaceful negotiations with Peking. They went to Hongkong but were held up there for more than a month and returned to Lhasa. India tried to plead with Peking for a peaceful settlement with the Tibetans. The Chinese, perhaps out of suspicion, natural in their isolation, questioned India's motives and called her all sorts of names in their press and radio broadcasts. Later when I went to Dairen I saw in a photo exhibition a snapshot of Ford and Bull, two British wireless operators in the Dalai Lama's service, with the caption "Indian spies in Tibet region of China." I felt a little disappointed and hurt at this unfounded accusation and told Chen Chia-kang, Director Asian Department in the Waichiaopu (Foreign Office) about it. He was a soft spoken, mild mannered communist of the Mandarin type, and told me to have patience and that all would be well. In the meantime, India's stand on Korea in the UNO and refusal to brand Peking as aggressor removed, to some extent, the Chinese suspicion that we were the "running dogs of Anglo-American Imperialism"—a description I had come across earlier in 1947-49 in Moscow. Anti-Indian propaganda on Tibet softened, as the Chinese troops advanced towards Lhasa. In May 1951, Peking and Lhasa signed the 17 Point Agreement. It ensured China's Sovereignty and promised a sort of cultural "autonomy" for Tibet which is conceptually different from "autonomy" as understood in liberal parlance.

Then came a communication from the Foreign Office in Delhi to Panikkar virtually asking him to send a note to the

Chinese Foreign Office amending Delhi's previous note re-
cognising China's Sovereignty over Tibet, and attributing this
to a cryptographic error. The supposed error was the word
"sovereignty" for "suzerainty." Panikkar was livid and drafted
a strong reply to Delhi. He showed it to me and I softened it a
bit and suggested he address it to the Prime Minister. He agreed
and sent it off giving reasons why such a communication should
not be sent. The Prime Minister agreed with him.

Many in India have criticized Panikkar's handling of this
matter. I have no doubt in my mind that Panikkar's action was
right on moral, political and strategic considerations and in the
short and long term interests of India. We had a hostile neighbour in Pakistan, backed by the USA and the West, especially
on the Kashmir question. The Soviet Union's relations with
India were still in the process of formulation and had not yet
become friendly. "Suzerainty" according to the Chinese was an
imperialist concept. India's insistence on "suzerainty" after
accepting China's "sovereignty" would not only have looked
ridiculous but meaningless and made no difference whatsoever in
the actual situation on the ground. It would only have further
aggravated Sino-Indian relations and increased China's suspicion of India.

Tibet never belonged to India and it was not for India to
"keep" or "give away" Tibet to China. Even the British had
accepted China's "suzerainty" over Tibet at a time when the
Peking Government was weak and China divided. This was
mainly to check attempts by Czarist Russia to increase her
influence in this region. The fact was that whenever the central
Government in China was strong it had exercised "sovereignty"
and effective control over Tibet; whenever it was weak, Tibet had
exercised internal autonomy and China's "sovereignty" had
become "suzerainty." In any case it was a matter to be settled
between Peking and Lhasa and no outside power could do anything about it, short of starting a war. America and the West
wanted India to pull the Tibetan chestnuts out of the Chinese
fire and watch the fun from a distance. They did not like the idea
of India and China getting friendly and tried to prevent such a
development. The CIA and the US Consulate General in
Calcutta made all kinds of promises to the Tibetan emissaries
and the KMT dropped leaflets and even arms and radio trans-

mitters to their agents in Tibet. The Government of India had no hand in this but suspicious, as the Peking Government was, it would not believe that.

India had to be patient and far-sighted. She was a big country with internal and external problems of her own. Similar situations might arise in certain parts of India, encouraged by outside powers, as actually they did in Jammu and Kashmir, Hyderabad, Nagaland, Goa, Sikkim, etc. The Government had to deal with them effectively and forcefully. The Tibetan situation vis-a-vis China may not have been identical with these, but the principle involved was similar, i.e. the right of a sovereign country to safeguard its sovereignty over all its parts and to ensure its territorial integrity.

Even on practical grounds, we could not have given any significant military help to the Tibetans and it would not have made any difference to the final outcome. It would only have precipitated a situation on the Sino-Indian border when we were least prepared for it. Talk of a military alliance with America, which some Indians advocated, would only have drawn India into the cold war, brought Russia and China even closer, and posed a serious threat to India's security and economic development. America would fight to the last Indian against China and not get directly involved herself. Its attitude on the Sino-Indian border, as declared by Secretary of State Christian Herter, was like Neville Chamberlain's on Czechoslovakia. Why then should India fight for American interests in China and endanger her own? On all grounds—political, economic, military, long term and short term—there was no other policy India could have adopted except to recognise China's sovereignty over Tibet and try to develop friendly relations with Peking. Nehru's policy on this question was the right policy and Panikkar did not "push" Nehru into it, as some believed.

However, there was one trait in Panikkar that created this wrong impression in some circles. As an intellectual, he tried to distinguish Chinese communism or "The Thought of Mao" from Marxism and justified it as a benevolent development not only for China but possibly for her neighbours. It certainly was good for China in many ways, in the concrete conditions prevailing at that time. But it also posed a potential threat to her neighbours in view of China's past history and her present

ambition to be the leader of Asia. During Khruschev's visit to
Peking after Camp David, Mao told him, "You can take the
leadership of Europe, but leave Asia to us." Khruschev replied:
"No one in Europe has asked us to take over the leadership of
Europe. Who in Asia has asked you to take over the leadership
of Asia?" Obviously, Mao did not like this reply and is
reported to have turned strongly against Khruschev personally
ever since. This was mentioned to me not by Khruschev himself,
but by one of his senior colleagues in the politbureau after his
fall and, therefore, seems more credible.

A far-sighted statesman that he was, Nehru foresaw the possibility of a strong, united, communist China trying to dominate
Asia. However, he wanted to befriend China, to remove her suspicions against India, so that peace in the region could be maintained and economic development take place quickly. He did not
mind China going communist, as long as it did not try to dominate its neighbours, but he wanted to gain time and prepare for
all eventualities. That is why he tried to befriend all countries
including the USSR and China, so that in case of need we did
not find ourselves alone or dependent on any one power.

8 India and China

Relations between India and China started improving from 1951 onwards. As far as China was concerned, Tibet was more or less a settled question. Attempts by some countries to raise the issue in the UNO were abortive. India's attitude on the Korean question and her strong support to the right of the Peking Government to represent China in the UN made an impression on China's leaders that India was not "tied" to the apron-strings of John Bull or Uncle Sam. Cultural delegations and performing troupes were exchanged. Trade agreements were entered into. The Indian Embassy in Peking was rated second in importance after the Soviet Embassy. Facilities denied to others were given to us to visit some "forbidden" areas. Panikkar visited the Tung Hwang caves in the north-west and the Loyang caves in Sian. I was permitted to visit Dairen, Mukden, Harbin and Port Arthur in the north-east, till then closed to all non-communist countries and even to some embassies of the socialist camp.

Chinese officials and some non-officials were permitted to accept our hospitality and they invited us. While our hospitality was extended at our homes, they invited us to restaurants where private rooms were booked by them. I partnered Mao's Master of Ceremonies, Mr Ma, in the Tennis tournament at the Peking International Club and we won the men's doubles. He was also a frequent visitor at the clubs's Saturday dances. He got into trouble once for giving a lift in his official car to some Chinese ladies. I learnt later that he had been criticized in the party meeting by his own chauffeur for this "bourgeois" habit and misuse of the official car and had to keep away from the club activities for a while. These were the days of San Fan and Wu Fan (the Three and Five Antis). I was relieved to find him back on the tennis court after a few weeks. The Chinese did not send people to their Siberia on mere suspicion, but tried to reform them and remould their ideology through discussion. This certainly was an improvement on Stalinist methods followed in the USSR in the late twenties and mid thirties.

Among the non-officials who accepted our hospitality I recall Professor Nan Han-Sen, a rural economist, Mr Ma, the President of Peking University, retired KMT General Dong and his charming old wife. She had been Lady-in-Waiting to the late Dowager Empress. Madame Dong was a tall, beautiful, slim lady of 75 and could still sing and dance and did so when requested repeatedly. Her skin had the most beautiful texture. She used an old recipe to make her own skin ointment. She came to our parties in a blue uniform but underneath it she wore the most beautiful Chinese silks and brocades, which she liked to show off. She had been a Manchu Princess and found it difficult to adjust herself entirely to the new puritannical rules.

When Panikkar was leaving Peking in 1952 to take up the post of India's Ambassador to Cairo, I went to see him off at Tientsin. He seemed already in the Court of King Farouq and Queen Nariman. He bought an old diamond watch fixed to a fan of ostrich feathers which he proudly showed off to me "for presentation to Queen Nariman." He had paid about two million JMP (or Rs 1,000 at the then rate of exchange) for it, but before he reached Cairo, the King and Queen had been overthrown. That was Panikkar—he would fit in any society-modern, medieval or ancient.

A high-level Indian Cultural Delegation, led by Mrs Vijaya-lakshmi Pandit, and including Acharya Narendra Dev, Prof Amaranatha Jha, Chalapati Rao, Frank Moraes, Shanto Rao, artist Bendre and V. P. Dutt and others visited China in 1952. They were well received and toured the usual places plus the Ta Tung caves where I went with them. Shanta Rao gave an enchanting performance of Bharat Natyam in the hall of Peking Hotel.

Mrs Pandit visited my home and raised her eyebrows when she saw photos of Gandhi, Nehru, Lenin and Mao bracketted together in one frame. She said, "What do I see?" I said, "You see right Madam. I admire them all for what they have done and are doing in their own countries." I do not know whether she believed me but I meant it.

Mrs Pandit had perhaps expected wild fanfare and frontline

publicity, at least a meeting with Mao. The Chinese were busy with their own struggle and still gave a lot of attention to the delegation, but she was not happy. She expressed her dis-satisfaction to me and Prof. Jha and we both tried to pacify her but she still sulked. I reported this to Panikkar. He succeeded where Jha and I had failed. He called her "*Madamissima,*" told her many stories and anecdotes. One of these related to the three Soong sisters: "One loves power (Madam Chiang Kai-shek); the second loves money (Madam Kung) and the third loves her country (Soong Ching-ling or Madam Sun Yat-sen)."

I had the honour of meeting Soong Ching-ling in her home in Shanghai where I went to see our Consul-General, P.R.S. Mani, who had good contacts and relations with the local. Chinese Shanghai was till then a little less austere than Peking. Madam Soong kept a vase with real flowers in it (for which she was criticized as a "*bourgeois*" later in Peking). She was a gracious, charming and patriotic lady, Vice-president of the Peoples' Republic, but not proud or arrogant like her sisters. She spoke to me in English (which was at that time frowned upon but is now preferred to Russian). Later when I visited her in Peking I noticed the difference in her style of living, though she still maintained her dignity. She visited India in 1955 and stayed with Nehru as his personal guest. The US press flashed wild and wishful reports that she did not wish to return to China, but there was no truth in them.

My first close view of Mao Tse-tung was on 26 January 1951, when he attended our Republic-Day reception at the Peking Hotel. A tall, loose-limbed figure, he entered the hall with a long brown woollen overcoat draped loosely over his shoulders reaching almost to his ankles, and a peak cap. Security guards removed the coat from his shoulders and he walked into the hall like a patriarch, smiling but not in the least self-conscious. The audience rose in his honour. Everyone stood still while the Chinese and the Indian national anthems were played. Mao took his seat at the head table on the right of Panikkar. Paranjpe, our able Chinese language expert, and Pu, Mao's Columbia educated English interpreter, stood behind. All eyes were fixed on Mao who rarely attended National-Day receptions. This was a signal honour shown to India in view of our improving relations. Such things assume far more importance in com-

munist countries than elsewhere because they do not represent
the personal likes and dislikes of the Head of Government
or State, but deliberate acts of policy, indicating changing
trends.

In India the Prime Minister and even the President, used
to attend National-Day receptions in the earlier years, until this
practice was changed in the mid-fifties.

Chairman Mao stood up to say a few words. He had a slight
stoop round his shoulders, his small eyes shone in his moon
face, and his smile (not a grin) lit up his whole personality. He
spoke, not like an orator or a demagogue, but in short, simple
sentences like, "India is a great country. The Indian people are
a great people," etc. His speech was translated into English by
Pu. Then Panikkar got up, beaming like a beaver and replied
also in short simple sentences, unlike his usual style. He seemd
to have been influenced by Mao's example. He spoke in English
and his speech was translated into excellent Chinese by Paranjpe.
Chou En-lai, who sat near me said "Paranjpe's Chinese is better
than any foreigner's I have heard." This was a great compliment
and well deserved. Paranjpe had spent four years at Peita
(Peking University) studying the language. I was coaxed by
Panikkar to translate his speech into Russian for the benefit of
ambassadors from the socialist camp. I yielded to the temptation
and did the best I could in my fluent but ungrammatical
Russian. The Russian speaking ambassadors were pleased they
had been shown special attention, though I was not happy with
my performance.

Toasts were proposed and drunk *Gambe* (empty the cup)
style. But Mao was very careful in his eating and drinking habits
—unlike other communist leaders in China and Russia, at that
time.

It was a great day for India. The ice between the two was
melting. The clouds were disappearing. Would the sun shine on
our relations or get covered by clouds again? The future
was unknown. There were straws in the wind and both
possibilities of a continuing thaw or a re-freezing of relations
existed.

Panikkar's term in China was over. He had tackled a difficult
and delicate situation with skill and imagination. He left Peking
at the peak of his diplomatic success. Chou En-lai gave a small,

intimate farewell dinner for him at his house. Chou's wife was also present and so were Chang Han-fu (Vice-Minister of Foreign Affairs), Chen Chia-kang (Director Asian Department), Han Shu (India desk officer and later number two in Moscow and now in washington D.C.) besides myself and Paranjpe. The atmosphere was warm and friendly and the Chinese meal was delicious. Chou En-lai was a great host and knew how to entertain his guests. He mixed courtesy, aplomb and diplomatic polish with a straight-forward, confident and clear Marxist mind. He was not dogmatic but very practical and came straight to the heart of the problem. First he mentioned how China had learnt much from India and called it "*Shih Tschang*" or "Heaven in the West" i.e. west of China. Then he described the Chinese dish that was served, known as "eight precious Indian noodles" and traced its origin to India. Unfortunately for Panikkar, and fortunately for the rest of us, there were no frog's legs, monkey's brain or python's heart. But, there was bird's nest soup, a dozen hors d'oeuvres, fish, chicken, Chinese vegetables and last of all plain boiled rice—about eight courses in all and unlike Indian dishes, served one by one.

At the beginning and end of each course there were toasts in the potent drink, *Mao Tai*. Chinese yellow wine (poured warm from a tea pot) and Chinese red wine were also served, but toasts were drunk only in *Mao Tai*. Chou En-lai described how *Mao Tai* (80 per cent proof) was made from rice and water from a spring in Kweichow. As with Vodka, one had to acquire a taste for it, especially as it has a bitter pungent odour and has twice the strength of vodka. You could light it with a matchstick. Panikkar was clever enough to avoid it and asked me to drink on his behalf. I was young and healthy and had some experience of drinking vodka "*Dodna*" (bottoms up) with the Russians in Moscow. Chou En-lai said to me, "If I, fifteen years older, can drink it why not you?" Not to appear unfriendly I drank six tiny glasses of Mao Tai with him. I thought I had done my duty and finished for the evening. Then came Vice-Foreign Minister, Chang Han-fu and said I must drink at least six more *Mao Tais* with him, since my Ambassador was not drinking it. I protested but Chou En-lai added, "I can assure you it will not give you a hangover." So, six more *Mao Tais* went down my gullet, giving a sensation of fire inside me. Panikkar was watching the fun and egging me on. The last straw was Chen Chia-kang's insistence that I could not let down my friend and opposite number in the Waichiaopu and again Chou supported him. I thought for a while and then decided to take the plunge. Six more *Mao Tais* inside me, making a total of 18 in about three hours.

The meal ended with mutual compliments. Next morning I found my head as clear as ever and Chou En-lai's assurance quite correct. However, I decided never to repeat the performance. Instead of *Mao Tai* sometimes Paikar is served: it looks similar and is equally strong, but poisonous. One thing I found rather pleasant with Chinese leaders—they never cheated you at drinks (like Stalin and Molotov did) and, except or very special occasions, never insisted on drinking *"Gambai."* They would say instead *'Sui-pien'* or, "as you please."

I had several occasions to meet Chou En-lai officially and otherwise when I was Charge for a few months after Panikkar left. From Chou you could always get a straight answer to a question. Not so with his Vice-Minister, Chang Han-fu, whom we called the "laughing Buddha." Chiao Kuan-hua, Chou's Special Assistant, with the rank of Assistant Minister, was another straightforward man and I used to exchange ideas with him informally. He became China's Foreign Minister later but was displaced when the "gang of four" was overthrown, possibly because he hesitated to come out in the beginning against them. My main contact however was Chen Chia-kang—historian, philosopher, marxist to the core, but not dogmatic. Always polite and pleasant, he was positive, constructive and tried to be helpful. What happened to him after he was recalled from Cairo in 1964, where he was ambassador, I do not know.

There were other leaders and important figures like Liu Shaochi, Chu Teh, Vice-Presidents U Lan-fu and Chang Lan, Marshal Chen Yi, Mayor of Shanghai and later Foreign Minister, Peng Chen, the Mayor of Peking, Wang Ping-nan, Secretary General of Foreign Ministry, Mao Tun, Minister of Culture and Madam Lee Teh-chuan, Minister of Health.

Perhaps a few words about Chou En-lai and some of these personalities would not be out of place. Chou En-lai was indeed the most outstanding of them. Handsome, smart, alert, quick to grasp a point and to react to it, he reminded me sometimes of

Krishna Menon, but he did not have Menon's biting tongue. Like Menon he analysed a problem bit by bit and tackled it step by step. He was polite even when he was firm and had the knack of making friends out of enemies rather than enemies out of friends, unlike Menon. He was polished and suave with a sense of humour that softened his direct approach. He knew some French and had a smattering of English which he sometimes used to correct his interpreter. I remember a long conversation with him in a meeting at my request where Shiv Shastri, our scholarly and able Public Relations Officer, accompanied me. I tried to probe Chou's sharp and practical mind by saying that China and India had many similar problems and could perhaps learn from each other's experiences. I mentioned the agrarain problem in particular. Chou looked straight in my eyes to grasp the real meaning behind my question. He said, without a moment's hesitation, that India and China were two great countries with tremendous problems. But, the concrete conditions in each country were different; even the various provinces of each country wrae in different stages of development. In China they could not adopt exactly the same model for land reforms in all the provinces. For instance, in the Tibet region of China, the Mongolian autonomous region (Inner Mongolia) and other less developed areas, the pace of land reforms was slower than elsewhere. In any case, the experiences of one country could not be transplanted on another. India had to find her own solutions to solve her peculiar problems, as China had to. However, both were under-developed countries and had suffered from imperialism and colonialism. They could wage a common struggle against these evils.

I referred to fears and suspicions, especially in some of the smaller countries, without naming them, about China's future ambitions. Would new China consider some means of removing these fears and suspicions? He asked "how"? I suggested, as an instance, making a public declaration that she respected the sovereignty and integrity of her neighbours and had no designs to interfere in their internal affairs. Chou again looked into my eyes and said without batting an eyelid: "There are no such fears or suspicions between India and China. There should be none. Some problems had been left over by imperialism, but these could be resolved peacefully through normal diplomatic channels." As for making a public declaration, he did not see the need for it at that time but if occasion arose he would think about it.

I then took up this question in greater detail with Chen Chia-kang, the Asian director in Waichiaopu. I mentioned the Sino-Indian border and its wrong delineation in Chinese maps which created misgivings in India as well as in some other countries. I suggested that they should correct these maps. Chen, unlike Chou, was evasive and in typical Mandarin style said that these were KMT maps, China had not had time to correct them, and would do so in due course when they surveyed the area and drew up new maps. He, however, repeated what Chou had said that if there were any differences, these could be resolved through normal diplomatic channels. I repeated my suggestion regarding a public declaration by China to remove the fears and suspicions of her neighbours. He replied that such a unilateral declaration would unnecessarily arouse the suspicion that perhaps new China had some designs and territorial ambitions. But he indicated that if necessary, such a thing could form the basis of a bilateral or multilateral declaration. I had Pandit Nehru's parting words in my mind and allowed these ideas to sink in the Chinese mind and simmer for a while.

Chang Han-fu, Vice-Foreign Minister, was a tough nut to crack and I hardly ever got any positive response from him. If Chen Chia-kang did not give satisfaction, I would broach the subject informally with Chiao Kuan-hua (Special Assistant to Chou En-lai) who spoke English fluently. (So did his wife Kung Pheng, who was the Director of Press relations in the Foreign Office). Chang Han-fu's wife, Shu Pin, younger sister of Kung Pheng, was a Deputy Director.)

I liked to pull Chang Han-fu's leg sometimes, but he took it too seriously. Once, while watching the May-Day Parade from the enclosure reserved for diplomatic representatives, I said to him jokingly, "I see here representatives and photos of leaders of communist parties of many countries, but India is conspicuous by its absence." He became serious and said, "We shall have to do something about it." On another occasion I said that they were in the habit of inviting members of various communist parties who were already converted and needed no persuasion; they should instead or, in addition, invite those who

were not communists and try to convert them. Chang Han-fu
again took this seriously and thanked me for the suggestion
which, he said, they would consider. When he did not have
a suitable reply he would laugh like the Chinese laughing
Buddha.

Although the Chinese script is the same, the pronunciation
varies so much from Peking to Shanghai, Shanghai to Canton
and Canton to Fukien that it is not easy for a man from the north
to understand the Chinese spoken in the south or south-east and
vice-versa. Chinese is a tonal language. Mandarin spoken in the
north has four tones, Shanghainese six, Cantonese eight, while
Fukienese has twelve. New China has, however, succeeded in
popularising Ko-Yu, or people's Chinese based on Mandarin,
with a vocabulary of about 3,000 words as against 40,000 odd of
classical Chinese. Each word is written as a character, based on
200 odd 'radicals' but it is by no means easy for a foreigner to
learn so many characters.

I tried to acquire a smattering of spoken Ko-Yu from a
Chinese teacher, Chang Shien Shang (Shien Shang meaning
"Mister"). He spoke only Mandarin and no foreign language.
His system of teaching, based on the Berlitz method, was excellent. After about three months with him I thought I had
acquired enough spoken Chinese to order a Chinese meal. I took
some visitors from India to a famous Chinese restaurant in
Peking and wanting to show off my Chinese ordered some soup
by its Chinese name "*Tang.*" Instead the waiter brought some
sugar because "*Tang*" has four tones and each tone has a
different meaning. Similarly when I asked for some salt "*Yen,*"
he brought me cigarettes. After that I gave up my Chinese
lessons. I must express my admiration for the persistence and
perseverance of Abid Hasan Safrani, our First Secretary, who
laboured each day for two to three hours and learnt the 200
radicals and to write his own name and a few others in the
Chinese script.

Chinese adaptation of foreign names is interesting. They are
usually based on the 100 famous Chinese classical names. For
instance, my surname KAUL was translated as KAU-ER (based
on a Chinese classical name meaning "the high or great"). When
a foreign name did not sound similar to any of the 100 classical

Chinese names, they would slightly distort it, e.g. Panikkar in Chinese became *Panichar*.

Liu Shao-chi at that time, ranked next to Mao in the party hierarchy. He was the interpreter of the "Thought of Mao Tse-tung" which he described in a nutshell as "Marxism-Leninism applied to the concrete conditions prevailing in China." Although Liu Shao-chi was considered by most as a dogmatist and doctrinaire, I think he was a theoretician who, unlike his Soviet counterpart Suslov, interpreted doctrine in a typically Chinese practical and pragmatic way, to make it less unintelliglble to communist cadres. He was a serious-minded, almost ascetic, personality and fell a victim to party intrigues and jealousies in latter years, when Lin Piao replaced him as the number two in the Chinese hierarchy.

Chu Teh was a pleasant, old soldier, who had been with Mao all through the Long March and later. He was not a dogmatist but a practical soldier—brave, courageous and patriotic. He was highly respected by all circles and given the honoured place next to Mao at all public functions. But his age and health prevented his taking any active part. He was more like an elder statesman and senior adviser and reminded me of Marshal Voroshilov in his later years.

Chang Lan, belonged to the old Democratic Party and was given a place of honour as one of the Vice-Chairmen in order to unite all anti-Chiang Kai-Shek forces in the new "people's democracy." He dressed in the old Chinese style and looked an impressive figure in his long Chinese gown going down to his ankles and his small skull-cap which highlighted his long pointed white beard. He did not care for modern table manners and enjoyed chewing chicken bone and spitting out the residue under his table. I envied and admired him for I have often felt like doing it myself, but never had the courage in public.

Shen Chen-ju, the Lord Chief Justice or the head of the Chinese Supreme Court, was another figure from old China. Short-statured (5 feet 2 inches) with a short pointed beard, he looked like God's own agent on earth to redress wrongs and dispense justice. Quiet, soft-spoken and mild mannered, his pronouncements were delivered in a stentorian voice.

Mao Tun, Minister of Culture, was a writer himself and spoke in beautiful Chinese. He came into disfavour perhaps because he was not in line with the new radicals who gained power and influ nce in later years. Madam Le Teh-chuan, Minister of Health, remii led me of Rajkumari Amrit Kaur at times. Sometimes she favoured family planning and birth control, while at other times she proudly proclaimed that China did not need these and could look after its entire growing population. I understand she became an ardent supporter of birth control finally.

Peng Chen, Mayor of Peking, ranked high in the party heirarchy and was a member of the Politbureau. He had a pointed red nose and seemed to suffer from a perpetual cold, but he was a strong man and controlled the nerve-centre of all activities in Peking. He also fell out of favour in later years. Ko Mo-jo was a Vice-Premier in rank but more useful as a frontman who made impressive speeches in domestic and foreign gatherings. He had been educated partly in Japan and had a Japanese wife at one time. Then there was the round-headed Wang Ping-nan, Secretary-General of the Foreign Office. His job was mainly administrative but he managed to survive all upheavals and is now the Chairman of the Society for friendly Relations with Foreign Countries, something like President of the Indian Council for Cultural Relations in India. He spoke German fluently and knew English.

I have tried to recapture my impressions and draw short pen portraits of a few Chinese leaders I came across. They are like us or anybody else, human but basically Chinese. In a one page note I sent to my Foreign Office after negotiating a rice deal in Peking I said: "Negotiations with China are like a game of patience. He who loses patience loses the game. China, whether communist or otherwise, will always remain basically Chinese." This is probably true of all ancient cultures—Indian, European, Russian, Chinese, Japanese or others, though national traits and character vary. Japanese are tough negotiators and can be blunt at times. Russians exhaust your patience, but sometimes get exhausted themselves in the process. Indians are always anxious to negotiate a deal successfully and in the process are generous and perhaps give away too much sometimes. The Chinese are polite, patient, never in a hurry and make the other side give in out of sheer exhaustion without getting exhausted themselves, unlike the Russians. They have a sense of history and destiny. If a bargain is to their advantage, they will strike immediately, if it is not, they will wait patiently for decades and persevere. Their tenacity is something one can learn from.

Sometimes, because of their isolation and introspective nature, they misjudge situations and other people and make mistakes, like we all do. They are apt to regard their own national interests as supreme and ignore those of others—hence all the trouble between them and India and the USSR. However, they are basically pragmatic people. With increasing contacts with the outside world, it is possible that their pragmatism may one day get the better of their dogmatic chauvinism and they may make a virtue of necessity and learn to live in peace, if not friendship, with their neighbours and others.

Neither Russia nor China, neither India nor America, has succeeded in creating a "new" man or changing the basic human character and values. It is, however, possible that one day the universality of man and the common interests of mankind may over-ride the individual profit motive, narrow national interests, chauvinistic and racial trends, colonial and imperialist ambitions. Then, perhaps, countries, big and small, capitalist, communist and non-aligned, may learn to live together in a peaceful and cooperative co-existence in One World. But, that day seems still far off.

9 China (Early Fifties)

Life in Peking in the early fifties was difficult in some ways, but not quite as difficult as in Stalin's Russia. Residential accommodation was available, there was no shortage of foodgrains, meat, fresh fruit and vegetables. Movement of foreigners beyond a radius of 30 Kms of Peking was forbidden though one could travel by train to Tientsin, Shanghai and Canton. The Chinese militia guarded all foreign Missions and questioned all Chinese before letting them in. Chinese domestic and clerical staff in the Embassy was helpful and polite, though they had to, as in Russia, make weekly reports to the Chinese authorities. But the secret police was not as "visible" as it was in Stalin's Moscow.

There was a sort of Asian puritanism combined with early Western evangelism pervading the party cadres, youth and students which was rarely seen in Moscow, except perhaps in the early days of the revolution under Lenin. Ideological remoulding camps for the anti-elements were held not in a routine way but with real revolutionary zeal. I was surprised to find my Chinese teacher, who belonged to the old school and wore a long gown and skull cap, reappear after an absence of a few weeks, in a blue cap and uniform worn by all the cadres. He gave a communist salute and said, "Please call me 'Thungchir' (comrade) and not 'Shien Shang' (Mister)." I was a little surprised and amused to see this man of over sixty, brought up and bred in the old Confucian tradition, transformed in a few weeks of ideological remoulding. They had not dealt with him harshly, in the physical or any other sense, but they had made him see the evils of bourgeois, capitalist Kuomintang rule. There was no doubt, as he said, that people like him now had to work harder but there was no theft, no fear of the policeman, gangster, or warlords any more; more necessities of life were available at fixed and reasonable rates. Life for the common man was certainly better and safer than it had been under the KMT rule.

For the intellectuals, softer but more subtle methods were adopted to "correct" them. In group meetings, in offices, educational and other institutions, they were first asked to make "self criticism." Then they were criticized by the group members who may be their colleagues, superiors or subordinates in rank. They had to answer the criticism and either confess or defend themselves. If they tried to justify themselves, then there was further criticism and this would go on and on until they made a full confession and recanted their past. The process was so gruelling that a few committed suicide in Peking, Tientsin and Shanghai. The vast majority confessed and tried to change their mode of thinking and living. The same process was adopted for housewives in their street meetings and factory bosses in their offices, and elsewhere, except perhaps in the higher echelons of the armed forces where political training was imparted through lectures on the "Thought of Mao Tse-tung" and his many theses on "Tactics and Strategy," "Principles and Practice," "Inner Party Contradictions," etc. No badges of rank were worn to indicate the status of an army officer; officers and other ranks ate in the same mess and shared the same food.

There was a nationwide campaign, affecting all sections of society, to weld them into one nation—politically, economically, socially, psychologically, culturally, and militarily. It was a colossal mass movement, unprecedented in human history, launched with "religious" fervour, fanatical zeal and puritanical perseverance, in a most ruthless and effective manner. It could have enormous potential for good or evil, depending on how long it lasted and what was its ultimate objective—national liberation or world-wide revolution, safeguarding of national sovereignty or expansion into and domination over neighbouring countries.

The Chinese leaders made loud noises about permanent revolution, inevitability of war, communist solidarity, internationalism, etc. The rift between them and the Russian leaders had not yet started. The sample atom bomb was not demanded by the Chinese and refused by the Russians until later. The bid for leadership of the communist world was yet to be made by China. They still used phrases like "the Socialist camp headed by the Soviet Union." Stalin was still alive (he died on 5 March 1953) and China honoured his portrait along with those of

Marx, Engels and Lenin in their 1 October and 1 May parades. China was busy with her own internal problems like land reforms, educational changes, consolidation of their hold on the outlying areas, border provinces and autonomous regions like Yunan, Sinkiang, Inner Mongolia, Tibet, etc. They had to deal with the KMT spy menace. On top of it all, they got involved in the Korean war.

China seemed to be going through a period similar to that of the pre-Stalin era in the USSR, though not identical with it. There were differences between the Russian and the Chinese experiences which were embodied in the "Thought of Mao Tsetung." China was lucky in having a military alliance with Russia and getting economic and technical cooperation from the Socialist camp. Russia had been alone at the time of its great October revolution and until World War II. In spite of this, the Soviet Union and communism had not only survived but expanded and emerged stronger in Europe after World War II. The Chinese had reason to believe that they would not only survive but be the dominating force in Asia and, possibly, in the communist world, after Stalin. This was not voiced openly until later, when Sino-Soviet differences surfaced, but there were some straws in the wind already.

For instance, the Chinese showed contempt for the Russians by calling them "the big-nosed brothers." Even street urchins would catch hold of their own small noses and run shouting "Big Nose" on seeing a Russian in the streets. Even some educated Chinese told us privately that the leadership of Russia in the communist world would not be tolerated by the Chinese and other Asian communists for long. There was a deliberate attempt to lump the Russians along with white Europeans and not regard eastern Siberia as part of Asia.

There was a joke going round in Tientsin, Shanghai and Peking at that time about "White Russians." There were quite a few of them scattered in those cities—remnants of the exodus that took place from the USSR during and after the October 1917 revolution. The Chinese said half seriously and half mockingly: "There are three kinds of Russians—Red, White and Carrots. The Carrots are those that are red from outside and white from inside." Carrots was a term of contempt used for those Russians who said they were communists but were adopt-

ing a *"bourgeois"* way of life. It was aimed mainly at the large
number of Russian women who used to flock to Chinese shops
on Sundays and buy Chinese silk, brocade, jade and jewellery.

Time would show whether the Russian *"bourgeois"* trends or
the Chinese "puritannical" way of life would prevail in the long
run. Already some Chinese officials and cadres were showing
signs of yielding to temptation and abusing their positions and
authority for personal gain. The Chief of Police in Peking was
publicly tried in a Peking park for accepting gold pens and
other presents as bribe. Mao Tse-tung had warned in his writings
of the "golden bullets" which the foreign and native *bourgeois*
elements would use to subvert the revolution. However, the vast
majority of the Chinese people were behind Mao and his party,
and lived a better and more secure life than ever before in the
Chinese history. Intellectuals, compradores and landlords may
have felt unhappy but they were only a few drops in the vast
ocean of the Chinese society.

I used to go to the central market on a Sunday morning
before sunrise and see the rickshaw pullers have their mooncake
and hot Chinese tea. They were a hardworking lot and plied
their pedicabs from dawn till dusk. Sometimes they would enter
into an argument with another fellow driver for taking the wrong
turn but they never came to blows. It was a civilized way of expressing yourself and talking out differences.

It reminded me of my negotiations with the Vice-Minister of
Foreign Trade who dragged on the talks until in sheer despera-
tion I told him the maximum price we were prepared to pay for
rice. He said he would have to telephone his Minister, went out
and asked me to wait. When I went to the toilet I saw him there
in a corner smoking a cigarette. He had not seen me and I turned back. He came into the negotiating room after a few minutes
and said he had consulted his Minister and "for the sake of Sino-
Indian friendship" the Minister had agreed to the price mentioned by me.

Even more dramatic and interesting was the "ritual" with
Chinese antique dealers who visited foreign homes on Sundays
to sell Chinese scrolls, paintings, porcelain, jade, etc. I would
ask the price and he would ask me to make an offer. I
deliberately suggested a very low price. He would pretend to feel
offended, wind up his "shop" and go up to the door, hesitate for

a while, look back and ask me to raise my bid. I would, in return, ask him to name his price. He would quote a figure twice the real price. This game would go on for an hour or so and then a bargain would be struck somewhere halfway between my first low figure and his first high figure. Both sides enjoyed this game but it was time consuming. The Chinese Government later opened a special shop for the diplomatic corps where they could get most things at fixed prices.

I recall visiting the house of Chi Pei-shih, the famous Chinese artist. He was about 90 then and died a few years later. He showed me some of his works, at my request, and presented me a scroll showing some birds in flight. I asked him the price but he would not accept any money. I then asked for another of his scrolls and insisted on paying for it, without any higgling and haggling. He told me the story of two American GI's in Peking during World War II. Each had bought a painting of his for the same price—one had five sparrows on it and the other six. The buyer of the five sparrow scroll who had in the meanwhile seen the other GI's scroll with six sparrows, came back to the artist and protested that he had been overcharged by a sixth. The artist smiled, picked up his brush and added another sparrow on to the scroll and sent the GI happy and satisfied.

I have mentioned these instances to indicate that national habits die hard. No matter whether China is communist or otherwise, the Chinese will always be Chinese, just as the Indians will always be Indians no matter what form of government they choose. It is true particularly of ancient cultures and civilizations. Perhaps, it is difficult for modern young civilizations, like that of the USA, to appreciate this—hence their failure to win the hearts and minds, respect and affection of ancient peoples.

Money cannot buy everything—certainly not command respect and affection. Power may instil fear for a while but it cannot bend a nation's will to subservience. A small but proud and determined nation, the Vietnamese, defeated the military and economic might of the USA. The Americans failed in Vietnam because they championed a wrong cause and compounded their mistake by misusing their military and economic power to humiliate and bring to heel a proud and ancient nation determined to safeguard its self-respect and independence.

Similarly, America failed to recognise the existence of the Peking Government from 1949 onwards and had to "open their eyes" and send their President to Peking and Shanghai in 1972. They forgot that they had refused to recognise the Soviet Government till 1933 when President Roosevelt corrected this mistake. In a similar misreading of reality and failure to appreciate the sensibilities of a proud and independent India, they dubbed "non-alignment" as "immoral" in the early and mid-fifties, but now regard it as a valid and viable policy for the developing countries.

Why did Stalin's Russia fail in its appreciation of the new Chinese Government's policy—or did it? Why did Stalin's Russia fail to appreciate the role of Gandhi and Nehru in India's struggle and consider India in the early fifties a mere appendage of British imperialism? And why did a resurrgent and revolutionary China break the Panch Sheel Agreement she had solemnly signed with India in 1954 and use massive force in 1962 to resolve the border dispute instead of using peaceful negotiations?

Is this because the new super-powers are apt to lose sight of the legitimate interests and aspirations of other countries and want to divide the world into their respective spheres of influence, as the old "great" imperialist powers did for centuries and then had to withdraw? Will the new super-powers learn the lessons of history or go on threatening each other and fighting their wars by proxy on other people's territory?

Is this an ideological war or one for merely gaining more territory and influence through brute force and economic influence? If it were basically an ideological war then there would be a real attempt to win the hearts and minds of the people and not use military and economic power to dominate them. If it were only an ideological battle, it would be inconceivable to find China pleading for the US forces remaining in the Pacific and the NATO forces not reducing their strength in central and western Europe, or taking sides with a pro-west military dictatorship in Pakistan against a democratic and non-aligned India. Most surprising of all is China calling Russia a "social imperialist" and considering it as her enemy number one. No less surprising is capitalist America wooing China and the Soviet Union leaning more towards "friendly" India than "fraternal" China.

All this seems to show that ideology is often used as a cover for one's national self-interest. International communism and international capitalism, freedom and democracy, are often used as catch words to idealise self-interest. The so-called "free" world of America's conception includes many countries with feudal and military dictatorship. Anti-communism is considered synonymous with freedom and democracy.

This is, perhaps, wherein lies the validity of the policy of non-alignment and peaceful coexistence, especially for newly independent and developing countries like India. But, how are they to safeguard their freedom, sovereignty, territorial integrity, independence and social and economic development as long as they are living in a world divided into two or three hostile military blocs? This was the dilemma before India soon after independence and still continues. Could India be friendly both with the USA and the USSR at the same time? Could India remain non-aligned and yet be equidistant from the great and super-powers, irrespective of their friendship or hostility to her? Was non-alignment the same as neutrality or did it mean the right to decide each question on its merits, as it affected one's national interests and the interests of world peace, independent of any big power pulls and pressures? How did India try to steer an independent course through the storms and upheavals of the early fifties, when she was suspect in America and the West, in Stalin's Russia and also in Mao's China? Was India non-aligned or merely sitting on the fence and playing the balancing monkey trick between two quarreling cats, trying to take advantage of both? Did non-alignment have any positive role to play in a world governed by military power and economic strength, ridden by ideological rivalry and military confrontation, and faced with the ghastly possibility of a nuclear holocaust?

The Korean war had ended in a cease-fire leading to an artificial division of one country, one people and one nation into two. The war in Indo-China was simmering still in spite of the Geneva Agreements of 1954. The Suez crisis was brewing and burst into war in 1956. Internally India was facing the hostile Naga underground movement in the North-East, backed and helped by China and Pakistan, the constant Pakistani attempts to create disruption in Kashmir, a move to divide India into linguistic states, a chronic food shortage, etc. In spite of all these external and internal difficulties, Nehru was able to maintain peace and progress internally, strengthen non-alignment abroad and enabled India to play the role of peacemaker in Korea, Indo-China, Congo, the Suez crisis, and elsewhere. How was it possible? Could such a policy and role last long? Would not internal pressures and external pulls tear it apart? How could such a policy be strengthened and made durable in a fast changing world? We shall try to examine these questions in the succeeding chapters.

Almost two-and-a-half years in Peking had been very educative and interesting. The early years of revolution are the most important, like those of a growing infant. I wanted to see something of ancient China too. Peita Ho, the seaside resort for diplomats, a few hours from Peking by train, was none too inspiring, and like any other seaside place, only less crowded. Tientsin with its brick houses and hybrid architecture still looked like a shanty town built by the foreign traders and occupation troops. Mukden (now Shenyang) was an industrial city with chimneys belching smoke all over the town—like Manchester or Birmingham in the 19th century. Shanghai which had been under occupation by the British, French, German and the Japanese troops was a hotchpotch of what had been before the liberation, a grand race course, posh night clubs, the main Shanghai club, tall buildings housing commercial offices, and the "other" Shanghai where lived the mass of China's industrial workers. The well-to-do Chinese still clung to their Spanish style bungalows, but knew they would have to quit and were sending part of their families and movable property to Hongkong, Singapore or the West, wherever they happened to have some relation or the other. Shanghai, in spite of signs of its erstwhile "grandeur" was a depressing piace. Canton was, perhaps, the worst example of colonial exploitation, with its Chinese population living in hovels or sampans, full of mosquitoes, dirt and disease. A few *pucca* buildings housed various offices and hotels for foreigners and high officials. Canton smelt of rotten eggs and decayed garbage. I liked it the least of all the Chinese cities and Peking the most.

The suburbs were, however, beautiful everywhere—fields cultivated intensively and with great care, not an inch of land wasted anywhere—especially between the Yangtse and the Yellow river. Temples and pagodas dotted the countryside. The Ming tombs were a monument not only to the Kings and Queens buried in them but even more to the sculptors who carved them. The Great Wall of Chiaa is deservedly a wonder of the world and a tribute to the tenacity, hard work and farsightedness of ancient China. It is a reminder that whenever China feels threatened she insulates herself from the rest of the world, draws inwards looking down upon "foreign barbarians." But when it is in an expansionist mood, high mountains and natural barriers do not stop its onward march—only superior might can.

I visited Hangchow and Soochow, not far from Shanghai, and found them beautiful. The lake at Hangchow and the view from the monastry on the hill-top was breathtaking. I had lunch with the monks in the temple. The dishes were all vegetarian but made to look like red and white meat and fish. It is said that the people of Hangchow and Soochow have the most beautiful complexion and texture, because of the temperate climate and sea air. As one goes up north, people look taller and tougher, the men have weather-beaten faces from the winter winds blowing down from Gobi desert. But most Chinese have a soft skin, a face without wrinkles and it is difficult to guess their age. Some attribute this partly to their racial genes and partly to their diet of pork. I would not hazard a guess.

I was impressed by the fact that no one was starving in new China. One reason, perhaps, was that they had no inhibitions regarding food and made delicacies and delicious dishes out of animals, insects, worms, birds, ducks, mice and even wild roots, leaves and the bark of some trees. There is a Chinese saying that you can eat anything that has its back to the sky. This is not something to be looked down upon, even though one may not agree with it. The Chinese culinary art, like their paintings, represents the height of civilization. It emphasises under-cooking so that the natural taste of an article of food is not ruined. But, it is not insipid like the British food or bland like the American food, nor tough like the Russian meat or over-spiced and over-fried like the Indian food. The Chinese food you get in some restaurants is really pseudo-Chinese, like "Chow-Mein." But you can get some excellent Chinese dishes in Kowloon, Singapore and China-towns all over the world. One should know what to order and wash it down with any number of cups of Chinese tea. The Chinese do not waste anything—feathers, skin,

meat, fat or bones. However, there are areas in the vast mainland of China which do use hot chillies in various dishes as in
Hunan (home of Mao Tse-tung), Szechuan and Kwangtung.
There is a simple concoction of powdered red chillies heated in
mustard oil (*La-Yo*) which when poured sizzling hot over plain
boiled rice makes it not only look appetising but also tastes delicious. Alas, the Chinese restaurants in Delhi, except the
Mandarin, do not cater to this simple but attractive appetiser.
Enough about Chinese cuisine; much has already been written
by others who are better qualified.

Peking, the immortal and inimitable "city of heaven," the
capital of the "Middle Kingdom," is the centre of China's
literary, cultural, political and other activities. It lends itself to
this role as no other city in China does. Nanking (the southern
capital) is a close second but not quite the same. Peking is ancient and has an enduring quality, like Varanasi (Banaras), Bodh
Gaya or Madurai in India. I felt sorry at leaving Peking but
happy that I was going back home.

Among the farewell parties by Chinese officials, diplomatic
colleagues and my own Embassy I enjoyed most the one given
to me by the Chinese peons and chauffeurs of our Embassy at
the famous Peking Duck restaurant. They waxed eloquent and
spoke in pure literary Mandarin and I was impressed by their
culture, wit and humour. They were genuine and sincere and I
was grateful to them for the help, cooperation and devotion they
had given me. I do not recall a single occasion when I had to
reprimand them. They were hard working and conscientious and
did their work without having to be reminded. This is a typical
Chinese trait which has sustained China through the ages. The
strength of a nation, like that of a chain, depends ultimately on
its weakest link.

Nehru visited China in 1954 and the USSR in 1955. On his
return in 1955 I asked him: "Sir, what are your impressions and
how would you compare the two?" He looked at me as if to say
"what cheek"! and asked "You have served in both the countries, how do you assess them?" I parried the question and said
my impressions were out of date and I was eager to learn the
impressions of a superior mind. He smiled, thought for a while
and then said: "The Chinese are a mystery to me. It is difficult
to know what is in their mind. They smile while saying the most

callous and ruthless things. Mao told me with a smile that
he was not afraid of an atomic war. If 300 million Chinese were
killed there would still be 300 million left to fight on. I wonder
if the translation of Marx in Chinese has the same nuances as
in other languages. Marxism may be capable of a different interpretation in the Chinese language, but war and death and destruction, science and technology, physics, chemistry and mathematics are not capable of different interpretations in different
languages." I asked "And what about the Soviets, Sir?" He
said, as if interrupted in his thoughts—"Oh, the Soviet leaders
seem to have settled down. They do not talk of permanent revolution and the inevitability of war. They are not isolated like the
Chinese leaders. They are more outspoken and can be provoked
to answer questions in a direct way. Their reactions are predic-
table and you can almost feel what is going on in their mind.
But, with the Chinese you never know and have to be prepared
for unexpected reactions. This may be partly due to their isolation but it is mainly the Chinese character I think." I have
quoted Nehru from memory and not from any document.

Finding Nehru in a reflective mood I ventured to ask how we
should deal with the Chinese in the given situation, particularly
after having signed the Panch Sheel Agreement with them.
Nehru said that it was a big question and we should deal with
each concrete problem as it arose without losing the larger perspective of avoiding war, safeguarding our national interests and
settling problems through peaceful negotiations. At the same
time we should be prepared for all eventualities.

This was in the days of "*Hindi-Chini Bhai-Bhai.*" Nehru had
hopes but no illusions about China. He was not certain how they
would act in the future, wanted India to be prepared for all
eventualities and at the same time pursue all possible avenues of
peace.

11   *Return of the Native*

There is something about the land of one's birth that goes deep down in one's blood and bones and can never be wiped out. It may not come to the surface or leap to the eye, but it is always there. Hence the unhappiness of Russian emigre's who always feel nostalgic about Mother Russia. The overseas Chinese, though less sentimental and more practical, still look upon China as their "Fatherland." Indians overseas are no exception and perhaps, even more attached to their motherland in spite of the relatively greater prosperity they enjoy abroad. I had been abroad less than six years since 15 July 1947, and felt the thrill and excitement of setting foot on the soil of independent India. It was one thing to interpret India's policies to foreign governments and peoples, but much more exciting to feel their direct impact, see them grow and develop at the very source and have a sense of participation in their formulation at home.

India had changed perceptibly in these six years. From Gandhi's India—struggling for independence and trying desperately to keep the sub-continent together and one, communal riots, the partition of India, the movement of almost ten million refugees—to Nehru's India,—more stable but reduced in size, trying to keep aloof from great power military blocs, creating a feeling of Asian solidarity, supporting anti-colonialism and opposing racist policies, laying the foundations of a new united India from Kashmir to Kanya Kumari (Cape Comarin), the merger of 500 odd "princely" states in the Union of India (thanks to Sardar Patel), the launching of the First Five year Plan in 1951 and the giant multipurpose dams for irrigation and power etc.

When Gandhi was shot dead by a Hindu fanatic, I was in Moscow and wept bitterly, alone in my hotel room. We felt lost and had not till then realised how deeply Gandhi had entered our hearts and souls. As Nehru said in his broadcast on the evening of 30 January 1948, "The light has gone out of our lives."

But Nehru proved a worthy successor and justified his nomination by Gandhi as his "political heir." The success of his foreign policy sometimes overshadowed his spartan work in building a new India—economically, politically, socially and culturally. He not only raised India's prestige abroad, as an independent peace-loving country, but created a new pride and awareness among Asian and African countries. He successfully launched the non-alignment policy and as it began to gain support among newly independent countries, it became a world-wide movement. But what was even more important, he laid the foundations of a democratic structure in India and tried to give it not only political meaning but also social and economic content, without which it could not survive. He was always a man in a hurry because he was dealing with stupendous problems involving the lives of more than 400 million people—most of them living below the poverty line or subsistence level.

After Gandhi's death, Nehru and Patel sank their personal and ideological differences and worked together until Patel's death in December 1950. Though a lonely man, Nehru was never alone. He had some able colleagues like Maulana Azad, Sardar Patel, Govind Ballabh Pant and others who had been with him through the long struggle for independence. But, what gave him more strength than anything else, was the love and affection, the faith and support he received from the vast majority of the Indian people. This sustained him through many difficult problems and periods. He in turn imparted his own faith, will and determination to the people. Nehru appealed to our minds and reason. It was a privilege and honour to work for and under such a man. I was happy to be back in Nehru's India which was pulsating with hope and action.

As Joint Secretary (East) in the External Affairs Ministry I had charge of East Asia. South-East Asia, Northern Divisions (Nepal, Bhutan, Sikkim) and NEFA (now Arunachal) and Controller General of Emigration. Soon after joining the Ministry, I undertook a tour of NEFA. It fascinated me, because of what I had seen and read about "minorities" in the USSR and China. I submitted a report which Nehru seemed to like, making some practical as well as idealistic recommendations. He ordered it to be circulated to the concerned ministries for follow-up action.

One evening, early in 1953, Nehru had invited some Indian and foreign dignataries to dinner including Lady Mountbatten, Sir B.N. Rau and others. I was asked to be present. When cigars were passed round after dinner I peeped into a box and found about one foot long Cuban cigars in it which a Cuban delegation had presented to Nehru. I ventured to take one and was rolling it in my hands before lighting when Nehru spotted me handling the long cigar. He said, "Young man, you seem to be doing well with this cigar. Is this also what they teach you in the diplomatic service?" I replied boldly, "I could not miss smoking a real Cuban cigar, sir." He smiled and said, "Report at Palam airport at seven in the morning. You have seen something of Russia, America and China. Now I want you to see something of India."

I reported at Palam five minutes before time because I knew Nehru was always punctual. Seeing me in a closed collar jacket and trousers he said teasingly, "Ah, so you have turned Chinese?" I replied the Chinese uniform had a detached double collar while mine followed the Indian collar, stiched and single. He examined my coat collar closely and said, "You may be right." He himself wore *churidars* (tight fitting trousers) and *achkan* (long flowing coat) on formal occasions and a home-spun Jawahar jacket (without sleeves) for informal occasions.

A few weeks later I found N.R. Pillai, Secretary General, External Affairs Ministry, barge into my office and say, "So, Tikki you are the culprit." I did not quite understand and asked "Why?" He looked at my closed collar coat and said, "You have influenced the Prime Minister in ordering your closed collared coat, and trousers as our formal dress." I had done nothing of the sort. It may have been that Nehru wanted to prescribe a simple and yet dignified formal dress instead of the flowing *achkan* and *churidars* (which were reserved for ceremonial occasions) or the proposed gold collar with stripes and a floral design. Pillai said with a chuckle "Wait till the sticky heat of the monsoons and then you will realise what you have done." He was right, but we found a way out by making the CCC (closed collar coat) of *Khadi* or home-spun linen which absorbs heat and moisture. And the CCC has now become the formal dress for almost all officials and non-officials including most politicians and even workers in the rural areas. It is much more tidy and presentable than the flowing *achkan* or the billowing *dhoti*. The credit for popularising it goes to Nehru's imagination, though he himself stuck to his Jawahar jacket and *churidars* (plus *achkan* for formal occasions). I often found him in an *achkan* or *kurta* with repairs and patches stitched or sewn on the texture. He was meticulous about everything, including his dress, but was not a snob. While he would not wear Gandhi's loin cloth, he never felt shy of wearing repaired clothes.

At the airport, Nehru ordered all his entourage to board the plane and came up the gangway last of all, as was his habit. He waved to his colleagues and others who had come to see him off, settled down in his seat and started reading a book. No sooner was the plane aloft, he kept the book on one side and surveyed the scene below. He took delight in pointing out to all of us the various places of historical, industrial and agricultural importance, just like a teacher, until we landed in Bihar near the Damodar Valley Project.

He performed the opening ceremony of the Konar Thermal Plant, but before pressing the button, he jumped down from the podium to pacify the huge disorderly crowd, asked them all to sit down, even pushing some down with his own hands. His security staff were perturbed but the people loved it and sat down in pin-drop silence to hear him. A hundred policemen could not have achieved in an hour what Nehru did single-handed in five minutes.

He started his speech, extempore, in Hindi, more like a teacher's monologue than an oration. His eyes lit up at "seeing" the silence of the huge crowd of villagers and workers. He started slowly, almost haltingly, but warmed up as he went on, "These are our new temples, mosques and churches—these huge structures that will give electricity to the villages, water for the fields, and employment to thousands of workers. We must work hard and construct them in every part of the country without which the country cannot progress." He went on in this vein for half-an-hour and his speech was interspersed with shouts of "*Pandit Nehru Zindabad*" (Long live Pandit Nehru) and "*Bharat Mata Ki Jai*" (Victory to mother India) from the large crowd. At the end of his speech he asked the audience to repeat thrice after him "*Jai Hind*" (Hail India) and the crowd joined with full fervour, louder and louder each time. Nehru was not a demagogue but spoke in simple phrases, intelligible to the common man and touching his basic needs. But, sometimes he would stray into the field of foreign policy and international affairs, and point out the horrors of atomic war and the need for disarmament etc. Most of this went above the heads of his simple audience at times, but they listened with attention and loved to see and hear him. Such was his rapport with the people.

It was a most heart-warming experience after the rehearsed orations I had heard in America or the boring, repetitive written speeches delivered in Stalin's Russia and Mao's China. Would the Indian experiment in democracy succeed where others had failed? Would Nehru be able to inspire the politicians and the bureaucracy, to enthuse the masses and give them a feeling of participation in the great adventure of building new India as he put it? I was keeping my eyes and ears open and absorbing an entirely new experience of Nehru's love for and faith in the masses.

From Konar we went for a boat trip on the lake beside Maithon Dam. Dr B.C. Roy, Chief Minister of West Bengal and Bihar Chief Minister S.K. Sinha, were also present besides Nehru's daughter, Indira Gandhi. She used to remain in the background those days and concerned herself mainly with looking after her father. It must have been a great education for her to travel with him everywhere and "discover" India at first hand, instead of merely reading about it in books. She was shy, unassuming, aloof and quiet and did not show much outward interest in party politics. It was only in 1959 that she was elected president of the Indian National Congress. She was a shrewd observer and Nehru seemed to show some consideration for her views even at that time.

We then flew to Jamshedpur where we saw the steel mill and molten iron being moulded into shape by flash light at night. There were some disputes between the management and labour and rivalry between various trade unions. The Tatas were somehow able to pacify them all for the time being. I wondered why we could not give the workers a stake and a share in industry so that they would not have reason to go on strike so often. No strikes occured or were permitted in Mao's China, and Stalin's Russia. Why should we always imitate only Western capitalist patterns and ideas which did not suit us? Why could we not give workers a say in management and a stake in industry so that there would be less incentive for strikes? However, I kept these thoughts to myself not wishing to appear presumptuous or opinionated. I did, however, mention to Nehru how some workers had been kept away from meeting him. He was furious, called the man in charge, and listened to the grievances of the workers and gave them some satisfaction.

We took off for Calcutta and from there for Imphal in Manipur. What a peaceful valley, what delightful, clean and simple people, what talent in music, dance and drama they possessed. We saw some of their cultural activities and visited the cottage industries centre where they wove beautiful patterns in multi-coloured threads. I was not interested in local politics but got involved in it when Daiho, the leader of the *Mau* Nagas and some *Kuki* tribal leaders met me. We had some Naga tribes in NEFA also and had to guard against the Naga Hills District agitation under Phizo spilling over into the Tuensang Frontier Division (then in NEFA). The *Kukis* and *Mau* Nagas did not get along with each other, nor with the *Maitis* in Manipur valley. In Tamenglong sub-division of Manipur, Rani Gaideleau was still popular and did not see eye to eye with Phizo. Violence had not yet erupted in Naga Hills District. Phizo had been launching a "peaceful" agitation till then. Things were left pretty much to the Assam Government who made a mess of it, by ill-treating the Nagas, sending Assamese or non-Naga officials to administer them. These officials looked down on the Nagas and there was not much love lost between the two. The Chief Minister and other Ministers had not gone beyond Kohima and Mokokchaung even once.

Nehru had invited U Nu, Premier of Burma, to visit the Naga areas of India and U Nu inivited him to visit the adjoining Naga areas of Burma. The aim was to exchange ideas and experiences and work out a cooperative and coordinated plan, suited to each area, so that the problems of one would not spill over to the other. U Nu, accompanied by his Chief Secretary, came to join Nehru at Imphal. The meetings at Imphal and Mau, on the way to Kohima, were good and tribal folk came in their ceremonial dresses to welcome Nehru and his distinguished guest. However, Kohima presented a different picture, thanks to the miscalculations, inefficient handling and wishful thinking of the Chief Minister and his staff. Although the Intelligence Bureau had information that the Nagas in Kohima might boycott the Prime Minister's meeting, the Assam Government was of the opinion that this was a false alarm. They probably thought that the Nagas would not be inhospitable to Nehru, who had done so much for them; they (Assam Government) wanted to exploit his pressence and that of U Nu for their own ends.

Nehru was a democrat to the core and did not want to question the State Government's judgment unless he had proof to the contrary. Some young Nagas, among them a public relations officer of the Phizo's NNC (Naga National Council) came to see me and invited me to their office where I drank *Zhu* (Naga beer) in Bamboo mugs with them. They told me that if Nehru did not allow the NNC to read out their memorandum, they would leave the meeting. I conveyed this to Nehru, but he brushed it aside, as the Chief Minister had assured him to the contrary. Things happened as the young Nagas had told me and as the Intelligence Bureau had forewarned. Nehru was naturally upset, especially in the presence of U Nu, but he took it in his stride. He said to the Nagas that they could have autonomy within the Indian Union, that they were as much part of India as any other state, any Naga could rise to the highest position and enjoy equal rights under the Constitution. Their tribal customs and cultural heritage would be respected, etc. But, 2,000 Nagas, under Phizo's influence, walked away from the meeting and only a few hundred remained to hear Nehru.

This came as a shock to Nehru who had addressed much larger and more hostile gatherings. He had converted to his side a million strong crowd on the Calcutta maidan when some elements even fired shots to upset the meeting. The Kohima incident opened Nehru's eyes to the mishandling and miscalculations of the Assam Government and its officials in Naga Hills District. He wanted to have a fresh took at the Naga problem. Phizo precipitated events by launching violence and the Naga problem was not sorted out until after Nehru's death.

We tried several times to arrive at a peaceful understanding with the hostile underground Nagas but Phizo's wing in the NNC thwarted them. I recall meeting Phizo's number two Imkongmeren Ao (Vice President of the NNC) in a jungle hideout, 10 miles from Mokukchang in 1955. I had received feelers from him and had taken Nehru's previous permission to meet him because he was a "proclaimed offender." When the Assam Government learnt about my meeting with Imkongmeren, the Chief Minister sent an angry telegram to Nehru saying he could have arrested me for meeting a proclaimed offender clandestinely. Nehru sent a brief reply that this was done with his previous approval. The stubborn attitude of the state government and the obstinacy of Phizo jeopardised the possibility of a peaceful settlement of the Naga problem in its earlier stages.

From Kohima we flew with U Nu to Sinkaling Khamti in the Burmese Naga area and landed our Dakota in a rice field. The Burmese Nagas were hardly literate as compared to our Nagas (who had 40 per cent literacy), less politically conscious, and had been left more or less undisturbed by the Burmese Government. However, the latter had taken precautions not to allow any foreign missionaries in the area unlike in our Naga Hills District where some foreign missionaries had played a subversive role. There was singing and dancing by the Nagas in which Nehru, U Nu and we all joined. A typical Burmese meal was served with the delicious *Dhurian* curry, smelling to high heaven. Nehru and I enjoyed it; other members of our party merely sniffed it and gave up. I even smoked the Burmese "atom bomb," a local cigar which set off sparks in all directions. Nehru did not approve of it, but was in a tolerant mood.

After lunch Nehru asked me to find out from the Burmese how they had tackled the problem of the ICS remnants in Burma and report direct to him whether we could adopt similar methods.

I learnt from U Nu and his Chief Secretary that they had adopted a very simple method. On gaining independence, they had retired all ICS officers with proportionate pensionary benefits and re-employed those whom they considered suited to the new set up on new Burmese pay-scales. Their problem was not as big in magnitude as ours. The number of ICS officers left in Burma was less than 50 or so, while it was ten times more in India. Burma did not have a civil service entrenched in power as in India. Indian political leadership was also more tolerant and Sardar Patel had assured the Indian members of the ICS that their previous rights and privileges would be safeguarded.

I consulted a few younger members of the ICS and we felt that safeguards and privileges were needed to protect the weaker sections of society and not those like the ICS who claimed that they stood on their merit and could compare with any other civil service in the world. As directed by Nehru, I recommended to him that we should follow the Burmese experiment in the principle. I was confident that the younger members of the Service would continue on new pay-scales, though some older and senior members might choose to retire. They would have the choice of being re-employed on new scales plus retain their full pension. It was, however, upto the government to employ only those whom they considered suited to the new requirements. This would remove the discrimination between the ICS and the other All India Services.

Nehru listened to me patiently, smiled and then said, "But can you persuade your seniors to voluntarily give up their privileges and endorse your recommendation?" For the first time in my service under Nehru I said "No" and added, "You are the only person who may be able to do this." He wanted a solution to emerge from the ICS itself rather than impose it on them. It was an idealistic and democratic approach, but I had my doubts about its success.

A few days later I was cold-shouldered by three senior Secretaries to the Government of India who called me a "renegade." Nehru had spoken to them about the matter. All that they and some senior members of the Service would voluntarily give up were petty things, like a free passage to the UK every three years, that were already obsolete and enjoyed only by the pre-1924 entrants to the Service. Thus ended an attempt by Nehru to integrate the ICS with the new All India Services. No privileged class would give up its privileges without some legal pressure, whether it was the landlords, the princes or the ICS. He knew this but was reluctant to exercise such a pressure on the ICS as Sardar Patel had given them a solemn assurance and Nehru did not want to go back on it. He was too much of a democrat and believed in the process of education and persuasion before using other legal means. The result was that many of his far-sighted policies were obstructed or even sabotaged in their implementation by vested interests among the bureaucrats and the politicians.

One Sunday morning, when Nehru always attended office, I

found him in a relaxed mood and asked, "Sir, why do you keep people in key positions of power who do not believe in your policies or ideals?" He thought for a moment and then replied, "Because, youngman, those who believe in my policies and ideals will always be with me; it is the others—and they are not few—whom I have to carry along with me." That was his way of doing things, but it became a drag in later years. Although he took a bold and courageous stand on amending Article 31 of the Constitution to effect land reforms, this legislation remained, by and large, only on paper and was not implemented in most of the states, where majority of the congress party members depended on or came from the landowning classes. But, his insistence on the passing of the Hindu Code Reform Bill was an instance where he succeeded in bringing about a silent and peaceful social revolution in Hindu society because he stood firm. On the question of untouchability, although Gandhi had brought about a virtual revolution in favour of the untouchables, the law remained practically a dead letter because of entrenched orthodoxy and casteism in the rural areas, and the lack of political will among the State Governments.

In spite of Vinoba Bhave's valiant efforts through his *Pad Yatra* (pilgrimage on foot from village to village) his *Bhudan* (land gift) movement got mostly barren and *Usar* (saline) land from the land-lords. Nehru visited Vinoba in a village in Bihar, during this trip, as he was lying ill with malaria and refused to take any allopathic medicine. Nehru pleaded with him to take anti-malaria mixture which, as Nehru pleaded, "is 99.5 per cent water." But Vinoba would not agree. He then introduced me to Vinoba as a "young diplomat just returned from China." I ventured to ask Vinoba, in Nehru's presence, whether it would not be worthwhile to try the experiment of collective farms (as had been done in China) on the *Bhudan* land he had received. He replied very gently, "It is not easy as the Indian tiller is wedded to his soil." As a com-promise I suggested cooperative farming where the individual ownership would remain, but expensive tools, implements and other services and inputs would be on a cooperative basis. He replied he would examine it.

I was deeply impressed by Vinoba's humility, simplicity, since-rity, honesty and dedication to truth and non-violence. But, I wondered whether his methods could really solve our huge agrarian problem. Was he not trying, as the communists had tried and failed, to change human nature and create a "new man?" However, he did produce a nation-wide consciousness about the agrarian problem, as Gandhi had done about untouchability. This could prepare the ground and create a congenial atmosphere for ushering-in and implementing land reforms on a nationwide scale.

The last leg of Nehru's week long tour, was in Silchar and Aijal, in the Lushai Hills, now called Mizoram. Unlike the Nagas, the Lushais or Mizos were soft-spoken and mild-mannered. They were fond of lilting, romantic and sentimental songs which they played on the guitar and danced to, unlike the war-like drums and dances of the Nagas. When we arrived at Aijal, a group of young men and women were playing a beautiful melody on the guitar and singing and dancing to it. I asked them what it meant and they translated; "Dear Nehru, we have been waiting a long time for you. You have come and gladdened our hearts. We are sad you are leaving early in the morning. Can't yon stay, stay on with us?" I mentioned it to Nehru and he was visibly moved.

A group of young boys and girls, surrounded Nehru on the lawns of the Circuit House at Aijal. He mimicked and made faces and established immediate rapport with them. They caught hold of each other's hands, made a ring round him and danced to their heart's content and his. Nehru had the capacity to feel like a child with children. They called him *"Chacha* (uncle) Nehru," and his birthday is celebrated as Children's Day.

In the afternoon and evening Nehru received numerous delegations and groups of people presenting their problems and grievances. There was no drinking water facility, no water for irrigation, their trade with East Pakistan had been closed by the Pakistan Government, etc. These were not difficult or complicated problems but real and needed an urgent solution. The Assam Government had done precious little about them. We were thus faced with a situation in Mizoram which became a serious problem, after a few years, when Phizo's influence penetrated there with the blessings of the Chinese and the Pakistan Governments. Nehru did his best, laid down excellent policies and issued far-sighted directives regarding the treatment of tribal folk and their problems. Alas, these were honoured more in their breach than observance by the local governments and authorities.

Late that night when Nehru was still meeting people, I yawned. Nehru looked sharply at me but said nothing. Then Indira came and asked me if I had a tablet for headache. I gave her one. Nehru saw me giving it to her and flared up, "What is the matter with you young people, taking tablets for a headache? I am much older, work harder and have never had a headache in my life." That was true and I felt ashamed of myself. Indira took his remarks in her stride. She must have heard them before. She swallowed the pill and retired. I had to remain in attendance till Nehru finished with his visitors at 2 AM.

We left next morning by road for Silchar and then flew to Calcutta and back to Delhi. It was an experience worth having. I understood my country's problems better in those seven days than I had in the previous seven years. The "prodigal" had returned home to become a "native" of his independent motherland.

So ended a trip of over a week with Nehru. I was struck by Nehru's faith in the people and his belief in the democratic, peaceful method of tackling serious problems. I had always admired Nehru from my student days when I had first met him at the University of Allahabad. I found in Nehru, the Prime Minister, the some old spark of revolutionary idealism, flashes of temper, and impatience with inefficiency, but a much more mellow and tolerant attitude to the tools and implements available to him. He could have been a dictator and delivered the goods much more quickly, but preferred the slower and peaceful democratic method.

12   Nehru's Policy and External Affairs Ministry
(Nepal, Bhutan, Sikkim)

Work in the Foreign Office was interesting enough but more so because of Nehru's inspiring leadership and guidance. He set the tone and example, maintained a very high standard of efficiency, disposed of files promptly, gave clear and cogent instructions, often dictated telegrams regarding various situations before we had had time to put up our drafts, and yet found time to tour extensively in India and abroad and receive visitors every day for 3 to 4 hours. He was both Prime Minister and Foreign Minister, apart from being Chairman of the Planning Commission and Minister for Atomic Energy. He worked 14 and sometimes 16 hours a day. And yet he was full of energy and never used the elevator to his office but jumped 2 to 3 steps at a time up the stairs. It was difficult to keep pace with him. His example inspired us and we tried to do the best we could.

Nehru encouraged initiative and drive and welcomed intelligent, honest and sincere advice, based on facts and supported by reason, even though he did not always agree with it. NEFA was directly under the administration of our Ministry, and the Northern Division (Nepal, Bhutan and Sikkim) depended largely on personal contacts with the rulers and people of these States. I had direct access to Nehru regarding these areas. He was business-like, precise and did not waste time in unnecessary conversation. But he was always polite, human and considerate and willing to hear your viewpoint. His method was to look at a problem in the world perspective, at it affected India's own national interests, India's relations with other countries and world peace. Maintenance of peace and peaceful methods of solving international problems was a passion with him. He often talked of expanding the "area and climate of peace."

Nehru appeared an "aristocrat" because of his lineage and education, but he was the greatest democrat of his time. His

famous anonymous article on himself, first published in 1936, is
a remarkable piece of self-criticism. His respect for Parliament
and parliamentary conventions was well known. He never missed
attending Parliament when in Delhi and spent the whole day in
his adjoining office room there. He would rush to the House to
the rescue of a colleague in difficulty, to reprimand unparlia-
mentary behaviour or to defend his own policies and portfolios.
He kept everybody on their toes, inside and outside Parliament.
He would often rewrite the drafts of answers to questions in
Parliament, put up by us, and his answers were always honest,
sincere, giving as much information as possible, and not evasive
or merely technical.

He found time to walk into the rooms of the Secretaries and
even Joint Secretaries in the Ministry, just to say "hello" and
see how they were working. One afternoon in 1955 he walked
into my room unannounced and said, "By the way, Tikki, what
do you mean by calling yourself "Samyukta Sachiva" on your
sign-board in Hindi? It means "United" and not "Joint Secretary." I replied sheepishly that this was the best equivalent I
could find unless he preferred "Saha Sachiva" which would mean
"Assistant Secretary." He quipped with good honour, "I don't
want to demote you, but try to find a better phrase." He was a
great stickler for precision and chose his words carefully and
well. Even in his extempore speeches, when he was thinking
aloud and ideas used to wander and ramble through his vast
mind, there was a link and cogency in his arguments.

His ideas came much faster than his words and to take a breath
he would use such phrases as "And so," "But," "as I was saying,"
etc., in his public speeches. I was once introduced to a young
Secretary in the US Embassy. When I asked her name, she replied "Oh, don't you know? Your Prime Minister is very fond of
using my name in almost every Hindustani speech." (Her surname was Lekin, which in Hindustani means 'but'). He always
says, "India is great, *Lekin* not militarily. We are making progress, *Lekin* we have a long way to go etc." It was true and we
had a good laugh.

N.R. Pillai was Secretary-General, R.K. Nehru, Foreign Secretary and S. Dutt, Commonwealth Secretary. They all belonged
to the ICS, as did most of the six Joint Secretaries like C.S. Jha,
Rajeshwar Dayal, myself. We were not trained diplomats but

had volunteered for the Indian Foreign Service at the time of independence, and had been "permanently" seconded to it. Some members were taken directly from the army, navy and air force, trade, commerce, law and some ex-princes, etc. They were appointed as ambassadors or in junior positions depending on their age, experience, qualifications, etc. The subordinate ministerial staff was also grouped together in various grades of IFS (B). Nehru tried to weld us all together into a homogenious family, but interservice rivalries and jealousies, the class structure and composition of the service, made it into a heterogenious hotch-potch. The new entrants who came in through open competitive examinations were a fine lot and very promising, but many of them soon imbibed the mannerisms and methods of their seniors and thought of themselves as an elitist group, a cut above the IAS and other services.

This was an unhappy trend but inevitable when the old bureaucracy was juxtaposed in a new situation requiring different qualities and a new outlook. Some of us tried to integrate the various branches of the Ministry into one Service. We also proposed an interchange between IFS and other All India Services, like IAS at junior levels. This would have given wider experience to the IAS and dug deeper the roots of the IFS into the soil of India, but vested interests prevented this. I hope that some consideration will still be given to this idea.

There was a communication gap between the Ministry and our Missions. People were posted abroad for 10 to 15 years continuously. They lost touch with realities and changing profiles at the grass roots in the country and thought that the whole world revolved round the country of their accreditation. They would indulge in loose talk, after a few drinks, and run down their own government's policies before foreigners. "Nehru is a Communist, he is too friendly with the Chinese and Russians; he is taking the country down the drain towards socialism," etc. were some of the remarks they made to please their foreign counterparts. Fortunately such people were not many.

These were some of our teething troubles and Nehru did not have time to look into these "toothaches." It was for the senior officers to remedy them. But, they were too busy with files and paper work. Parkinson's law was in full operation. The more officers and staff, the greater the volume of paper work created and produced, and the less work done. There was too much concentration in the Central Secretariat and even in the States on "keeping the record straight" rather than on action or performance.

I was glad to be dealing with NEFA, Nepal, Bhutan and Sikkim where paper work did not impress anyone because urgent problems cropped up almost every week demanding immediate action. I spent almost half of my time touring these areas.

One day the Nepalese Ambassador called on me with a complaint that our people on the Indo-Nepal border had "abducted" some Nepalese rhinos and wild elephants. He wanted these animals to be returned. I replied that if his men could "identify" they were welcome to take the animals back. The Ambassador saw the point and laughed. I heard no more such complaints.

Nepal has close cultural, religious, historical and traditional links with India. Most of its trade and commerce, imports and exports were with or through India. Black marketeers and smugglers on both sides had thriving business because of the long and open border. We tried to check it but vested interests, on both sides, opposed any checks.

The people of Nepal are proud and patriotic. The Gurkha soldiers in the Indian Army are some of the finest. A small landlocked country like Nepal, wedged between two big neighbours, India and China, found it tempting to play one against the other and exploit their differences. This was, however, a short-sighted policy, not likely to last long. China, Pakistan and some western embassies in Nepal also tried to rouse anti-Indian feelings there and succeeded upto a point. But, the main fault lay with India and Nepal for not coming to a mutual understanding of their common interests.

There is psychological fear in a small country against a big neighbour. While Nepal was afraid of China, she took India for granted. The people of India and Nepal are like kith and kin and any attack by India on Nepal is inconceivable. Nepal's stability, and security are important for India's own security and vice-versa. India extended full cooperation to Nepal politically, economically and in defence matters.

China did not seem to like this and protested to Nepal against the presence of the Indian Military Mission in Kathmandu and technical personnel at their border checkposts. We offered Nepal reciprocal facilities in India, but they were so frightened of the Chinese protests that we had to give in to their demand for withdrawal of our Military Mission and technical personnel. Unlike the British, we had helped Nepal to gain international recognition of their sovereign independent status and membership of the UNO. We respected their wishes. At the same time, Nepal expected India to pull her chestnuts out of fire, internally and externally. A one-sided relationship was not durable and had to change. She could not apply double standard towards India and China. While the Chinese project aid to Nepal was mostly in the form of cheap Chinese consumer goods, Nepal insisted on discrimination against Indian manufactures. However, we had to appreciate Nepal's delicate position and did not press the matter.

A very ticklish problem was that of the Nepali Congress leaders who came to India for safety and security against threats of assassination by the King's agents in Nepal. Soon they began to organise and arm the Nepalese guerillas for raids into Nepal. The King's government did not like this and thought we were aiding and abetting them. The truth was that we were not giving them any arms and were discouraging them from indulging in violent, political activities. But, there was widespread sympathy for them among the Indian people; most of these Nepalese leaders had been educated in India and had also participated in India's struggle for freedom. We did not arrest them or force them to go back to almost certain torture and death but tried to informally impress on the King and his advisers to come to some political understanding. This was misconstrued as "interference" in their internal affairs. We gave up the attempt.

One evening I had a talk with JP (Jayaprakash Narayan) who asked me why arms and other assistance was not given to the Nepalese exiles in India and their followers in Nepal. I pointed out that this would be against international law and morality and might divide Nepal into two hostile camps—one pro-India and another pro-China, which would give an excuse to China to send arms to the anti-Indian elements in Nepal. JP appreciated the position and did not press the matter.

On another occasion, JP made a similar proposal of giving arms to the Tibetans. I pointed out the possibility of its doing more harm than good and asked if he would have accepted such a proposal if he was the Prime Minister of India. JP kept quiet and did not raise the matter again.

The last such occasion was when we met in my office in April 1971. He wanted the Government to recognise Bangladesh immediately and treat the emigre' government of Tajuddin as its lawful government. I replied that we would certainly recognise Bangladesh as an independent country when the Bangladeshis had established their control over a sizeable part of their country. To do so in April 1971, would seem like putting up a puppet regime which would not carry conviction anywhere in the world. JP did not quiet believe me then and said he would sound world opinion and go on a world tour. The Prime Minister encouraged the idea and gave him every assistance possible. The late Prof. Sisir Gupta of Jawaharlal Nehru University accompanied him. JP came back from his tour disillusioned and disappointed. He had the courtesy to meet me then and again in December 1971, when we had recognised Bangladesh. He had doubted our word in April but had the generosity to admit in December that we were right.

Nehru had always encouraged me to meet JP whom I found to be a man of great integrity, honesty and dedication. Nehru wanted and needed him. It is a pity he did not accept any office of responsibility because of which his ideas were, sometimes vague and impractical.

Coming back to the External Affairs Ministry, I may mention a few points regarding Bhutan and Sikkim. Both had special treaties with India, which were different in form and content. Sikkim was a "protectorate" of India while Bhutan was treated as a sovereign country which had agreed to be guided by India in the conduct of her external relations. The future evolution of the two would depend on their internal developments and their relations with India. In the case of Sikkim it was inconceivable that she could continue as a "protectorate" of India for long or that India would like such a mill-stone round her neck. After the developments in Tibet and its absorption by China, the Sino-Indian border became a live one and the importance of Sikkim for India's defence and security vis-a-vis China increased greatly, India could not be indifferent to what happened in Sikkim and helped her in economic development and political stability. Under letters exchanged after the Treaty of 1950, India was responsible for "good government." The Maharaja of Sikkim had been a member of the Indian Chamber of Princes before India's independence and had never enjoyed "sovereign" status as Bhutan and Nepal had. Had India wished Sikkim's merger it could have easily done this in 1947-48 when the people rose against the ruler, surrounded his palace and he virtually asked for merger. But, at that time, there was no Chinese threat to India. Tibet was still a buffer between India and China and it was thought desirable to leave Sikkim as another buffer, like the British had done. With the merger of Tibet with China in 1951, and the consolidation of Chinese hold over Tibet, the situation had changed. Sikkim could no longer be a buffer, with Tibet armed to the teeth by the Chinese troops. India had to strengthen her defence, communications and security in and through Sikkim.

Large-scale internal autonomy was still enjoyed by Sikkim and this could perhaps have continued as long as defence, security and communications were looked after by India and Sikkim cooperated fully. But the new ruler, Palden Thondup Namgyal, under the influence of his newly-wedded American wife and her friends started giving pin-pricks to India on matters, big and small. He antagonised 75 per cent of the population which was of Nepalese origin and stifled democratic elements among *Bhutias* and *Lepchas* also.

I knew Thendup personally since 1953. I tried to argue with him day after day and night after night in Delhi and Gangtok. He would agree with me but as soon as he went back he would change his mind. He did not get along with any one of India's several able Dewans and representatives in Sikkim—from John Lall and Rustomji to Baleshwar Prasad and Apa Pant to Bahadur Singh respectively.

One of my last efforts as foreign secretary was in September 1972 to have a democratic autonomous Sikkim as long as defence, communications and security remained with us, and remove the incongruous and ugly appellation of "protectorate" from the Treaty. A draft agreement was drawn up and approved. Thondup said he would send it back duly signed from Gangtok within a week. He never did, because some foreign advisers misled him into believing that he had a cast-iron case for independence. I sent word to him, after a week, that the opportunity would not recur, but he showed no response.

What happened after that is common knowledge. He tried to

divide and suppress his people and set up a puppet Sikkim Youth Forum comprising a few of his pet officers. The people rose in revolt. The Government of India in my opinion, acted with caution and hesitatingly accepted the result of the referendum in Sikkim and the unanimous resolution of the duly-elected Sikkim Assembly wanting merger with India. There was nothing wrong or immoral about it. It hardly lies in the mouth of China or other countries to criticise us on this. They have merged much larger areas and territories than Sikkim with their own, in times past and recent, through violence, force, terror and war. India accepted the merger of Sikkim through peaceful, democratic and constitutional means.

Thondup was a good friend but given to bouts of depression. His first wife Tsangde La, was a fine person and kept him steady. But his American marriage, perhaps, made him believe that through extraneous influence he could ensure American and Canadian support for his claim to independence. Some junior representatives of the USA and Canada also encouraged him in this. He can perhaps still play a positive and constructive role if he recognises realities and does not entertain dreams of becoming an absolute monarch.

I recall several trips to Nathu La, the border pass between India and Tibet (height 13,500 feet). My first one was on 23 December 1953, with George La (Thondup's younger brother) when a blizzard overtook us at the pass and we had to run down for our lives, three kilometres below. My last visit was in 1966. I recall greeting the Chinese commander standing across the barbed wire at Nathu La. To my *"Ni Khao Ma"* (how do you do), he replied brusquely *"Wo Khao-Ni Khao"* (I OK-you OK?) He was greatly agitated at my presence and muttered something in anger. I asked him in Chinese *"Way Shamma"* (Why, what is the matter?). He pointed to my presence and the barbed wire. I pointed to the Nehru Tableau on the pass and said, *"Indo Jan Chungko Jan Lao Phengyo"* (Indian and Chinese are old friends) —a phrase I had heard often in Peking—and left him wondering who I was and why I was there.

I should like to pay a tribute to the Indian Jawans and their officers whom I saw living in snow-covered bunkers at a height of 10,000 to 13,000 feet ready to defend the integrity and sovereignty of India at Nathu La. They had a keen sense of humour.

Whenever the Chinese put on their usual propaganda on the loud speaker across the border for our troops, our jawans would put on loud Indian music. Ultimately there was a gentleman's agreement to put on Chinese and Indian music only alternately and no propaganda stuff. Thus ended the Battle of Loud Speakers at Nathu La!

Nehru once said that if he were a young officer, he would love to be posted to Sikkim. I venture to disagree with him. My first choice would be Bhutan and second the Mongolian People's Republic. Both are similar in many ways, with mountains and rivers, flora and fauna; but more than anything else, the people are similar—cheerful, smiling, looking one straight in the eye, and standing erect. They are hardy and strong because of the difficulties of terrain and nature, but they enjoy life in their own way through slow moving dances and lilting songs, eating and drinking. Both are Buddhists of the Lamaist school, eat meat and drink alcohol.

I loved Bhutan at the first sight. Thimpu, Paro, Wangdiphu-drang, Bumthang, are beautiful places. Rhododendrons in all colours of the rainbow literally grow wild on the hillside. The rivers are unpolluted and provide excellent fishing. The water is crystal clear, reflecting the blue sky, which is more blue than even in Kerman (Iran). Above all is the view of the Chomalhari peak (24,000 feet high) on the border with Tibet. It is as beautiful as the Kanchungjunga or Mount Kailash. The people in the villages weave lovely designs in cottons, silk and wool. Silversmithy is well developed. The *Dzong* or fort-cum-monastry is the centre of religious, social and administrative activities. The best developed art is that of painting frescos on the walls of monastries and Thunkas or scrolls which are hung on walls of private homes and chapels. The people lead a simple life and in spite of the hardships, always have a smile on their lips and a twinkle in their eyes.

Unlike Sikkim, but like Nepal, Bhutan was treated as a sovereign country by India. But it was completely cut off from the rest of the world because of lack of roads or airstrips. India looked after its foreign relations, such as they were. Bhutan, in the old days, had a trade representative in Lhasa, but he was recalled later. When India built the beautiful 200-kilometre long mountain road from Phuntsoling in North Bengal to Thimpu the

capital of Bhutan, and airstrips at Paro and Thimpu, various
Ambassadors posted in India and others started visiting Bhutan.
They threw feelers to the King for establishing diplomatic relations but he politely refused. He was a shrewd and wise man.
He knew that his people were not yet ready to resist the machinations and intrigues of diplomatic missions. Also, there were
hardly any buildings or other amenities available to house the
foreign embassies. The simple economy of Bhutan could not
stand the inflationary pressures of large-scale building and other
activities. At the same time, the King wanted to assert his
sovereignty and satisfy the urge of his people, especially the
educated ones. Their numbers were small but they were very
influential at the palace and in the administration. The King
adopted the formula of allowing a few countries like the USA,
the UK, Australia, Switzerland, etc. to accredit concurrently
their Ambassadors in Delhi to Thimpu. But they were not encouraged to visit Bhutan more than once a year. Their "generous"
offers of aid were politely declined.

The King, His Majesty Jigme Dorje Wangchuk, the father of
the present King, told me all this in my very first meeting with
him, without any provocation. He was in his early forties, shav-
ed his head clean, always dressed in the Bhutanese *Baku* and was
a chain smoker. He said he regarded India as the natural and
best friend of Bhutan and Nehru as his *Guru*. He did not believe
in playing India against China and vice-versa, as Nepal did, and
put complete faith in Nehru's India. In turn Nehru gave him
and Bhutan complete respect and cooperation which the King
valued greatly. He resisted feelers from many countries for aid,
etc., because he did not want Bhutan to become the battle
ground for conflicting ideologies and interests. He said publicly
that India was the best and closest friend of Bhutan and he
received enough aid from India and could not absorb any more
from anywhere else. However he selected a few areas in which
he accepted aid from some of the middle, small and distant
countries like a rice-research station from Japan, transport trucks
from Australia, etc.

· After the assassination of his able Prime Minister, Jigme
Dorje, in 1964, there was great pressure on the King to join the
UNO from the Queen and the educated class. The Queen (now
Queen Mother) was made to believe by some that India might

absorb Bhutan one day, especially after Nehru; it was, therefore, best to have Bhutan's sovereign status recognised international- ly. She was quite frank with me and said this in her soft, subtle and diplomatic way when I called on her. The King had already told me about her views. The Queen told me "You think we don't trust India. That is not true. We believe that India is the only country that can help us to achieve our natural aspirations. But, any hesitation on India's part to get us into the UNO naturally raises suspicion among our people. I can assure you that once India gets us into the UNO, there will be no suspicions, but complete trust between us."

I listened with respect and attention. She was educated in Darjeeling and spoke beautiful English. I told her of the King's desire not to rush into the UNO of which she was already aware. The King wanted to take his own time and go step by step— membership of the Universal Postal Union, Colombo Plan, etc., before joining the UNO. He wanted to try his people out in these forums before letting them into that Tower of Babel, the UNO. Pressure on the king was increasing. I reported all this to Nehru. He had no doubt that Bhutan should be in the UNO, but agreed with the King's step by step approach.

I used to visit Bhutan at the King's invitation twice or even thrice a year. He would confide in me even his personal problems and difficulties which he felt hesitant to mention to an elder like Nehru. His Queen did the same and I soon found myself in the position of a friend to both. I respected the confidence of each and in turn received theirs.

I tried to convince the Queen that India did not wish to stand in the way of Bhutan's membership of the UNO. India wanted to prepare the ground and canvass support for it to ensure that it did not fall through, as had happened regarding Bhutan's membership of the Universal Postal Union in the first attempt. The Queen was adamant and said as long as Bhutan was not in the UNO, people would think India did not want it there. When Bhutan did enter the UNO in 1971, with India's full support, the Queen told me that from then on there would be no suspicion against India. So far this seems to have proved correct and the main irritant in our relations is out of the way. Whether this will lead to closer cooperation and friendship depends largely on India and Bhutan, in spite of the intrigues and machinations of some countries which had, for a time, succeeded in spoiling relations between India and Nepal.

We should avoid the mistakes we made in Nepal and not take smaller countries for granted or act as their big brother. They are sensitive, even touchy, on small things, proud and easily hurt. We must respect their sensibilities, honour their national aspirations and win their trust and confidence. They are subject to many pulls and pressures, stresses and strains, internally and externally, and cannot bear these alone without the understanding and respect of a friendly neighbour like India.

It is a matter of satisfaction that relations between India and Bhutan are friendly and are developing along the right lines. They could become a model for relations between a big country and a small neighbour. We should make every effort, honestly and sincerely, towards this end.

The New King of Bhutan, His Majesty Jigme Singhe Wangchuk, who ascended the throne in 1972, is a chip of the old block, shrewd and intelligent like his father, but more modern minded. Bhutan has come of age and we can depend on the new King and his people to reciprocate our efforts in further strengthening friendly relations.

13　The Panch Sheel Agreement

Panch Sheel or Five Principles, is an old Sanskrit phrase. It was revived by President Sukarno when he gave a similar name (Pantaja Sila) to the five principles of his national policy. These were not the same as the Five Principles embodied in the Sino-Indian Agreement on Tibet of 29 April 1954.

Panikkar who happened to be in Delhi suggested to Nehru to give the old Sanskrit name to the Five Principles. Nehru liked the idea and made the phrase "Panch Sheel" internationally known and widely respected, especially in India and the Third World.

How did the idea arise, how were the Five Principles of peaceful co-existence evolved? Whose brainchild was it? Different people have given different versions and made conjectures about it. I should like to mention what I know first hand.

As mentioned in Chapter IV, it was Nehru's idea to evolve a method of peaceful and friendly co-existence with the Peoples' Republic of China, in spite of our different political, social and economic systems. Such a *modus vivendi* between a communist and a non-communist country had not been mentioned by any well-known Indian or other statesman till then, in such specific terms. The Kellog Pact, The Charter of the UNO, and similar documents were of course there. They were more in the nature of international declarations, not bilateral agreements between two sovereign independent countries. Lenin had mentioned "peaceful co-existence" and Woodrow Wilson had enunciated his 14 Points, but their successors were engaged in a cold war of acute tension and indefinite duration, Gandhi had empha-sised the need for peace and non-violence as an ideal. Nehru was the first world statesman to formulate these ideas and ideals into a code of conduct governing bilateral relations between two sovereign countries following different social ideologies and forms of government.

The credit for formulating and popularising the Five Principles goes to Nehru, if any one person can claim it. But, it was
really a consensus that evolved, developed and took shape in
the discussions and negotiations preceding the Sino-Indian
Agreement on Tibet. Apart from earlier discussions, negotiations were held in Peking from the last day of December 1953,
till the end of April 1954.

There were two main trends of thinking in both India and
China regarding the development of Sino-Indian relations. In
India, one school which looked upon China as the main
threat to India's security in the north and north-east. It was
further developed by some into a thesis that India should align
herself with America and the West to meet this threat, as she
could not meet it alone. This latter trend ignored the fact that
no other country, not even the USA, would like to get directly
involved in a war between India and China, though they might
try out their obsolete or not so obsolete weapons by proxy in
such a theatre. It also ignored the fact that a country like India,
with its tradition, history, culture, policy of non-alignment, and
its size and potential, could not become the client-state of any
other power. The proponents of this trend brushed aside the
danger of further dividing the world into two war camps and
the certainty of China and Russia coming closer, if India
joined the Western camp. They forgot the facts of geography
and geo-politics that India was physically much closer to China
and Russia and their combined hostility could prove a much
more serious threat to India than only China's or that of the
West.

The other school was represented by the doctrinaire wing of
the Indian communists who saw in the liberation of China the
panacea for India's troubles, and therefore, wanted India to go
the Chinese way. They wanted to have an alliance with both
China and Russia and go communist. They were supported by
some camp followers and fellow travellers who waxed eloquent
on the sentiment of Asian brotherhood and *"Hindi-Chini Bhai-
Bhai."* (Indians and Chinese are brothers).

Nehru belonged to neither school of thought. He was a
realist, proud of India's heritage and conscious of its destiny.

He believed in non-alignment because his pride in India would not allow any other country or group of countries to dominate our policies. As a realist, he saw the danger of antagonising both Russia and China which were physically close to India. He wanted to befriend both, and not to antagonise the West either. He drew a blank in the West. The USA and the West had supported Pakistan against India on Kashmir (The US-Pak Military Assistance Agreement, SEATO and CENTO, had not yet come into being but were in the offing). Dulles pronounced non-alignment as "immoral." The West, led by the USA, was taking a negative attitude on colonialism, imperialism and racialism inside and outside the UNO. Besides, America's China policy was totally opposed to that of India.

Stalin's Russia still believed that India was the "running dog" of Anglo-American imperialism. Although Stalin died on 5 March 1953, his ghost still ruled in the Kremlin (as Yevtushenko—the young Soviet poet—has forcefully brought out in his poems—"Stalin's heirs", "Fears" and "Poets of Russia"). But things were bound to change in Russia and China—for better or worse—and Nehru wanted to keep his options open and not precipitate a crisis. We were virtually at war with Pakistan and he did not want to open a second or third front. His stand on the Japanese Peace Treaty and insistence on signing a separate treaty with Japan in 1952 giving up the right to reparations, was in sharp contrast to the treaty signed by the USA and her allies at San Francisco. This had impressed Moscow, to some extent, and even more so Peking, that India was perhaps not a client state of the USA or the West.

Mao's China, though communist, had its own brand of communism which had not yet become dogmatic as in Stalin's Russia. The Tibet problem was, for the moment, out of the way. India's attitude on Korea and refusal in the UNO to brand Peking as aggressor, had made an impact on the Chinese leaders. India's leading role in repeatedly pressing for the right of the Peking Government to represent China in the UNO was a principled and consistent stand which China appreciated. India's efforts to bring about a cease-fire in Korea impressed China of India's helpful and positive role in international affairs. Also, there were straws in the wind of possible differences between Stalin's Russia and Mao's China over the joint railway in north-east China and the control of Port Arthur. China was a big country and capable of taking an independent stand, independent of the West and, if need be, independent of Russia. So was India. At the same time, there was danger of a strong, united, isolated and expansionist communist China dominating her neighbours. India would be the main obstacle in this. But Nehru argued that if India and China could work out a *modus vivendi* of respecting each other's sovereignty and integrity and non- interference in internal affairs, it would be a step away from the cold war and prevent its penetration into Asia.

Nehru was not sure of China's attitude but felt that the attempt was worthwhile. China was not yet a super power and, like India, needed peace to rebuild its social and economic structure. This was the best time to make a rapproachment with China. It might still be possible to reach a tacit understanding on our border and other problems peacefully.

It seemed there were also two main trends of thought in China. One, represented by Chou En-lai, hoped for a peaceful, cooperative co-existence with India. The other represented by the so-called "radicals" wanted to humiliate India. Mao was perhaps, somewhere in the middle.

Nehru wanted India to keep her options open. Any agreement with China would not prevent or deter India from having similar agreements with other countries; on the contrary it might create a climate of peace, favourable for similar agreements with others.

I have tried to recapture Nehru's thoughts—not in his words but in my own. He would often think aloud and give vent to these ideas in private discussions and sometimes even in public. Many meetings and discussions were held and it was decided to sound the Chinese. Not unexpectedly they welcomed the idea. It was decided to send a small delegation to Peking to discuss the matter and reach an agreement, if possible. The spade work had already been done by Panikkar, Raghavan and me in Peking. The new Indian Ambassador to China, N. Raghavan, was appointed the leader and I the Deputy-Leader of the Indian delegation. Director, Historical Division, External Affairs Ministry, the late Dr. Gopalachari, was a member. His knowledge of history and facts of the Sino-Indian border was an asset. We were authorised to coopt such other members of the Embassy as we found necessary. It was a small delegation, as delegations go, but convenient and closely knit. I had worked with Raghavan for a few months before returning from China in 1953. We got on well together.

Before our departure for Peking, the following broad guidelines were fromulated (I am recalling from memory).

Negotiations would be restricted to trade and cultural intercourse between India and the Tibet region of China. However, it was important not to lose sight of the broader perspective and larger interests of putting Sino-Indian relations on a proper footing. The border question was not to be raised by us. We would not express any doubts about the border. If the Chinese raised it we whould affirm that the border was traditional, historical and well defined by treaties, geographical and other features. An attempt was to be made to make the Chinese agree that this agreement would resolve all the problems outstanding between India and China.

If any matter was raised on which there was doubt, it would be referred to Delhi by the negotiating team.

Dr Gopalachari and I flew to Peking via Hongkong and Canton in the last week of December 1953. It was good to see the progress Peking had made during the last few months in improving roads, beautifying, parks, in housing, health and hygiene. Raghavan was different from Panikkar, though both hailed from Kerala. He had lived mostly in Malaya where he had come in contact with the typical Chinese wheeler dealer. He once told me that Chou En-lai reminded him of a Chinese insurance agent in Malaya who was fond of higgling and haggling about his commission before striking a deal. I politely suggested that he keep an open mind as there had been a social, political and ideological revolution in China. New China exuded confidence, conviction and enthusiasm. Chou En-lai had been one of its leaders with Mao through the Long March and after. I had found him straightforward who left the higgling and haggling to others and came straight to the crucial point himself.

The delegation called on Chou En-lai. He warmly welcomed and wished us success in our discussions. He said he would be watching them with keen interest and keep in close touch. He reiterated his oft-repeated statement: there are no problems between India and China which cannot be solved through normal diplomatic channels, as between two friendly neighbours. We thanked him and expressed the hope that successful negotiations would lead to the solution of all problems outstanding between us. He was quick to grasp our point and said that some of these problems had been left over by imperialism. Neither independent India nor liberated China was responsible for them. But they could be resolved in a peaceful and friendly manner, through normal diplomatic channels. The current negotiations could certainly solve problems, which were "ripe for settlement," he added. We repeated that it could solve "all outstanding problems" and left it at that.

Chou then went on to say that India and China had never waged war against each other. Their friendship was centuries' old and would not only continue but get stronger on the basis of mutual respect, equality and mutual benefit, respect for each other's sovereignty and territorial integrity, non-interference in internal affairs and peaceful co-existence. He had been echoing the thoughts of Nehru which had been conveyed to him by Panikkar and me before, and putting them in the language mentioned in China's Common Programme of 1949. Chou added the phrase "mutual non-aggression." Raghavan was a little surprised but I was not, for I had often discussed these principles with Chen Chia-kang before and heard them repeatedly. Nehru's words uttered in October 1950, were fresh in my mind and what he had said again in 1953. Raghavan was a little hesitant and asked me if we could accept this basis and should we not refer to Delhi first. I said it was all right (I knew Nehru's mind) and we could accept them, and I took full responsibility. Raghavan trusted me and replied to Chou that these principles were a sound basis for conducting negotiations and guiding our relations. On that happy note the meeting came to an end. Delhi welcomed these principles.

The Chinese delegation was led by Vice-Foreign Minister, Chang Han-fu and included Chen Chia-kang, Asian Director, Han Kung-su, Chinese Liaison Officer in Lhasa (he was later appointed Consul-General in Calcutta), Han Shu (he later became number two in Moscow and is at present number two in

Washington D.C.) and an interpreter. On our side we had Raghavan, myself, Dr. Gopalachari and Paranjpe (our Chinese language expert), and Om Sharan, my old Private Secretary in Delhi and Peking. Om was excellent at taking accurate notes in shorthand and Paranjpe was able to get the nuances of what was said in Chinese. I took down my own notes and used to finalise the verbatim record of discussions on the very day or night after the talks, and send a telegram to Delhi summarising the day's discussions. Whenever any ticklish problem arose, the discussions were adjourned and I would try to thrash it out with Chen Chia-kang informally.

To cut a long story short, the negotiations started well, went on smoothly for about two weeks and then got bogged down. China was directly involved in Korea and indirectly in Indo-China. India was trying to set up the NNRC in Korea and bring about a peaceful settlement in Indo-China. Chou En-lai was busy in the Geneva Conference and Chang Han-fu was reluctant to take decisions in his absence. He stuck like a leech to each and every detail and would not give in even on minor points. I had to tell Chen this was not the spirit in which Nehru and Chou had inspired and directed us. If Chang Han-fu's attitude represented the real Chinese view, it was better to call off the negotiations. Chen was friendly and amiable, tried to pacify me and frankly admitted that they had been busy with Korea and Indo-China and Chou had been absent and unable to give his personal attention to our negotiations. I suggested that if there was any difficulty or the Chinese did not have time, we could postpone the negotiations. He said he would get in touch with Chou and suggest that he ask Chang to expedite matters.

We met after a few days but again Chang's attitude was stiff; so was Han Kung-su's. It appeared as if they were not quite sure of the various trade marts and border passes in Tibet and were making enquiries from the local authorities. They delibe- rately put up a stiff stand to gain time and wanted to make a show of "concessions" later. This was typical of Chang Han-fu and the traditional Chinese tactics.

Raghavan and I put our heads together and decided that instead of wasting time with Chang, I should discuss matters informally with Chen and then put up joint conclusions for formal acceptance before the two delegations. This worked for about a month and the process, though laborious, did produce some agreed points. But, we were stuck on the following:

(i) Duration of the Agreement: We had suggested 25 years while the Chinese wanted only 5 years. Ultimately it was agreed to have it for 8 years. This made us somewhat suspicious of the Chinese motives and we reported this to Delhi, but Delhi accepted eight years.

(ii) The Chinese side insisted that the Five Principles need not be a part of the Agreement, but could be incorporated in a joint press statement when the Agreement was signed. They said this was their practice with other countries and they would not like to depart from it. We, however, insisted that this was the essence and the most important part of the Agreement, and should form a separate article in it. Through Chou's intervention it was agreed to have it in the Preamble. Delhi welcomed this.

(iii) Chang Han-fu would not agree to the mention of the "six (border) passes" in the middle sector between Tibet, UP and Himachal Pradesh. I requested Raghavan to tackle him and ultimately Chang gave in and said "This is the sixth concession we make to our Indian friends."

(iv) Lastly, they objected to the mention of Demchok (in the Ladakh Province of Jammu and Kashmir) as a (border) pass for traders. Their hesitation, as Chen confessed to me privately, was about making any mention of "Kashmir." They did not wish to take sides between India and Pakistan, he said. However, their real objection was, I believe, to strengthening our claim to Aksai Chin (in the Ladakh province of Kashmir) which they needed for linking Sinkiang with Western Tibet. An agreed formula—"the customary route leading to Tashigong along the valley of the Indus river may continue to be traversed in accordance with custom" was worked out and Delhi approved it.

All these talks took four months. A last minute minor hitch was created by Chang and resolved between him and Raghavan. The Agreement was signed on 29th April 1954. Dr Gopalachari and I left Peking on May 2 after attending the May Day Parade at Tien An Men, the previous day.

The main highlights of the Agreement were:

(1) The Five Principles or Panch Sheel.

(2) Recognition of the six (border) passes in the middle Sector.

(3) Establishment of Consulates General (India's in Lhasa and Shanghai, China's in Calcutta and Bombay).

(4) Setting up of trade agencies (India's at Yatung, Gyantse and Gartok and China's at New Delhi, Calcutta and Kalimpong).

(5) Establishment of ten trade marts in Tibet for customary border petty trade by Indian traders (without any on the Indian side).

(6) Ensuring entry and security of Indian and Tibetan pilgrims to each other's holy shrines (Bodh Gaya, Sarnath and Sanchi in India; Kailas, Mansarower and Lhasa in Tibet).

By letters exchanged the same day India gave up the "extra territorial" rights in Tibet (forced by the Younghusband expedition on Lhasa in 1904) viz. military escorts in Gyantse and Yatung; posts, telegraph and telephone services and 12 rest houses which the Chinese agreed to maintain as rest houses, between Yatung, Gyantse and Lhasa. These were anachronistic in 1954 and in any case not of much use after the Chinese exercised full control in Tibet. But, more important was the fact that they were vestiges of imperialist domination and violated the principle of equality. Nehru's policy was not a replica of British policy and he did not want any irritants of no practical value. (Raghavan had kept this card up his sleeve and gave it as a 'concession' to Chang in his last meeting with him.)

There were also some interesting side-lights of the negotiations. For instance, in our Hindi translation, we had put *"Chhota Mota Vyapar"* for "petty trade." *"Chhota"* means small and *"Mota"* fat. The Chinese Hindi expert could not reconcile these contradictory words, not realising that it was an idiomatic Hindi phrase for "petty" widely used in India. It took us two weeks to convince the Chinese about it, and only when they had checked with their embassy in Delhi did they finally agree.

Another interesting and revealing episode was the intervention by Chang Han-fu calling Paranjpe's translation incorrect. When Paranjpe insisted his translation was correct, Chang retorted, "I am Chinese, you are not." Paranjpe replied, "I have studied Chinese at Peking University for four years and know a little English also." Chang failed to bully Paranjpe.

On the whole, the Chinese were polite, pleasant, courteous and cooperative on details but adamant on the main points of interest to them. They made a show of "generosity" on little points. Chang Han-fu would never miss an opportunity of saying, "This is a concession to our Indian friends." We were more frank, straightforward, but equally adamant on principles though much more graceful on details.

The Panch Sheel Agreement, as it came to be known after its christening by Nehru in Parliament, represented an attempt, the first in post-World War II history, to put bilateral relations between the two big countries of Asia on a principled basis. Its success would depend on the intentions and motives, the national aspirations and interests, the leadership and implementing machinery on each side.

Both sides were aware of the possible conflict between their respective national interests and the irritants left over by imperialism. The Agreement was an attempt towards reconciling our national interests and aspirations and finding a peaceful method of resolving the irritants through peaceful means and diplomatic negotiations, directly between two great neighbours.

It was not a perfect agreement. No agreements between two great countries are ever perfect. There was give and take and a spirit of compromise on details. On the Five Principles there was broad agreement which formed the essence of the Agreement. Its success would depend on the spirit and the manner in which it was implemented, applied and extended by both sides, to guide the conduct of bilateral relations.

Territorial disputes have existed between near and distant neighbours through the ages. The question is whether they can and should be resolved by war, threat, use of force or through the more civilized and peaceful method of negotiation. The Agreement was an attempt to rule out war and ensure the peaceful settlement of international disputes. Both sides still profess their faith in the Five Principles, and therein lies perhaps some hope for the future.

The world is still divided into not only two, or even three worlds, but many worlds. Ideologically it may be said to consist of only three—the capitalist, the communist and the Third or non-aligned world. Economically, we are using the terminology of the "Fourth" world or the most seriously affected countries (MSAC), the least developed countries (LDC) or the "poorest countries."

But within each such world there are further divisions and sub-divisions that cut across social, political and military ideologies. The communist world is divided at least into three camps —the pro-Soviet, the pro-Chinese and Euro-communists, like our own Communist Parties in India, CPI, CPI (Marxist) and CPI (ML) (Marxist-Leninist). The capitalist world has almost as many hues as the major countries in it—American, British, French, West German, Japanese, etc. Even the non-aligned world represents many different shades and nuances of non-alignment which cut across political and ideological concepts— ranging from socialist and mixed to free market economies, from parliamentary democracy to military or feudal dictatorship, multi-party to one-party rule.

The concept of "One World" is still a distant dream, in spite of the rapid development of communications, science and technology. Although physically closer the world is experiencing new forms of imperialism and colonialism of the more developed over the less developed countries. There is an attempt to create ideological, political, economic and military spheres of influence by them. The threat of a thermo-nuclear war hangs like the sword of Damocles over our heads. It is being avoided by what Nehru called "the balance of terror." Wars and direct confrontation between the nuclear countries are avoided, out of the sheer necessity for survival. Nuclear weapons and technology are becoming a monopoly of some powers who want to use them for increasing their own influence and domination over others. Wars are being fought by proxy and new weapons are being tried on other people's lands.

How long can such a world last? How can the developing and non-aligned countries exist and survive in this world? Can they play any positive and useful role in bringing more sanity and order in their own internal situations and relations inter-se and preventing the further expansion of Great Power military rivalry? Can they avoid their being sucked into it? Non-alignment and peaceful co-existence are positive dynamic concepts. Panch Sheel points the way. Will the world take to it or destroy itself? As Nehru said, in the final analysis the only alternative to peaceful co-existence is violent mutual destruction.

Immediately on my return to Delhi I was summoned by Nehru and asked to give him a brief note for his statement in Parliament. I got down to it straightaway. Nehru accepted my broad analysis but raised it to a much higher level. He emphasised the importance of the five principles mentioned in the Preamble. He also defended the giving up of our "extra-territorial" rights in Tibet. There was not any significant criticism in Parliament, except by some of the extreme rightist elements. A new wave of enthusiasm and euphoria about Sino-Indian friendship spread through the country. One was a little overawed by it, for it might create undue hopes and expectations that might not be fulfilled.

The discussions in Peking revealed the need for paying more attention to the development, administration and security of our frontier areas in the north and east which had been neglected during the British rule. After some serious thought and discussion at the highest levels it was decided that we should concentrate on the economic and social development of border areas, build communications, ensure effective administration, and establish and reinforce checkposts at all salient points along the border.

NEFA (North East Frontier Agency) was under the administration of the External Affairs Ministry and the Governor of Assam excercised direct control over it as the agent of the President, with an adviser appointed by the External Affairs Ministry. The civil administration was exercised by officers and staff borrowed from Assam Government. This arrangement was not satisfactory and the Prime Minister approved the formation of a separate cadre of a new service, to be known as the Indian Frontier Administrative Service (IFAS). A selection board with the Foreign Secretary as Chairman was set up and interviewed the candidates. The cadre came into existence in 1954, and after a brief orientation course in Shillong, the officers took charge of the six frontier divisions and a dozen sub-divisions. This was a record in setting up a new service and was possible through the cooperation of the various Ministries concerned.

K.L. Mehta, ICS, who had had experience of border areas in UP and Himachal Pradesh and as Chief Commissioner Ajmer, was personally selected by Nehru as the new Adviser to the Governor for NEFA. The post of a Special Officer Frontier Areas (SOFA) was created in the External Affairs Ministry for touring all the border areas from NEFA to Ladakh and making suggestions for the rapid development of these areas. Nehru was keen to ensure respect for tribal culture and customs in NEFA (which had about 30 tribes speaking different dialects in 33,000 square miles of territory, with a population of less than a million) and at the same time, attract them into the mainstream of India. Nehru asked me to invite late Dr. Verrier Elwin and if I found him willing, sound him about accepting the post of Adviser Tribal Affairs to the Governor for NEFA. Nehru had warned me that Verrier was an unorthodox chap but had done good work among the *Gonds* and *Murias* in Madhya Pradesh. He was glad to accept the offer and volunteered to apply for Indian citizenship. To help him in formulating the programme and evolving a common script for the 30 main tribal dialects he was assisted by Dr H. Ghoshal, an eminent linguist and B. Das Shastri, an able philologist, in the linguistic and philological fields and a few others.

We got the IFAS cadre going in full swing. The new officers were a dedicated and entusiastic lot. They underwent great hardship in the farflung, inaccessible and almost uninhabited areas. They lived in bamboo huts, ate and drank with the tribal folk, joined in their songs and dances and travelled throughout the areas on foot. We gave them various concessions and a special frontier allowance. All the same spending ten years at a stretch in this difficult terrain, almost without any contact with the outside world, made some of them liable to heart trouble, high blood pressure, etc. Nehru directed that, to compensate them for the hard life, they should be considered for suitable posts at headquarters in Delhi and in some of the Indian diplomatic Missions in the neighbouring countries like Bhutan, Nepal, Afghanistan,

The author with Jawaharlal Nehru (1954)

Nehru and Prime Minister U Nu of Burma leading a procession of Nagas (1953)

President Ho-Chi-minh toasting the author in Hanoi (1953)

Lunch at the House of Commons (1961)

The author with Nehru and M.C.Chagla
at India House, London (1962)

Mrs Indira Gandhi with Mrs Khruschev
at Indian Industrial Exhibition, Moscow
(1963)

Mrs Gandhi with late King of Bhutan
at Thimpu (1968)

Kosygin greets Lal Bahadur Shastri at
Tashkent (1966). The author is in the
centre

Indian Delegation at the Tashkent Conference (1966)

Mrs Gandhi being received at Bumthang for the funeral ceremony of the late King. pix. shows Mrs Gandhi, the author, Queen Mother and King of Bhutan (1972)

etc. However, the directive was not liked by the IFS who resented "outsiders" poaching on their preserves. I suggested that some of the IFS officers could exchange posts with IFAS for a temporary tenure of two to three years, but only one IFS officer volunteered. The difficulty was later overcome by inducting suitable IFAS officers into the IAS.

We undertook a crash programme of building roads, setting up airstrips and ensuring effective administration right up to the frontier in NEFA. It was a difficult task but since we had a free hand in the External Affairs Ministry and the Prime Minister was also the Foreign Minister, we were able to do quite a bit. In other areas progress was slow.

The Chinese had constructed the road from Sinkiang through eastern Aksai Chin to Western Tibet by the middle of 1956. They had positioned about ten divisions in Tibet and constructed a network of roads and air strips. Their objection in 1954-56 to our summer outpost in Bara Hoti (in the middle sector) which they insisted on calling *"Wu Je"* in Chinese, aroused our suspicion. However, we did little to strenghten our defences to meet the impending Chinese threat. This was a mistake which weakened the effectiveness of the Panch Sheel Agreement. A weak border is a temptation to a strong, militant and expansionist neighbour to encroach on it. No agreement on paper can ensure safety and security unless it is backed by strength—military, economic, social and political.

These difficulties were under-estimated, sought to be covered up or ignored because of the *"Hindi-Chini Bhai-Bhai"* euphoria, and by mistaken interpretations of Gandhian philosophy. Gandhi's *Ahimsa* (non-violence) was a weapon of strength and not of weakness. But, some of our "Gandhian" experts and followers thought they could convert the Chinese through a Peace March to Peking; others did not believe there was an imminent threat from China in view of Chinese assurances in the recent past; opinions of experts were not given due weight until China's aggressive policy became obvious in 1959.

Nehru tried to defuse the tense situation through diplomatic démarches, and did his best to find peaceful ways of solving the problem. But, the Chinese had their own internal and external compulsions. Their difficulties and differences with Russia were increasing and coming in the open. Russia had refused to give them a sample atom bomb and insisted on repayment of past credits for military hardware and technical assistance. The Korean war had proved costly for China but they had to go in there to safeguard their security. The "liberation" of Taiwan (Formosa) had become a national slogan but they could not fulfil it because of the superior US military strength. They had to show success somewhere to satisfy their people whose hopes and expectations had been raised. They could not do much in "Outer" Mongolia because of the Soviet-Mongolian Peoples Republic Military Pact. The easiest targets were northern Burma, northern Nepal and Aksai Chin. The main stumbling block was India and they had an unfounded apprehension that India might be made a base by American anti-Chinese elements to create trouble in Tibet. This apprehension was enhanced by some infantile elements of the CIA in the US Consulate-General and pro-KMT Chinese in Calcutta, who did more harm than good to the Tibetans.

Conditions inside Tibet were not stable. The Mimang Movement was spreading. The Tibetans were alarmed and angry at the large-scale influx of Han soldiers and there contempt for Tibetan culture and religion. The Chinese took large numbers of Tibetan youth for indoctrination as party cadres and "released" the numerous serfs from the bondage of their Tibetan overlords. They introduced electricity, drinking water and modern agricultural facilities. They were thus able to reduce the influence of the Dalai Lama and the Tibetan monks and nobles on the people. They probably would have succeeded in converting the vast majority of Tibetans to their side, but for their desecration of Tibetan monastries, and contempt for Tibetan religion and culture. This produced dissatisfaction and discontent and the Dalai Lama in disguise escaped to India in March 1959, along with thousands of his followers. They sought asylum in India; it was granted on the condition that they would not indulge in political activities.

This enraged the Chinese though they themselves had earlier given asylum to K.I. Singh of Nepal and others from Malaysia, Thailand, Burma, etc. They could not question, under International Law, India's right to give assylum to refugees fleeing from religious persecution. The flight of the Dalai Lama and thousands of refugees to India hurt their pride and tarnished their image in the world. It worsened the already deteriorating relations between India and China.

Indian public and parliamentary opinion had already been inflamed by the unprovoked attack of Chinese soldiers on Indian border police at Kongka Pass and Kurnak Fort in Ladakh in 1959. Sympathy for the people of Tibet was widespread in India. Nehru was under great pressure in and outside Parliament. *"Hindi-Chini Bhai-Bhai"* became a hollow and unpopular slogan. Nehru tried his best to lessen the tension through diplomatic channels but the Chinese were in no mood to listen. The radical hawks in China were getting stronger. They adopted an openly hostile and aggressive attitude and went on making incursions into Ladakh. They got closer to Pakistan and demanded self-determination in Kashmir while rejecting it in Tibet. The principle of self-determination cannot be applied to parts of a sovereign country. India's stand was consistent and in accordance with international law but China applied double standards. Their press and radio launched a propaganda war against India. They started giving aid and asylum to Indian Nagas (and Mizos with the help of Pakistan), training them in China and sending them back for hostilities against India. The Panch Sheel Agreement was honoured more in its breach than observance by China.

Why did the Chinese do this? What would they gain by it? They had already built their road across eastern Aksai Chin to link Sinkiang with western Tibet. They built two more roads over the Karakoram through Pakistan-occupied Kashmir to link Singkiang through Gilgit to Pakistan. Is it possible they were afraid that the USSR was not helpful to them, but getting more friendly with India, with some ulterior designs in Sinkiang and Tibet? Hardly, because the USSR had enough territory of its own. India had a border dispute but no designs on the Chinese territory and could not possibly want a hostile terrain like Tibet to fight China. The only valid, logical and reasonable surmise seems to be that China's radicals, isolated and beset with internal and international problems, wanted to divert the attention of their people by securing successes somewhere. They wanted China to become the leader of the communist world and the "Big Brother" in Asia, with a string of client states around it. They had published maps in their school text books depicting Ladakh, the NEFA, Malaya, Burma, Nepal, Sikkim and Bhutan as part of China. India was gaining importance in the Third World and China tried to reduce India's prestige there by offering all kinds of inducements to the developing countries. India seemed to be the main obstacle in extending China's hegemony over Asia and then assume the leadership of the Third World.

The "Great Leap Forward" had been a flop. China's economy became stagnant. Its industrial production was nearly at a standstill. The Soviet pipeline of aid and cooperation had almost dried up. China was too proud to ask for aid from the West, even if it was available. Relations with the USA were still strained. The militant, radical leadership of China wanted some "victories" somewhere to divert their peoples attention from internal troubles. Nehru's India was the main obstacle to their ambitions and, therefore, the obvious target.

First China tried to soften India's immediate neighbours. They neutralised Burma, instigated Nepal and provoked and encouraged Pakistan's hostility towards India. Then she started nibbling India's territory, bit by bit, to provoke her into some kind of military activity in a terrain where India had all the disadvantages and China all the advantages. This was China's "forward policy" against India. She wanted to show the Third World that India was militarily weak, socially decadent and economically dependent on Western aid.

China's "friends" in India also misled her into believing that India was "ripe for revolution" and would fall apart at the first military reverse vis-a-vis China. The north-eastern belt and the eastern states would fall like a ripe plum into the Chinese orbit. The south, with memories of Telengana, would secede: Kashmir would go to Pakistan and the Punjabi *Suba* (province) become an independent Sikh Republic of Khalistan. India would be reduced in size to a small Hindi-speaking area—socially backward, economically weak and militarily of little consequence. The militant pro-Chinese eastern and north-eastern states would then overpower Orissa, Bihar and UP and the Gangetic plain would also become a pro-Chinese communist State in due course.

Once India broke up, Nepal, Burma, Malaysia, Singapore, Indonesia, Thailand, Philippines, etc., would fall like nine pins. There were already sizeable Chinese populations in most of these countries. As for the Indo-China states, they were already going the communist way. China's physical proximity to them would exercise a centripetal pull towards China. Hongkong, Taiwan and South Korea would in the long run present no serious problem. Japan would be difficult to conquer, but trade and other inducements plus the cultural and ethnic pulls would exercise a pro-China influence. At best Japan would remain "neutral" in a conflict involving China. China would thus become the overlord of Asia.

Such seemed to be the dream of the Chinese expansionists. They were led to it by their own wishful thinking, old expansionist tradition, new radical militant leadership and by the miscalculations of their "friends" in Asia. If China could turn from an ally to an enemy of the USSR, what chance had India of resolving differences with her in a peaceful way in accordance with Panch Sheel? This was the question India was faced with after the Dalai Lama's flight from Tibet and China's "forward" movement against India.

Nehru tried to avoid direct conflict, but public opinion in India demanded some action. Chou En-lai wanted to visit India and Nehru invited him. He came in April 1960. What a contrast to his visits in 1954 and 1956 when he had been welcomed as a hero, a friend and a brother!

I recall Chou's visit to Delhi in July 1954, on his way back from the Geneva Conference on Indo-China. I was the only Indian aide present with Nehru during these talks, while Chou was assisted by Chiao Kuan-hua. Chou expressed China's gratitude to India, appreciation of India's policy of peace and non-alignment. He said India's policy was a model for other Asian countries and China would like the states of Indo-China to follow a similar policy of non-alignment. The Five Principles (Panch Sheel) were reaffirmed.

His visit in 1956 was an even greater success. He allowed the Dalai and Panchan Lamas to visit India which showed trust in Nehru. He was touring south India when Nehru sent me with a special message to him in Madras. He warmly responded to the message. It seemed then that China and India might make a success of Panch Sheel.

But between 1956 and 1960 relations deteriorated to such an extent that neither Chou nor Nehru could do much to repair them. Chou's visit to India in 1960 was perhaps the only chance of settling the border problem peacefully. India felt she was the aggrieved party and could hardly make any concessions. China was in a position to propose a peaceful settlement on the basis of tradition, factual position and give and take. Instead of suggesting a settlement recognizing NEFA within India and Eastern Akasai Chin' as China's, as had been indicated earlier, Chou harped on his "six points" and wanted to reopen the whole border question a new (similar to their attitude on the Sino-Soviet border). Nehru could not accept this. He was willing to discuss specific points but not treat the whole border as "disputed." All that the visit achieved was the setting up of a joint team of officials from both sides to consider and examine the facts and evidence on each side and present a joint report to the two governments.

The Chinese provoked us by advancing beyond even their "actual line of control" of 1959. This went on for some time. The officials' teams met but failed to produce a "joint" report. This was only to be expected from a team of officials who had no political authority to give in on any point, however small. Each side tried to outsmart the other in legal quibbles and academic interpretations of historical, traditional and strategic facts.

Nehru paid a visit to Iran in 1959 when I was Ambassador there. I suggested to him the freezing of the actual positions, the creation of a demilitarized zone and the appointment of a high-level joint boundary commission to settle the main points on the spot and make recommendations for a final settlement to the two governments. Nehru agreed in principle, but found it difficult to implement this. Not that this would have solved the problem unless there was political will on both sides. But, it might have prevented its getting worse and assuming serious proportions, There were precedents for this in history. However, the proposal could not get off the ground. I am not sure that the Chinese would have agreed either. It was worth finding out. The atmosphere in both countries was so tense that any such move was a non-starter. Only Nehru or Chou could have proposed it, but even they found it difficult to do so in on atmosphere of tension prevailing then, between and within China and India. The officials' teams presented separate reports to their respective governments.

I was the Deputy High Commissioner in London when Nehru came there in the first week of September 1962, for the Commonwealth Prime Ministers' Conference. I suggested to him, that since the officials' reports had been submitted, time had come to take the initiative and suggest an early meeting between the two sides at the highest level to consider the reports. Nehru agreed and even approved a draft message to this effect. But the Chinese troops precipitated the situation. News came of their unprovoked attack across the Thagla ridge in NEFA on 8 September 1962. They had been making preparations for this for some time. Nehru tried to defuse the situation by treating it as a local incident and made the statement that the Chinese would be driven out (from this area). But, when Chinese troops advanced further on a massive scale, it could no longer be treated as a mere local incident.

The radical, militant Chinese perhaps, wanted a show down to humiliate and defeat India and lower her image in the eyes of the world. They perhaps believed that India would crumble, go to pieces and ask for a cease fire. Instead the people of India were galvanised into one nation. Almost all political parties sank their differences and rose together calling on the nation to defend itself. The Chinese advanced and outflanked our badly equipped and hastily grouped forces and inflicted a defeat on us in NEFA although they suffered more casualities than we did (10,000 against our 4,000). Our soldiers put up a resolute fight but they were heavily out numbered. In Ladakh where they had been acclimatized for a longer period, our troops fought better.

Many books have been written on our "debacle" in NEFA. It is unfair to blame our armed forces or their commanders whose repeated requests for more and better equipment had been ignored. But, a military defeat claims its own scapegoats to satisfy the public opinion. The two who suffered most were Krishna Menon who had to resign as Defence Minister and Lt. General B.M. Kaul who had been recalled from leave to become the Corps Commander in NEFA. Both were patriots, but were treated unfairly and cruelly by those who wanted to pin the blame for our defeat on a few heads. Nehru tried his best to defend both, but public opinion had been raised to a fever pitch. Krishna Menon was a politician who, in the best tradition of our democracy, resigned. General Kaul need not have done so—his Chief did not resign. But Bijji Kaul was a man of honour and wrote a very dignified letter of resignation. Nehru offered him an ambassadorial post but, unlike some, he declined as he did not want to embarrass Nehru.

Krishna Menon stood the shock and strain in spite of his age. He lost the 1967 elections to Parliament but won in 1972 as an independent. He had left the Congress and was a disillusioned man. I used to meet him often, especially after his resignation. He had a very sharp mind and thought leaps ahead of others. His biting tongue hid a very tender heart. It is a pity he had to resign and could not come back to power again. India lost a great patriot and able politician in him.

Bijji Kaul was an outspoken and straightforward person. He wrote two books—one to redeem his honour and therefore subjective ("Untold Story") and the other, ("Confrontation with Pakistan"), a more objective one where he predicted another conflict with Pakistan, Bijji was a dedicated, patriotic and brave man whose worth was not appreciated by some of his jealous colleagues. He died a sudden death in 1972 after he had suffered a great personal tragedy. I hope some day his real contribution will be assessed fairly and justly.

Coming back to the Sino-Indian conflict of 1962, whe the Chinese discovered that India had not crumbled or sued for peace and their own lines of communication had become too long and vulnerable, they made a virtue of necessity by declaring a "unilateral cease fire" on 20 October. This was meant, perhaps, to lull us into a sense of complacency, but it had the opposite effect. China launched a massive attack on 24 October and yet another on the night of 15 and 16 November. Nehru wrote to heads of all friendly governments, asking for moral, material and political support. But he did not offer to join any military bloc or military alliance as some have tried to prove. He adhered to his policy of non-alignment but as he put it, "You cannot be non-aligned towards a threat of war to your own country."

The Anglo-Americans sent a military team to assess our urgent requirements, gave us some mountain warfare equipment, but not much to make any significant difference. When Duncan Sandys and Dean Rusk came in December 1962, they tried to put pressure on India to make concessions to Pakistan in Kashmir and enter into a joint defence pact with her. Nehru refused to be blackmailed. When the Pakistan Government "gave away" 1,500 sq. miles of Indian territory in Pak-occupied Kashmir to China in December 1962 under the Sino-Pak Provisional Agreement, Nehru threw the Sandys-Rusk proposals into the waste paper basket.

I was recalled from London and asked to go as India's Ambassador to Moscow. I reached Delhi in the third week of October 1962, and left for Moscow within ten days. Those ten days were the most heart-warming and yet most sad. Nehru's dream of possible friendly relationship with China had been shattered. The Panch Sheel Agreement had been reduced to a mere scrap of paper. Nehru was a sad and disillusioned man, but he was calm and patient and never lost his nerve. He kept the war hysteria under check. Though responsive and respectful towards public and parliamentary opinion, he played it cool. A man's or a nation's strength is tested in times of adversity. Nehru and Nehru's India stood the test well in 1962. Instead of treating it as a humiliating defeat, Nehru considered it as only a battle lost. He utilised it to unite the nation, and turn public enthusiasm into positive and constructive channels.

Defence, which had been sadly neglected, was given its due importance. A nation-wide campaign of austerity, hardwork and sacrifice was launched. Public response was total and wholehearted.

This is what kept Nehru going in those sad and difficult days. I can never forget his advice to me on the eve of my departure for Moscow. It was a sad and realistic Nehru in October 1962, unlike the optimistic and buoyant Nehru who had spoken to me in October 1950 on the eve of my departure for Peking. He was pensive and spoke slowly but deliberately in a soft and gentle voice. I listened with rapt attention. This is, in brief, what he said to me:

You are going to represent us in one of the most important countries in the world. You are going at a difficult time. Don't be impatient and never lose heart. The Russian leaders may not come out openly on our side, but their sympathy is with us. Try to work on this and tell them the facts. Try to convince them of the justness of our cause. There is no conflict of national interests between them and us; on the contrary there is much in

common. China's expansionist and aggressive policy is a threat
to Asia and the whole world. We will not yield or submit to it,
nor shall we barter away our policy of non-alignment and peaceful co-existence. We shall stand alone, if necessary, but we
expect friendly countries like the USSR to understand and
appreciate our stand. The peace and stability of Asia can be
helped by friendship and understanding between India and the
USSR.

I have tried to recapture the trend of Nehru's thoughts to the
best of my recollection. He asked me to meet some cabinet
ministers also. Suddenly he smiled, stood up, put his hand on my
shoulder and said, "Do you know who are the three Indians most
popular with the Soviet people?." I replied, "Gandhi, Tagore
and Nehru." He laughed and said, "No—first Nargis, second Raj
Kapoor (the famous film stars) and last Jawaharlal Nehru." I
joined in the laughter, thanked him for his trust and confidence
in me and promised to do the best I could. I took his permission
to write directly to him, if need be.

I met Bijji Kaul (who was lying seriously ill with pleurisy),
Krishna Menon, my own colleagues, senior cabinet ministers,
leaders of various political parties, journalists and others before
I left for Moscow by Air India on 2 November 1962.

This was my second posting to Moscow. My recollections of
Stalin's Russia were a mixed bag and none too pleasant. I wondered what Khruschev's Russia would be like. I kept an open
mind and went without any prejudices, or pre-conceived notions.

On 2 November 1962—the flight from Palam to Sheremeteva airport in Moscow took only six hours. The difference in temperature on the ground between the two places ranged from plus 20°C to minus 20°C. I was fully prepared for the Moscow winter, having experienced it before. My colleagues in the Embassy, the Protocol Department, representatives of a few friendly Missions and some Indian nationals greeted me. I found the customs clearance procedures much simpler than in 1947-49.

I recall an incident at Leningrad airport in September 1947 when I was on my way from Moscow to New York for the UN General Assembly session. The passport checking was done at Leningrad instead of at Moscow. The customs official discovered that while my exit visa had Molotov's signature it did not have the seal of his office; so they would not let me go. When I asked if Molotov was their Foreign Minister and if they identified his signature on my exit visa, they replied in the affirmative. But, they said, they could not let even Molotov himself go unless his exit visa had the seal of his office. I asked them to telephone Moscow which they did after an hour or so. In the meanwhile the plane for Stockholm took off and I asked to be flown back to Moscow. Then the customs authorities came round and said Moscow had cleared my exit and offered to send me to Helsinki by train. I refused and insisted on being flown back to Moscow which they could not refuse. Next day in the Foreign Office in Moscow I demanded an apology from the chief of the visa section but all he would say was that there had been a "misunderstanding." It was a clear case of neglect on their part and I demanded a proper exit visa immediately which they gave me. I left by air next day with Mrs Pandit who was leading our delegation to the General Assembly.

Life in Stalin's Russia for Russians, foreigners and diplomats, in particular, had been hard. Things did look better now—a more relaxed atmosphere, better dressed people, shops full of consumer goods, a few private cars and taxis on the road, less jostling on the auto-buses, many more apartment houses, hotels and restaurants. Anyone who had not seen Stalin's Russia could not notice these changes. Most diplomats compared things in Khruschev's Russia to the USA in the sixties which was not a fair comparison. America had not suffered any war damage on the ground as the Soviet Union had. Besides, a country's progress is to be measured in comparison with its own past and not with that of other countries, though Khruschev sometimes boasted he would overtake America in seven years.

With this first impression on my mind I settled down without delay in the embassy which was to be my home for the next three-and-a-half years. My colleagues, Rikhi Jaipal (Minister Political), now our Permanent Representative in the UN in New York, O.P. Malhotra (military attache) now Chief of Army Staff, N.P. Jain and B.S. Das, First Secretaries, Second Secretary Purushotam and others had made all the necessary arrangements to make me feel at home. It was a relief after the 1947-48 days to find a ready home to receive you on your arrival instead of having to live in a hotel for months.

My colleagues were all anxious to know about conditions back home. I told them of the enthusiasm among the people and the determination of the government not to kowtow to China. I also impressed on them the importance of our tasks in Moscow. They promised me their wholehearted cooperation and devotion to duty and I was happy to see their patriotism and team spirit. I also called a meeting of Indian students and nationals in Moscow and gave them an upto-date picture of India. They had been deeply moved by events back home and some of them wanted to return and fight for their country. I assured them there were enough volunteers in India and they were doing an important job in Moscow and should continue there.

My most important task was to establish contact with the Soviet authorities. This I started straightaway by a call on the Acting Foreign Minister (Gromyko was in the UN) and the Chief of Protocol. I presented my credentials to President Brezhnev within a week of my arrival. The Soviet Chief of Protocol, Molotchkov (he had also been the Chief in 1947-49 but had gone as Ambassador to Berne in between) prided himself on the fact that the USSR followed the Austro-Hungarian protocol of the last century.

During the half-hour chat after the ceremony, Brezhnev was pleasant and polite, completely at ease and made me feel at home. I had not met Brezhnev before but had heard of his warm-hearted manner and hearty, husky laughter. We talked briefly about the conditions in South Asia, India, South-East Asia and China. He referred to his last visit to India in December 1960, when he had congratulated India on the liberation of Goa. He praised India's policy of peace and non-alignment and said the Soviet Union would always be friendly towards India. Indo-Soviet friendship was a bulwark for peace and progress in South and South-East Asia, he said.

I mentioned that India faced a serious threat to her peace and integrity at the hands of China. In spite of the Panch Sheel Agreement, China had embarked on a massive invasion instead of negotiating through diplomatic channels. Brezhnev did not say much on this beyond expressing the hope that the matter would be settled peacefully and soon. He was at that time President and not First-Secretary of the party. Khruschev was both First-Secretary and Premier and could talk with greater authority. I did not press the matter further and took leave of Brezhnev. I was impressed by the friendly atmosphere and warm manner of Brezhnev, compared to the cold and formal approach of Stalin's days.

The visit of Khruschev and Bulganin to India in 1956, following Nehru's visit to the USSR in 1955, had opened the eyes of Soviet leaders to the realities in India. The blinkers of dogmatic Stalinism had been removed from their eyes. Soon Soviet academics, like Dyakov, who had branded India as a "lackey and running dog of the Anglo-American imperialism" in Stalin's days, changed their tune and called India a "great, peaceful, progressive, democratic and non-aligned country." Even the Great Soviet Encyclopaedia changed its assessment of Gandhi and Nehru and recognised the important role they had played in India's struggle for independence and thereafter. An Indian who had seen Moscow in Stalin's days could not but notice the difference in Khruschev's Russia, particularly towards India.

Even the ubiquitous Soviet militiamen were different now.

Instead of the sulky, sour and hostile looks they greeted you
with a salute and a smile even if you violated a traffic regulation. I drove my own private car in 1947-49 and also now. In
the earlier period they frowned upon diplomats driving their own
cars and insisted on their taking the driving test, but this was
only a device to fail them all and compel them to engage a
Russian chauffeur. I had then refused to take the test and insisted on my rights as the holder of an international driving license.
The Soviet authorities protested verbally but would not send a
note in writing, as they were not sure of their ground. But even
as a First-Secretary in 1947-49 I was harassed and followed
everywhere. Once a traffic policeman scolded me and said, "You
are violating the rules by blinking your light." I said, "I am
sorry I am a foreigner." He snapped back, "then you have no
right to drive in our country." As against this, I recall a Sunday
afternoon in the summer of 1963 when I was returning with my
daughter from a suburb of Moscow to the embassy in my private
car. I turned into the main street from a side street when there
was a bus coming from about 150 yards away. The policeman
whistled, stopped me, saluted and asked for my "documents."
When he saw my identity card, he said, "You come from the land
of Gandhi and Nehru. What would they say if you violated a
traffic regulation in your own country?" I begged his pardon and
said I was sorry. But he would not let me go until he had finished his polite but telling speech.

This simple incident symbolized the difference between
Stalin's and Khruschev's Russia. Stalin allowed Beria to rule with
an iron hand, through his secret police and militia, by creating
fear, terror and suspicion. Khruschev used the same apparatus,
but ruled through persuasion, education and discussion, at all
levels. Stalin was dogmatic and ruthless while Khruschev was
reasonable and open to persuasion and discussion. Stalin sent
people to exile in Siberia or hard labour in the Karaganda
mines or had people kidnapped, imprisoned without trial, or
liquidated on mere suspicion. Khruschev treated his opponents
more humanely, democratically and in accordance with the
Soviet laws. Stalin used Leninism-Marxism to suit his own
purpose and to keep himself in power. Khruschev used the party
Congress in 1956 to expose the ugly face of Stalinism and

ushered in a more open, democratic and peaceful road to communism in each country.

Not that everything Stalin did was wrong and everything Khruschev did was right. Stalin's linguistic and minorities policy made a great contribution to unifying the Soviet Union. He placed the Soviet Union's national interests, as he saw them, even above "international" communism. He led his people to victory in a war that was heavily weighted against Russia in the beginning. But his methods were cruel and dictatorial, merciless and inhuman. Khruschev, on the other hand, created a feeling of security and confidence, dignity and human rights. I saw with my own eyes, towards the end of October 1964, just after Khruschev's fall from power, a crowd of people gathered round a drunken man in a park. They were telling him "Go home quickly otherwise you may be sent to jail—Khruschev is no more in power." Khruschev made his mistakes too, but they were not deliberate, cruel or inhuman like Stalin's. His rebuking senior colleagues in public, his thumping the table with his shoe in the UN General Assembly in 1960, his insistence on sowing Kukurozei (maize) even in soil that was not suited to it, his peasant-like contempt for the intellectual and the academician, the artist and the writer, his giving undue importance to his son-in-law, Adzubei—were some of his mistakes which contributed to his fall. But, these were human errors of judgment, genuine and bonafide. That is why when Khruschev fell from power on 24 October 1964, the common man in Russia felt sorry, while Stalin's death had been silently hailed with hope and relief.

This was Khruschev's Russia to which I was accredited as Ambassador of India. I took the earliest oppportunity of seeking a meeting with him to apprise him of the situation on the Sino-Indian border and sound him about selling us urgently the needed military equipment. I had not met him before. My first meeting with him was on 9 November 1962. It was almost at the height of the Cuban crisis. Khruschev and Kennedy had withdrawn from the brink of war. Each was trying to test the nerves of the other, but neither wanted to risk a war. Nor did Khruschev, at this time, want to pick a public quarrel with China for the sake of India. I had gone prepared to meet

Khruschev expecting little positive response in the first meeting.
The meeting was somewhat stormy. After greeting me
Khruschev burst out: I do not understand the point of this
senseless war between India and China. My Marshals inform me
that you are fighting for and at places where a man's bottom
freezes when he shits. These were his exact words and his interpreter, after a little hesitation, translated them literally.

I was a little taken aback by his peasant-like, down to earth
description of the conflict. I replied very politely but firmly, that
every inch of Indian territory was sacred to us as Soviet soil was
to the Soviet Union. We were not fighting for the sake of fighting. A war had been thrust upon us. It was our sacred duty to
defend our sovereignty and integrity. I then explained the
situation on the ground with the help of maps I had taken with
me.

Khruschev listened to me patiently and then burst out again,
"You can explain these maps to my Marshals. I am interested
only in peace and a peaceful settlement of disputes. This is a
most unreasonable war." I told him we were also interested in
peace and the peaceful settlement of international disputes. That
was why we had taken the initiative in signing the Panch Sheel
Agreement with China in 1954. Chou En-lai had always assured
us that all our outstanding problems could and would be resolved peacefully through normal diplomatic channels. We had
relied on that and not strengthened our defences. That was perhaps a mistake because China had been increasing her military
strength and took advantage of our military weakness. We were
determined to resist aggression and would not yield to force. We
wanted to remain non-aligned. We would seek moral, political
and material support from all friendly countries, but we would
fight our battles ourselves. Would the Soviet Union give us such
support?

Khruschev thought for a moment and then asked in a calm,
gentle and thoughtful tone, "You are our friends and China is
our brother. How can we take sides?"

I felt a little more confident at his change of tone and replied
immediately, "If my brother hits my friend, I shall not stand by
and watch but do something about it." Again Khruschev said in
a gentle tone, "We foresaw this coming. We warned both sides
to settle the problem peacefully in our Tass statement of

The author with President Tito in Belgrade (1969)

Signing of the Indo-US Joint Commission Agreement in New Delhi (1974)

*The author with the King of Bhutan
in Bumthang (1972)*

*Reception at White House. The author
shaking hands with Henry Kissinger while
Mrs Ford and Mrs Kissinger look on.
President Ford can also be seen in the
Picture (1976)*

*Famous conductor Zubin and Mrs Mehta with Senator and Mrs Javitts at Indian
Embassy, Washington, D.C. (1975)*

President Sambho of Mangolian People's Republic with Indian and Mangolian delegations at Ulanbator (1970)

The author (extreme right) with Prof Haridas Mazumdar, Prof George Sudershan and Y. B. Chavan

*The author with Mukesh (a day before
the latter's death) and Lata Mangeshke
in Washington (1976)*

The author with Jimmy Carter

*The author with Prime Minister Pidling
the Bahamas (1976) at Nassan Baham*

9 September 1959. You must remember that China is our brother but not a small brother. We cannot hit him as if he was a little brother."

I said that we did not want Russia to hit China. She had given China many weapons—tanks, planes, etc. not to fight India but to resist imperialist aggression. The west was giving arms to Pakistan which were being used against India. We had to get arms from somewhere and hoped the Soviet Union would consider our needs and requirements urgently.

Khruschev said that I should see Malinowsky about it. He again stressed the need to settle the problem peacefully and not through war.

I took leave and said that I might have to see him soon again. He said I was welcome. I was impressed with Khruschev's common sense, down to earth approach. He was under great pressure in Cuba and could not openly side with India, a friendly non-communist country, against a communist fraternal country, China. He left the door open, which was the most we could expect at that juncture of the Cuban crisis.

Pravda had come out with a somewhat anti-Indian and pro-Chinese editorial on 25 October 1962. Meanwhile there was a thaw in the Cuban situation and the threat of war seemed to have receded. I attended the party celebration meeting in the Great Kremlin Hall of Congresses on 6 November. The meeting was positive in tone and realistic in content. I attended the 7 November parade in the Red Square and Malinowsky's speech, though strong in tone, was comparatively mild in content.

Pravda came out with a second editorial (5 November) on the Sino-Indian conflict. It was neutral and not pro-Chinese or anti-Indian. The Cuban crisis had been averted and Russia felt more free to look at the Sino-Indian conflict in its proper perspective. Internal differences between China and Russia at the party level had been brewing for some time, though state to state relations were correct albeit cold. How long could or would the Soviet Government ignore realities and their own interests which were involved in the Sino-Indian conflict? Did communist solidarity mean that, right or wrong, one communist state must help another communist state in any conflict with a non-communist state? Would the defeat of non-aligned India at the hands of communist China be in the Soviet interest? Would it not make China even more recalcitrant and antagonistic to Soviet leadership of the communist world? Would it not further increase Chinese influence in Pakistan and the Third World and pose an additional threat to the southern underbelly of Russia? And, if India also went into the western and or the Chinese camp, like Pakistan, would it not make the Soviet position in central Asia and its Asian Republics rather difficult?

These were some of the questions that must have been in the minds of the Soviet leaders. Also, the possibility that India might be forced to join the western camp, if the Soviet Union did not give her any help. This would strengthen the Western ring around the Soviet Union from Europe to East Asia. The Soviets are realists. They were waiting for the Cuban crisis to subside. In the meanwhile the situation on the Sino-Indian border would also be clearer. They were watching to see whether India would fall for the Chinese declaration of unilateral withdrawal and ceasefire or keep on the struggle. The Chinese had precipitated the situation by launching another massive attack on 20 October and yet another on the night of 15/16 November. The Russians were impressed by our resistence to it.

I had several meetings with Malinowsky and his Marshals and explained the situation in detail to them on maps. They had their own assessment through their embassy in Delhi and their experts in Moscow and the Far-East. Malinowsky was a great tease. In one of my meetings with him he asked why I was speaking to him in a foreign imperialist language, English. I said I would be glad to speak in my own language, Hindustani, but regretted that neither he nor his interpreter spoke it. He laughed and from that day we became friends.

My second meeting with Khruschev on 24 November, was less stormy than the first one and more fruitful, as I had hoped. The Soviets take a long time to come to a decision especially where other countries are concerned. A collective leadership comprising doctrinaires like Suslov, politicians like Khruschev, technicians like Kosygin and military men like Malinowsky, is inclined to look at such a situation from different points of view and it takes time to reach a consensus. I had a feeling that Khruschev was broadly sympathetic to our cause, Malinowsky was definitely for us but I was not sure of the others.

I congratulated Khruschev on the resolution of the Cuban crisis. He gave me a lecture on it justifying the Soviet stand and then suddenly burst out, "It should be a lesson to you to resolve the Sino-Indian conflict also in a peaceful way." I tried to point out that while the USA and the USSR were evenly matched, China had superiority of arms and man-power over us and a favourable terrain to fight in. In any case, their second massive attack on 20 October followed by another on 15/16 November had proved, if any proof was necessary, what their real intentions were—to defeat and humiliate India in the eyes of the world, to frighten her smaller neighbours and to gain hegemony over Asia. We would never submit to it, come what may, even if we had to stand alone. India was a great country, we were proud of our history and culture. It was not possible for any country, however big and powerful, to conquer India. Our resistence in Ladakh against heavy odds had proved this. If Russia wanted an early peaceful cessation to fighting, she should make it clear to China that she was wrong and redress the military imbalance against India. Any hesitation on Russia's part would only encourage China to increase the tempo of war.

Khruschev let me talk and listened with a twinkle in his eyes and a smile broadening on his lips. He was testing me. I felt I had passed the test of convincing him that Indians did not have feet of clay, that they would fight bravely and resist strongly. Khruschev replied gently, "Mr Ambassador, I am impressed by what you say. But what can we do? Supply of military equipment takes time. We shall keep our contractual obligations and try to expedite supplies. The end of the Carribean crisis has opened possibilities because of relaxation of combat-readiness. I suggest that you discuss the matter with Malinowsky and others and come to me again, if necessary."

I gave him a list of our urgent requirements and let it rest at that. I would take up the details with Malinowsky and others now that he had given the green signal. I did not expect him to say "OK" there and then. I was not sure how expeditiously the bureaucracy and the State Committee for Economic Cooperation with Foreign Countries under Skatchkov would clear our demands. But, a hurdle had been crossed. The Soviets were prepared to discuss details. If not in the immediate short run, it would produce results in the long run. One had to be patient and preservering. As a parting shot, Khruschev said to me, "I hear you are arresting in your country a whole range of communists." I replied smilingly, "They are all Stalinists." He laughed and we sort of understood each other.

Disturbing news came of our rout in NEFA. I did feel isolated and disheartened at times. One night I sat listening to AIR, BBC and the Voice of America and could not sleep. I drafted a long personal letter to Khruschev and showed it to my number two Rikhi Jaipal, first thing in the morning. He was deeply moved by it and said, "I do not think our own Foreign Office or the Soviet Foreign Office will appreciate it. This is a historic letter which need not be sent but may be published when you write a book." I accepted his advice and reproduce below the text unchanged, as I had drafted it on that November night in 1962:

Personal

Moscow
November 27, 1962

Dear Mr Khruschev,

You have been good enough to see me in my capacity as Ambassador of India twice on the 9th and 24th of this month. What you have told me has helped me and my Government in understanding the Soviet Government's position and point of view in the present most unfortunate conflict between two great countries of Asia—India and China.

The common man and woman in India are not fully satisfied—they cannot understand how a country like China, which has had no wars with India for the last 2,000 years, could have launched such a premeditated, unprovoked, expansionist, chauvinistic and large-scale invasion on a peaceful, democratic and non-aligned neighbour like India. This becomes all the more difficult to understand when such a large-scale invasion has been launched by the Government of China which claims to be the follower of Lenin and Marx. The Communist Party of India is, not unnaturally, puzzled by it, angered by it, and is groping for an explanation. I enclose an article by Mr S.A. Dange, Chairman of the Central Committee of the Communist Party of India which was written even before the second large-scale onslaught by the Chinese on the night of 15/16 November. If even communists cannot understand it, you can well imagine the shock and resentment of people like me who are not communists but who believe firmly in our socialistic pattern of society, in peaceful friendly and cooperative co-existence between different social, economic and political systems and in a policy of non-alignment as an instrument of peace and friendship in the world.

Mr Chairman, I was associated in the negotiation of the Sino-Indian Agreement of 29 April 1954, on trade and cultural intercourse between India and the Tibet region of China, which in its very Preamble, laid down the famous five principles of peaceful co-existence or Panch Sheel—for the first time. Like Nehru, we believed in the bonafides of the people's government of China and its leadership that they would adhere to these principles in their bilateral relations with us. This was one of the main pillars of our foreign policy. We still believe in these principles but we can no longer believe in the word of the present leadership of China after what they have done to our country. It is not what they claim, which is bad enough, but the violent, aggressive and brutal manner in which they have tried to enforce their claim that has shocked us and the whole world, especially the non-aligned countries of Asia, Africa and Latin America.

I raised these questions with you during our last two meetings but I did not wish to take too much of your precious time in an ideological discussion. And yet, I believe, that unless this matter is frankly and fully discussed and all the doubts cleared, our relations with China, can never be the same as before. What is more, unless you help us in understanding this and clarifying the attitude to this problem, of Leninists-Marxists, whom you so ably represent, there is bound to be doubt and suspicion in the minds of our common people with regard to the future.

The Government and the people of India are genuinely impressed by the progress and developments in your country and your great efforts in maintaining peace and avoiding a nuclear war in the world. They feel, therefore, all the more puzzled how another country that claims to be Marxist-Leninist also, can flout the very cannons of Leninism and Marxism by launching an unjust war against a peaceful and friendly neighbour and thereby endanger peace in Asia and the world. The people of India, Asia and the world expect you, Mr Chairman, as the head of the government of the leading socialist country in the world, to remove their doubts, to remedy the wrong committed by "an ally" and a "brother" of your country against a "friend." It is important to do so not only from an ideological point of view, but because of its grave practical consequences and serious implications. It is even worse than what the KMT and the old imperialist Chinese Governments ever did to their neighbours. It is a symptom and an eruption of a deep rooted disease that must be properly diagnosed and cured completely—otherwise it may threaten to destroy the whole of humanity.

Mr Chairman, I hope you will pardon me for this frank and perhaps "undiplomatic" expression of my views. I am not writing this letter to you in my official capacity as the Ambassador of India, or under the instructions of my government, but as a simple, ordinary human being who believes in the friendship and brotherhood of man. If you care to reply to this letter, I should be grateful. If you would give me an opportunity to discuss this vital problem of the future relations of the communist and the non-aligned world with you, I should be even more grateful. In any case, I hope that you will give some consideration to what I have said which reflects the doubts, hopes and aspirations of the ordinary man and woman in India and, I believe, in a large part of the world.

Please forgive me for writing to you so frankly. I do so because I believe that you and your country have a vital role to play in maintaining peace in the world and in building greater friendship and understanding between the peoples and governments of our two countries and others.

I thought of sending the letter to newspapers under the title "A letter written but never sent," but resisted the temptation.

My apprehensions about bureaucratic delays by the Soviet civilians were confirmed in the days and weeks following. Malinowsky and his Marshals and Generals were sympathetic. The bureaucrats in the State Committee were cautious, careful and slow. The Soviet Foreign Office was "diplomatic" and non-committal. We, therefore, launched a major offensive at various levels of the Politbureau and the government. We also adopted the unorthodox method of briefing the Soviet press and speaking out at Indo-Soviet Friendship meetings. We adopted tactics that we thought Khruschev would appreciate. It seemed to produce some effect because everything was reported to higher ups.

My colleagues and I worked hard and approached the Soviet official and non-official elements at all levels. What impressed us was that they listened with attention and sympathy. They did not have to be convinced. They were aware of how China had paid them back for their own cooperation and assistance. They were quite disillusioned with China already. They were not quite sure of India's ability to stand united. They had their own doctrine and dogma from the past which they had not quite got over yet. We felt time was on our side.

Then came the news of the Chinese "unilateral" withdrawal from some of the forward areas in NEFA. This made an impact on the Russian mind, not of "China's generosity" but of her inability to frighten India into submission. There was praise for India's courage and determination not to yield to pressure from China or the West. China was merely making a virtue of necessity as she could not maintain a long line of communications inside India. Also, she had received no support from any section of the Indian people who had united overnight. This impressed the Soviet Union.

The annual session of the Supreme Soviet was held on 12 December 1962. I had a meeting with Khruschev on 15 December. It was interesting to hear his frank tirade against the Chinese leadership and their imperialistic and expansionist policies. He called them "laughing Buddhas" who are impervious and insensitive to the feelings of their own people, let alone others. He did not mince words and told me that the Soviet Union had already made her views known to the Chinese leadership about their unjust attack on India. The Soviet Union would not stand by idly but give material and political support to India. He would personally see to it. His colleagues were with him and there was no difference of opinion on this. But, India should take care not to prolong the war. Wars were costly and cast heavy burdens on the people. He went on in this vein for over half an hour and I listened with great interest. I had already read his speech at the Supreme Soviet wherein he had said, "There may, of course, be people who will say that the Peoples Republic of China is now withdrawing its troops actually to the line on which this conflict began. Would it not have been better not to have moved from their positions on which troops stood at one time?...We absolutely do not admit the thought that India wanted to start a war with China."

The tide had turned. The Soviets now openly said what they had privately believed. India seemed to have in the Soviet Union a dependable friend; our interests coincided and did not clash. A strong stable, democratic, non-aligned India, in friendship with the Soviet Union, would strengthen stability and peace in Asia, and stop China's hegemony and expansion, and not be a threat to any country. It would also be a bulwark against attempts by the western countries to dominate the non-aligned world. The Chinese invasion of India might yet prove a blessing in disguise and make India more realistic and conscious of her defence needs. A strong, stable, non-aligned and independent India could play a positive, constructive and progressive role in Asia and the world.

These were the thoughts that raced through my mind after my meetings with Khruschev. If only Stalin had seen similarly, things might have been different today in China, in India, in Russia and the world. But, one learns by bitter experience. The Sino-Indian conflict of 1962 was something that would shake up India and awaken it to its real needs and role, internally and externally. I conveyed some of these thoughts to Delhi and some I kept to myself. Sometimes, one has to be diplomatic even with one's own Foreign Office. But, I did write "personal" letters to Nehru who, I knew, would appreciate them. I was heartened by his prompt replies and encouragement which kept up my spirits in those dark and difficult days and nights of the Moscow winter of 1962-63. In one of his personal letters to me in December 1962, Nehru wrote of Khruschev's meeting with Vice-President Radhakrishnan in Delhi. In the course of the talk Khruschev said much against the USA but he ended up by saying that in 10 years time the chief enemy would be China. This was said in 1956—how right Khruschev was!

In one of my letters to Nehru I gave my assessment of Khruschev: One can strike a personal equation with Khruschev more easily than with most other heads of government. He is an outspoken extrovert though he is also a clever actor and can simulate grim seriousness as well as light-hearted laughter, as he pleases...the Russians are much more human even when they are communists, while the Chinese are much less communicative even when they are not communists. This was in December 1962.

I had acquired a smattering of Russian in 1947-48 and could speak it ungrammatically, but fluently. I utilized this in many national day receptions and those at the Kremlin where one could go up to the Soviet leaders and enter into an informal conversation with them, even without an interpreter. Some of them talked more freely than others, especially when there was no interpreter around. I got to have a nodding acquaintance with almost all members of the politbureau and called officially on those who were also in the government apparatus, like Khruschev, Brezhnev, Kosygin, Podgorny, Polyansky, Mazurov, Shelepin, Molinowsky and Voronov. All of them, except Brezhnev and Podgorny, and the party secretaries like Suslov, Andropov, Ponomoriev, Kirilenko accepted our invitations and came to lunch, dinner or receptions at the embassy. Some of them even gave me their "private" telephone numbers, where I could contact them, if necessary.

This would have been inconceivable in Stalin's Russia. The style of working both in the government and the party had changed significantly. Khruschev was the most outspoken and outstanding in the new set-up. Although not very popular with intellectuals, artists, writers and academicians, because of his unorthodox manner and approach, the people loved him. He had freed them from Stalin's terror and Beria's tortures.

There were many stories going around Moscow, some based on facts and some made up. I heard from the Russians themselves that Beria would fancy a girl in the street or a shop, have her "picked up" and kept in his special house for pleasure. He used to keep hundreds of rouble notes there which he would offer them and even jewellery which he had "confiscated" from some other unfortunates. Wives were taken away from their husbands, and daughters from their parents, at the whim and fancy of Beria.

I did not hear any such stories about Stalin. Some writers and intellectuals told me that they used to keep a bundle of clothes ready to take with them whenever there was a knock at the door at night. But, they blamed Beria and not Stalin for this. Stalin went only for his opponents or possible rivals. The intelligentsia had looked upon Stalin as the saviour of their country, next only to Lenin. They had cried when he died because they did not know who would succeed or follow him. They were shocked at the revelations made during the 20th Party Congress. They blamed Khruschev and others for their "conspiracy of silence" as Ilya Ehrenberg called it, during Stalin's rule, but they also admitted there was little anyone could say in those days. One had to obey and carry out orders. Stalin was not easily accessible and was suspicious of all, except one or two. Beria took full advantage of this and settled many private scores even without Stalin's knowledge. Khruschev told a high Indian dignitary in my presence, "Stalin warned us all that the Americans would twist our necks like those of chickens after him. Stalin is dead but nothing like that has happened."

The intelligentsia said that Khruschev had given them freedom. They could now move about and talk freely among themselves, without the fear of a mid-night knock. In Stalin's days and Beria's rule they did not know who was their friend or foe and would not discuss things even privately. People were not sent to Siberia or Karaganda mines on mere suspicion any more. Of course, Khruschev had his "hare brained" ideas about literature, art, music, agriculture, etc., which were not scientific or "cultured" (*Nekulturni*); they could openly talk about such things among themselves and made fun of him. They could not, however, publish what they liked. Once the party laid down a particular line, they could not deviate from it, but they had freedom to discuss and criticize before a decision was taken.

This was a great change from the days of Stalin when Zhdanov issued his infamous decress against "rootless cosmopolitans." There were still "anecdotes" about Jews, as in other western countries, but they were in good humour and not racist or malicious. Malinowsky told me once: A Jewish educated youth approached the local party boss and said he wanted to join the party. The boss said "Youngman you will have to make many sacrifices, as a member of the party. You may have to

give up smoking, drinking and women." The youth said he
would do so. The boss said "You may have to give up your life."
The youngman replied, "Life would not be worth living after
giving up smoking, drinking and women." Jokes apart, there
was no organized movement against the Jews as such; only those
who showed any extra-territorial feelings and gave vent to them
were punished. There were some Jews holding important positions in the government and many in the professions—arts,
science, literature, etc.

Though restrictions on Soviet citizens meeting foreigners
continued, they were enforced less strictly and more humanely
than in Stalin's Russia. Diplomats were always suspect and many
of them were still shadowed, but more Russians were allowed to
meet them than before. If you spoke Russian, you could carry
on a conversation with a Russian on the street or in a park or
elsewhere and he would not try to avoid you as in the old days.
But, if a Soviet citizen went to an embassy, he had to show his
invitation or "document" (identity card) before he was allowed
entry. Most of such "invitees" were still expected to make a
"report" on such meetings and conversations with diplomats or
foreign nationals. Not unless there was evidence of any anti-
Soviet act or secret information given away by a Soviet citizen,
was he punished. However, some writers who did anti-Soviet
propaganda in their writings or through foreigners were rounded
up. Those who did not tow the party line could not publish their
works in the Soviet Union.

Some embassies, were more "popular" than others, depending on current relations of their countries with the Soviet Union.
India was amongst them. We had the pleasure of having many
distinguished Soviet writers, artists, scientists and professors at
our small and big parties. Among them were Ilya Ehrenburg,
Madame Kempe (of Riga) and her husband, Yevtusheuko, his
first wife Bella Ahmadudlina and her second husband Yuri
Nagibin, Professor Kapitza, the famous nuclear-physist, Symyr-
nova, the Director of Bolshoi Ballet School, famous ballet
masters and ballerinas from the Bolshoi, professors of Moscow
State University (where my daughter was doing a short course
in Russian), curators of museums and others. They would sing,
eat, drink and dance or just chat or engage in serious conversation. We also had the pleasure of having high and low officials

from all the ministries with whom we had dealings like Minister of Foreign Trade, Patolichev, a most delightful, able and outspoken man; Madam Furtseva, Minister of Culture, who was the wife of Vice-Foreign Minister, Firubin; Malinowsky, Minister of Defence, his Deputy (later successor) Marshal Gretchko, the irreplaceable Foreign Minister Gromyko and his amiable wife; Kuznetsov, the able First Vice-Foreign Minister (now Vice-President), Skatchkov, Chairman of the State Committee for Economic Relations with Foreign Countries, Yelutin, Minister of Higher Education, Romanowsky, Lapin, Malik and others. Also there were the six famous 'observers' who used to write for Pravda and Iznestia, especially Yuri Zhukov, Olga Chichetkena and Matviev. They told us of the rivalry between Izvestia, the government paper and Pravda, the Party paper. There was a current joke that "there is no Pravda (truth) in Izvestia and no Izvestia (news) in Pravda."

What a contrast to the Moscow of 1947-49. Mrs Pandit would perhaps have enjoyed it now. She promised to pay me a visit but never managed to come. We had quite a number of Indian visitors and guests—both official and non-official—especially in the summer and spring when it was hot in India, and sometimes in the autumn too, but hardly ever in winter. Most of them preferred to stay at the embassy rather than in Soviet hotels where service was slow, privacy limited and no Indian cuisine available.

I suggested once to Khruschev and to Patolichev to open an Indian restaurant in Moscow. I would help them to get Indian spices, cooks, etc., but the project did not materialize. There was a Chinese restaurant set up in the days of the Sino-Soviet honeymoon in Hotel Peking. When relations between them deteriorated, the Chinese cooks went home and the food there was more Russian than Chinese. The most delightful restaurants, for us Indians in particular, were the Georgian and Uzbek, where the food was spicy and more to our taste. Aragvi restaurant was popular with all foreigners and Russians because of the gay Georgian music and their "sword dances." Whenever we went there, the band would play catchy Indian tunes, which Russian reprints of films of Nargis and Raj Kapoor had made popular throughout the USSR, like *"Awara Hoon"* (I am a vagaband) from the film "Awara" or *"Eachak Dana, Peachak Dana."* After a while, when the atmosphere got more friendly, Georgians from adjoining tables would invite us and then join us in drinking numerous toasts according to Georgian custom, to our health, then to our families, country, etc. Aragvi was there in Stalin's days too but it was then more like a mausoleum than a restaurant. We held an Indian industrial exhibition in Moscow in the summer of 1963, which was inaugurated by Khruschev. The most popular stall was that of Moti Mahal selling *Tandoori* Chicken. Queues, a mile long, waited to get in. Perhaps that was one reason why our proposal to set up an Indian restaurant did not fructify. It might have become even more popular than Aragvi.

Russians are fond of eating and drinking, always have been, partly because of the climate and partly to relieve the boredom of their life. They miss no opportunity of drinking toasts, "*dodna*" (bottoms up) in neat Vodka, Cognac and even wines. After that they thaw a little, then warm up and either sing or talk. I recall one evening when I had eight Soviet Generals from Skatchkov's State Committee at my house, along with three of us—O.P. Malhotra, Jaipal, and myself. It so happened that all the eight Generals were Ukrainians. I mentioned that I had just received a case of "Gorilka" (Ukrainian Vodka with two green or red chillies in the bottle) from the Ukrainian Foreign Minister. They jumped up with joy for Gorilka was not easily available in Moscow. The 12 bottles were opened, one by one, and consumed in about three hours. I must pay tribute to their capacity to hold liquor. None of them got drunk or unpleasant and they talked sense, related anecdotes and, in between, transacted business. That evening we solved many problems and crossed many obstacles that were holding up our military supplies. May be they had already come prepared with their answers and just wanted to celebrate.

Unlike the British, the Russians do not just hug a glass of whisky, diluted with water or soda, or drink without any snacks. They eat and drink. The Russian Zakuska (*hors' doeuvre*) is a must and is almost as variegated as the Swedish Smorgesbord. It helps to line the stomach with fat to neutralize the alcohol. Some of them even eat butter or drink olive oil before coming for a drink party. They do not mix their drinks and whatever they drink is drunk neat. Vodka they gulp down and chase with mineral water (Narzan or Borjom) and a slice of black Russian rye bread which they always sniff before eating it.

I could not stomach these Russian habits easily and evolved my own technique when I had to drink with them. I hated eating fatty snacks with drinks; I would drop a tablet of Alka Seltzer in a glass of water or soda and drink it up before, during and after a party. Marshal Zakharov once asked me at the table, *"Chto Eto Tablichki"* (what is this tablet)? I told him and he tried it and found it useful. After that I always sent him a present of Alka Saltzer tablets and gave him some when he visited India.

Marshal Malinowsky was the hardest drinker of spirits and wines but never lost his sense of humour, even though it was sometimes at the host's expense. At my lunch in honour of our Secretary-General R.K. Nehru, Malinowsky and Gromyko were both present. Malinowsky took every drink "dodna" before, during and after the meal, while Gromyko only sipped his. After Vodka, white wine and red wine had been served, champagne was passed round. Gromyko looked at Malinowsky and hinted to me that no more drinks need be passed round. I gave the signal accordingly to my Indian bearer who was in charge of drinks. Malinowsky noticed this departure from the usual custom at the Indian Embassy and said to R.K. Nehru, "It seems, Mr Secretary-General, you do not pay your Ambassadors enough for the drinks they have to serve." I felt embarrassed and ordered more champagne and Malinowsky drank to his heart's content, just to show off to Gromyko, it seemed. He stayed behind after the other Soviet guests had left and gulped half a dozen cognacs with coffee. And he was in his office after that, sober like a judge. But, whenever his wife was present she would not let him drink too much. At a dinner at the embassy when she was present, Malinowsky said to me: *"Chto Delat"* (what to do?) pointing to his wife. She was the head of a library and a very cultural lady.

Even Khruschev liked his drink when his wife was not present or when she was looking away. At a luncheon I gave for Indira Gandhi when she was the Minister for Information, Khruschev, his wife and his daughter Rada were present. Khruschev told his wife "look at that fine painting" and while she was looking at it, he gulped down a glass of red wine. She pretended not to notice but gave him a broad smile. He said to Indira Gandhi, "We are dominated by our womenfolk. They outnumber us." But Khruschev did not drink spirits, only wine, under doctor's orders, I was told. Mrs Khruschev was most kind-hearted, gentle, understanding and motherly. Her sweet smile conveyed the suffering, hardships and survival of the human spirit against all odds. She could have been a great leader in her own right and would have become a heroine in any other country. But she was happy and content to be a modest wife, mother and grandmother and remained always behind her husband. She continued to teach at a school even when her husband was number one in the Soviet heirarchy.

Khruschev was the delight of the diplomatic and press corps. Short, roly-poly, with a round clean-shaven head, badly dressed with loose fitting clothes, shoes, half worn out at heels, with hands crossed behind his back and his thumbs twiddling, he would stand up, speak extempore, and answer questions off the cuff, to the shock and surprise of some of his colleagues and the amusement of his listeners. His language was simple but telling. He had a peasant's earthy sense of humour. He did not mince his words or try to beat about the bush. He came straight to the point and said what he felt. But, he was no fool. He had strong common sense and knew how far to go with or against foreign dignatries. He sized up a situation or a person quickly and threw feelers to watch the other person's reaction, struck when he thought he would succeed or parried a question if he was not certain. His 1961 bout with Kennedy in Vienna was an exercise in sizing up the young new President of the USA. His "brinkmanship" in the Cuban crisis was an attempt to test Kennedy's nerves. He found in Kennedy a match to his own toughness and respected him for it. I recall when Kennedy was assassinated, Khruschev came to the funeral service in the Church in Moscow with tears in his eyes.

There was something human in Khruschev that endeared him to all his people and those foreigners who came in contact with him. His fault, perhaps, was that he went a little to far in showing his contempt for some of his colleagues and aroused their jealousy, enmity and wrath against his uncouth and arbitrary methods. He was not born to be a dictator nor did he want to be one. He was a proletarian democrat at heart and his sympathy was always with the common man. He was impatient and could not tolerate bureaucratic delays or the expert's habit of going into details and missing the wood for the trees. His way of dealing with people was rough and sometimes even crude and that cost him his office in the end.

I heard a story about Khruschev's first visit to Siberia. He met an old man of ninety and asked him: "Grandpa, are you happier now than you were before the Great October Socialist Revolution?" The old man replied, "I do not know about being happier now or then, but before the revolution I had two pairs of boots, two overcoats, two suits, two fur hats and two pairs of fur gloves. Now I have only one of each and even that is torn and tattered." Khruschev said, without batting an eyelid: "Never mind Grandpa. Don't you know, in China, India, Asia, Africa and Latin America, they don't have even that and go naked?" The old man scratched his head and said, "Then they must have had their great socialist revolution long before we had ours." For once Khruschev did not have the last word.

Kosygin was quite the opposite of Khruschev—courteous, careful, weighed every word he uttered, went into each and every detail, never promised more than he could do, nor did more than he promised. He was a technician *par excellence* having qualified and worked as a textile engineer in Leningrad. He was shrewd, businesslike and had a dry sense of humour, unlike Khruschev. He seldom laughed but he gave a hint of a smile when he appreciated some remark. He was one of the few Soviet leaders who had been a minister and an alternate member of Stalin's politbureau in 1941 and had survived unscatched. I found it sometimes difficult to get Kosygin to agree wholeheartedly with anything, though he would always leave the door open, never say "No" and always meet us part of the way. He was a good administrator, knew his job and the Soviet civil servants were very happy with him and his method of work. He would not say a word more than necessary, listened patiently, carefully considered each and every point, had it examined thoroughly and only then committed himself.

Anastas Mikoyan was the clever Armenian, an expert on foreign trade, shrewd, calculating, with a deep insight into men and affairs and a tough but pleasant negotiator. Like Kosygin he would never be number one, but always remained in the inner circle, close to his number one, whether it was Stalin, Khruschev or Brezhnev. He was sent on most difficult missions, like the one to Japan. Although he did not succeed in converting the Japanese to his point of view, he came close to it. Perhaps the solution he proposed to the Japanese about the four northern islands is the one that can solve this ticklish problem: the two southern islands should go to Japan and the two northern ones which the Soviets consider vital to the defence of the Bay of Kamchatka, should remain with them, unless of course Japan is prepared to become neutral and do away with the Japanese-US military alliance. Who can foretell the future in the fast changing situation in the Far-East?

When President Radhakrishnan visited Erevan, the capital of Armenia, I was following in the car behind him and the crowds lining the streets looked at me and shouted *"Vot Mikoyan"* ("There goes Mikoyan"). I mentioned it to Mikoyan and we had a good laugh over it. Armenians and north Indians have similar features. I heard a story about Mikoyan attributed to Khruschev. They both visited the Vatican and the Pope ordered his best gold and silver plate to be laid for a dinner in their honour. During the meal the conversation drifted to Christianity and communism. The Pope said "We Christians believe in miracles. Do you communists have any miracles to believe in?" Pat came Khruschev's reply, "Of course, we do. I will show you one right now. Here I take one of your best gold spoons and put it in my pocket. Lo and behold—there it is in Mikoyan's pocket already."

Armenians are supposed to be very clever at business and making money throughout the world and Khruschev would never miss an opportunity to have a dig at his friend and colleague Mikoyan. Once at a luncheon in the embassy I served fresh Alfonso mangoes I had received through the courtesy of Air India. Mikoyan and Khruschev were both present. Khruschev took off his jacket, rolled up his sleeves and began eating his mango in the typical Indian fashion. He had probably learnt it during his visit to India in 1956. Mikoyan hesitated and Khruschev pulled his leg: "Anastas, you save your mango, it may double itself by the time we go home." It was said in good humour and Mikoyan never minded Khruschev's jokes. He had been with Stalin and suffered worse things and yet survived.

Andrei Gromyko, Foreign Minister (now also member of the Politbureau) is a most skilled diplomat. I first saw him in 1947 in the UN when he used to have a sour, glum look on his face.

Gromyko in the sixties was a much more seasoned diplomat, smiled when necessary and showed a subtle sense of wit and humour. He spoke excellent English and I spoke very bad Russian. Once he suggested that we carry on an official conversation in Russian and do away with the interpreter. I suggested we may do so in English as his English was perfect and my Russian was ungrammatical. To my surprise, he said in Russian "Grammar—that is necessary only for interpreters and not for ambassadors." I added, "or for Foreign Ministers" and we had a good laugh. He could be very serious at times, pull on a long face, look grave as if war was going to break out any moment. On the whole, I found him very pleasant to deal with. He was business-like, cogent, to the point and reasonable. If he could not say "yes" he would not say "no" either, but "we shall report to our leaders." That meant "we shall consider—the matter is not closed." The old days when he always said "*Net*" (No) in the UN were gone.

Among the Vice-Foreign Ministers I found Kuznetsov the most pleasant and knowledgeable. Jacob Malik was the most interesting with a ready wit and humour. I recall having seen Malik preside over a Security Council session in 1950. It was past six in the evening when Gladwyn Jebb, the British representative, stood up and said in a solemn and serious tone, "Mr President, I have a historic statement to make." Everyone was tired at the end of the day. Malik sensed the mood and quipped, "If future history will not suffer, may I request the distinguished representative of Great Britain to postpone his historic statement till tomorrow." Everyone laughed and Jebb sat down. A story Malik himself told me was when he was the Soviet Ambassador in London. The Soviets had just launched their first Sputnik. At a party Princess Margaret asked him, "what does Sputnik in Russian mean." Malik replied that its ancient meaning was a boy following a girl, but its modern version was a device in orbit. Princess Margaret said, "Oh, I prefer the ancient version to the modern, don't you?"

Nikolai Firyubin, was the smoothest of all. He should have been an actor and might have done even better in that profession, but he was doing very well as Vice Foreign Minister for South-East Asia. At a party I invited both "Mr and Mrs Firyubin." Mrs Firyubin was no other than Madame Furtseva.

Minister for Culture. She refused to come unless she was invited in her own right. I did so. She came and I naturally gave her precedence over her husband. On the other hand, Mrs Gromyko and Mrs Kosygin were never conscious of their position and behaved naturally and came whenever they could manage to leave their household duties. In Stalin's Russia, wives hardly ever attended official parties with their husbands, unless they could come in their own right. But in Khruschev's Russia this rule was no longer observed. One of the most pleasant evenings we had at the embassy was when I invited about a half-a-dozen Soviet interpreters from the Foreign Office to a game of volleyball followed by dinner. Their wives also came. They were a gifted lot, sang, danced and talked most intelligently. The new Soviet diplomat is a match to any other in the world.

Among the Soviet Ambassadors abroad I liked the following: Pegov, who was with me in Iran and later Ambassador to India; Menshikov (smiling Mike as the Americans called him) who was Ambassador in India, then in the USA, and later Foreign Minister of the RSFSR; Antoli Dobrynin who was Ambassador in the USA when I was there (1973-76) and is still there; Chief Editor of *Pravda* Zamianin, whom I knew in Hanoi. These four were the best Soviet diplomats, I met, each different from the other but all clever, cultured, pleasant, friendly, helpful and communicative.

Skatchkov, Chairman of the State Committee for Economic Relations with Foreign Countries, was over-cautious, careful, "conservative"; he would not agree to anything unless he took approval from above. A good, honest man but difficult to get anything from without approaching his superiors. I had to do this on more than one occasion and seek Khruschev's, Kosygin's and Malinowsky's intervention to get things expedited. At a banquet in the Soviet embassy in Delhi for Skachkov and his delegation, I proposed a toast to "Skachkov, the greatest and best bureaucrat in the world," much to the amusement of his colleagues, but he did not seem to relish the compliment.

Among the Vice-Premiers, Dimshits was the most friendly towards India having headed the Soviet team at the Bhilai Steel Plant, a few years earlier.

As for the other members of the politbureau whom I got to know, Brezhnev struck me as a "refined Khruschev." He had all of Khruschev's good qualities but not his bad ones. With bushy eyebrows, a warm smile, a hearty laugh and deep husky voice, he had the knack of winning friends. He was fond of his drink, a chain cigarette smoker, and liked to drive fast cars. Once during a meeting, after Khruschev's fall, he told me in Gromyko's presence "India always charmed me. I ran away from home at the age of 15 and wanted to go to distant, mysterious India. My father brought me back and wanted me to prepare for the Soviet Diplomatic Service. I insisted on doing engineering, otherwise I would have suffered the same fate as Gromyko! Don't you think I acted wisely?" When Shastri visited the USSR in May 1965, Brezhnev told him, "There should be no formalities between us. Whenever you feel like it, come to us for a cup of tea at Tashkent or Moscow and return to India the next day. We shall do the same." This was a more subtle way of saying what Khruschev said in 1956 in India, "Whenever you need us, shout to us across the mountains of your Kashmir."

Brezhnev has natural qualities of leadership and was the one who was acceptable to all members of the politbureau at the time of Khruschev's fall from power in October 1964. There was a little delay in making the announcement but a compromise was worked out by appointing Kosygin as Premier and electing Brezhnev as First Secretary.

Mrs Gandhi, then Minister of Information and Broadcasting, was in Yugoslavia and came to Moscow on her way back to Delhi. She wanted to size up the situation and I was able to get an appointment for her to meet Brezhnev. We arrived at the party office punctually at 10 am, were taken up in the lift and seated in a reception room. There was a little flurry and I noticed Ponomoriev, secretary incharge of Asian communist parties at that time, in the corridors. We were then taken to a room where we expected to meet Brezhnev, but instead there was the gentle, mild-mannered, scholarly looking Suslov. He stood up, apologised and said, "Comrade Brezhnev has influenza, has sent his apologies and asked me to receive you, Mrs Gandhi, on his behalf." I was a little surprised but Mrs Gandhi rose to the occasion and replied, "Please convey our best wishes to Mr Brezhnev for speedy recovery. It is a pleasure to meet you, Mr Suslov." Suslov felt a little embarrassed but Mrs Gandhi put him completely at ease. She can be charming when she wants to.

We talked about China, India; the USSR, America and the world, but I wondered at the time whether Brezhnev was really ill or there was some trouble inside the politbureau. My doubts were soon resolved, but I still could not understand why they had not informed us before 10 am that Brezhnev was unwell. Perhaps they are as "efficient" as we in India about such details, or may be they were as anxious to sound Mrs Gandhi who had come from Belgrade about the reactions to Khruschev's fall, as she was to sound them.

Suslov is a quiet, soft-spoken, tall, slim, academic rather than a dogmatic theoretician. His scathing and scientific criticism of Chinese leadership during Khruschev's time, and even later, showed him as a staunch believer in Marxism-Leninism and consistent in his analysis. The new collective leadership did try, soon after Khruschev's fall, to make up with China, but failed— not for want of effort on their part, but because of China's dogmatic stand and perhaps misreading of the new situation.

I recall the triumphant manner in which a Chinese delegation led by Chou En-lai came to Moscow a fortnight after Khruschev's fall, to attend the 7 November celebrations. I had gone to Vanukovo airport to meet Pham Von Dong who was heading a Vietnamese delegation. Chou En-lai got down first, recognized me in the line of ambassadors and shook my hand firmly. Pham Van Dong was gentler and more affable and talked to me for a minute or two. In the evening at the Kremlin reception, Chou was the cynosure of all eyes, especially of the foreign press corps. He behaved like a hero celebrating the downfall of Khruschev rather than the Soviet National Day.

The ambassadors were standing in the front line facing Chou En-lai and Pham Van Dong. I went up to Pham, we talked about Vietnam for about five minutes and then I returned to my place. Chou stared at me but I did not make any move to go to him. However, when the ambassadors were asked "one by one" to clink glasses with the chief guests, I wished Chou "good health" and was about to pass on when he held me by the wrist and asked, "Why are you avoiding me?" I replied that he was the chief guest and I did not want to stand between him and others. He laughed and said *"Womun Lao Pbungyeo"* (We are old friends) and added: "Have you forgotten the past?" I asked: "which past? The Panch Sheel Agreement?" Then he asked: "Let us look

forward to the future" and I asked "which future, what future?"
He replied: "Don't be evasive. You know what I mean." I said
I did not. By then the Foreign pressmen were coming closer and
surrounding us. Chou took me aside and said: "I mean the forth-
coming Afro-Asian Conference at Algiers. We could meet and
talk there." I made no response. Our relations were strained.
We had been shocked at their violation of the Panch Sheel and
massive attack across our borders. I had no authority to make
any response nor had I expected Chou to make this gesture.
However, nothing came of it because the Algiers Conference was
postponed.

Curious ambassadors and inquisitive journalists, both foreign
and Soviet, asked me what had transpired between Chou and me.
I said that I had known him in Peking and we exchanged plea-
santries. Chou's gesture, however, intrigued me in more ways than
one. Was it a hint that Sino-Soviet relations might improve, after
Khruschev's fall, and we had better make up with China and not
rely too much on the Soviet Union; or could it be a genuine
move to meet us half way and settle the border issue? I think it
was more the former than the latter because if China wanted to
make up, they would not have made such a gesture in Moscow
rather in Peking or Delhi. We had not broken diplomatic relations in spite of the 1962 conflict and maintained senior Charge's
at each other's capitals. I did not attach too much importance to
this little encounter.

Chou behaved like a hero come home, expecting perhaps that
Khruschev's successors would now accept Mao as the leader of
the Asian communists, if not of world communists. The Soviet
collective leadership tried to make up with the Chinese leadership, but they would not accept Mao's leadership or make a
complete turn-about from Khruschev's line, which had been their
collective line. Khruschev may have used blunt language but the
policy was collective and the polemics a cover for more fundamental differences over national interests and policies.

Not being able to make much headway with Chinese leadership, the Soviet party came out with a strong, principled defence
of their stand and criticism of Chinese policies. Suslov had made
his famous report to the Party which was now widely publicized.
It criticized China and upheld the Soviet stand. Then came a
barrage of Chinese propaganda attacking the new Soviet leader-

ship which was described as "Khruschevism without Khruschev."
Khruschev must have had a good laugh in his Moscow flat where
he was living with his wife as a retired private citizen.

Other Soviet leaders I met were more outspoken in private
than in public. Polyansky, the amiable young protege of Khruschev, and still a member of the politbureau, and Vice Premier,
was very critical of China. Incidentally, he told me that he was a
child of the October Revolution. His mother gave birth to him in
Leningrad when the guns were booming on 7 November 1917.

Mazurov, who also belonged to the "younger" generation, was
close to Kosygin and his first deputy. Serious, sober and soft
spoken, he reflected Kosygin's mind in his own way. I found
him, like Kosygin, a helpful, cautious and useful man. He always
tried to do more and not less than he promised. I thought he
would make a good successor to Kosygin.

The most ambitious and outstanding among the younger
members of the politbureau was Shelepin, who held charge of
trade unions, security as well as party affairs. He spoke as if he
wielded power, influence and authority. He held too many portfolios, was too ambitious and earned the jealousy and suspicion
of his colleagues and was finally denuded of some of his feathers
and left with his role in the trade unions. Is it possible that he
may come up again? I wonder.

With the rest of the Politbureau members—Voronov, Pano-
moriev, Kirilenko and others I had a mere nodding acquaintance and not much contact. Podgorny who became President
after Brezhnev, impressed me as another Khruschevian type
though less ebullient, blunt and outspoken. During Khruschev's
days he wielded more influence, I thought, than after his fall.
Brezhnev emerged as the real number one in the Party combining
eventually both posts of President and First Secretary. New
and "younger" leaders are coming up and it is not easy to fore-
cast who will succeed Brezhnev. Whoever succeeds him, the
trend towards collective leadership is likely to increase.

Among the scores of Soviet Marshals and hundreds of
Generals I should like to mention a few I came across. Malinowsky heads the list. I once asked him what would happen to
the hundreds of Soviet Generals when there was complete disarmament. I added teasingly, would they not be unemployed? He
replied without a moment's hesitation, "There is no fear of that

because we shall need thousands of supervisors and inspectors of high rank to ensure and control total disarmament." He was Ukrainian, short, portly with a keen sense of humour and a warm smile. I once asked Khruschev what sort of defence preparedness we needed against the Chinese threat. He replied: "I am not an expert. I cannot say whether there will be sunshine, rain, thunder or lightning and whether you need an umbrella, a mackintosh or a winter overcoat. Why don't you ask Maliowsky?" So I did. Malinowsky said what India needed was a strong, mobile, well equipped (with latest weapons) army, air force and navy. Instead of a prestigious overhauled old British aircraft carrier (which he called the fifth leg of a dog and an easy target) we should go in for a submarine fleet to guard our long coastline, etc, etc. That was Malinowsky, a practical soldier who talked sense and gave it straight from the shoulder.

His deputy and successor, Marshal Gretchko, was quite the opposite—tall, slim, quiet, serious and a man of few words. What little he said was pregnant with potentialities and meaning. Unlike Malinowsky, he drank little and was not given to bantering. Air Chief Marshal Vershinin was a tall, slim, pleasant and delightful conversationalist. He was not tense and like Malinowsky, frank, friendly and outspoken. I remember once sitting between him and Menshikov at a Kremlin New Year banquet, where the two of them polished off a couple of bottles of Armenian cognac (75 per cent over proof) while I stuck to Vodka (40 per cent). Admiral Gorshkov, Chief of the Navy, is a typical naval officer—hail fellow well-met type—a good host, a delightful guest and a man who keeps his word. The most outstanding soldier was Voroshilov who always recalled his younger days when he had been at his height. The most impressive in appearance was Budenny, with a moustache like Stalin's and the best horseman in the USSR. I got along well with the Soviet military men and found them generally well informed and well disposed towards India and much more frank than the civilians.

One is apt to judge or misjudge communist societies, by their leaders. That may have been true during Stalin's rule when the Soviet people had little voice in their affairs. It is not true today. The Soviet people have tasted internal freedom and like it. The post World War II generation and youth, in particular, did not experience and do not remember Stalin's dictatorship.

Like youth everywhere, they like good music, good food, good
clothes, travel, fun and games. They talk critically and not res-
pectfully, much less worshipingly, about the older generation.
They get bored with repetitious party propaganda and monotonous hackneyed speeches. They like to get in touch with people
from other countries and travel abroad. There was much
evidence of this between 1962 and 1966. It is a sign of growing
strength and stability within the Soviet Union, maturity among
its leadership, and more confidence among its people. They are
not afraid of German revanchism or American imperialism.
They make jokes about China's chauvinism and, what is more
important, have developed the capacity to laugh at themselves.
They are no less talented and patriotic than their leaders, but
they are more relaxed. They desire peace not merely in it's sense
of absence of war but more positively as plenty, prosperity and
progress. They are keenly interested in the development of
science and technology in other countries. They listen to foreign
music, read foreign magazines, when they can get them, study
new modes and fashions and are much more internationally
minded than their predecessors.

Yevtushenko, Voznesensky, Bella Ahmadullina, Akujawa and
others are their favourite poets and singers, Neizvestny their
favourite sculptor and Glazunov their popular though controversial artist. There are many more but I have mentioned a few
I came across.

It is the younger generation in all countries—the USA,
western and eastern Europe, the USSR, Africa, Latin America,
India, South-East and South-West Asia and Japan which is the
hope of the future. Even in China the youth are showing signs
of coming into their own, but they will need more time perhaps
to assert themselves. When the present leadership of these
countries passes into the hands of the younger generation, there
will perhaps be greater scope for international understanding
and peace on the basis of mutual respect and mutual accommodation.

I recall my shock in 1948 at hearing from some Soviet intellectuals that they would rather lose 99 friends than risk having
one enemy among them. But in 1962-66 I found that though all
foreigners, especially diplomats, were suspect, there was no open
hostility to them. There was more contact and less fear. Foreign

tourists and students came in thousands to the USSR. Contact is bound to increase between the youth of all countries and likely to create greater trust and confidence, less fear and suspicion and thus strengthen the chances of peace and international understanding. It will take time but no one can stop this trend throughout the world.

I found this growing desire to know other countries and come closer to other peoples, throughout the Soviet Union—from Riga and Kiev to Tiblisi and Erevan, from Moscow to Tashkent and Dushanbe to Irkutsk and Khabarovsk. I had opportunity to travel to 20 out of the 28 Republics of the Soviet Union between 1962 and 1966, and was impressed by the progress made towards unity, stability and prosperity. Progress in education, culture, science and industry was phenomenal compared to the Czarist days or Stalin's Russia. Agriculture had not made the same progress but with increased irrigation facilities, digging of the long canals from north to south, and south-east to south-west and the diversion and inter-linking of various rivers and inland seas, agriculture is likely to progress further. I was deeply impressed by the development of power and industry in Siberia, especially in the Baikal-Irkutsk-Bratsk region. I often visited this area on my way to Ulan Bator where I was concurrently accredited as ambassador.

The new town of Bratsk was inhabited by a population averaging 29 years only and run by youngmen and women who came from the western regions to participate in the building of new Russia. They were given additional incentives and attractive salaries and appeared to be the future backbone of this vast country.

The Soviet Union has the largest area in the world. Its population is the third largest. Its natural resources are perhaps the largest but not yet fully tapped. With the development of science and technology, it is bound to become the leading country in the world by the end of the century—leading not necessarily in armaments but in the generation of power and production of steel, timber, gas and non-ferrous metals, etc. It has a vested interest in peace and against war. So has America, India and the rest of the world. But it will take time for them all to work together for the welfare and prosperity of all mankind. Countries like India can play a constructive role as a catalytic agent towards this end. Herein, lies one of the bases of Indo-Soviet friendship, and mutality of interest. Being geographically and geopolitically close to each other, they cannot afford to go apart and must get closer in their own interests and in the interests of peace in Asia and the world. Indo-Soviet friendship has prevented war and stabilized peace in south Asia and could play a similar role in South-East and South-West Asia, in cooperation with the countries of these regions. Will China and the USA realise this and join them or try to divide Asia into various spheres of influence? India wants to be friendly with all countries on the basis of equality and reciprocity and can never be the stooge of any country, however big and powerful. But friendship is a two-way and not a one-way street. It could be developed into a multi-lane highway to peace.

Jawaharlal Nehru was the most popular foreigner among the people of the Soviet Union. His visit to the USSR in 1955 had endeared him to the masses. Even dogmatic communists admitted to me that "though Nehru is not a scientific Marxist, his humanism transcends ideological barriers and unites people with different ideologies." Soviet leaders and people were genuinely concerned about his deteriorating health and often asked "after Nehru who?" and "after Nehru what?" Most Indians and other foreigners also asked the same question.

I had gone home for consultations in February 1964, and met Nehru several times. The Chinese invasion of 1962 had not only shattered a long-cherished dream, but also his health. He was making a valiant effort to recover. At a private luncheon in his house I saw him struggling to lift his left hand to the table. I pretended not to see this struggle. After lunch I mentioned to him what some eminent Soviet doctors had told me, "Nehru should lie down in bed and rest for two or three months." He flared up, "Let them go to hell. If I lie down in bed for even a week, I know I will not get up." Perhaps, he was right. He had never rested in his life, except in prison. Activity in pursuit of his goals was the only "rest" he knew. This was "the meaning of life" for him, as he had said in reply to a questionaire from Will Durant, the American philosopher many years before he became the Prime Minister.

I met him again after a few days. He was alone sitting on the sofa and reading. He was pensive but calm. He encouraged me to talk. I talked briefly about Sino-Indian, Sino-Russian and Indo-Russian relations. He listened patiently. He reaffirmed his faith in India and her destiny. I ventured to ask why he had not nominated or suggested a successor to lighten his own burden and groom someone to take his place, and added that the whole world was asking, "After Nehru who and what?" He did not seem to like my question and looked at me sharply as if to say "What cheek!" But, he softened his expression and said philosophically, "I do not believe in nominating a successor. Lal Bahadur is already acting as my Minister without Portfolio and has lightened my burden. To nominate him would only jeopardise his chances. Remember what happened to Eden when Churchill nominated him. Democracy must be allowed to work its own way. The people will choose whom they like. Somebody will emerge and be thrown up by the democratic process."

I felt sad at seeing the active, ever youthful Nehru, getting old. I had no idea his end was so near. He died on 27 May 1964. I had returned to Moscow. We were all shocked and stunned. Hurriedly we put up his portrait with a garland of flowers and a condolence book on the table in the entrance hall of the Embassy.

Khruschev was the first foreign dignitary to call. As he stood in front of Nehru's portrait, with his head bowed, tears rolled down his cheeks. He tried to console me. "A special delegation is being led by Kosygin, to attend the funeral. You can go in the same plane with them if you like," he told me. I accepted the invitation and informed Delhi I was coming with the delegation, without waiting for their approval. There was no time for it and, in any case, they were busy with more important matters.

We were off—Kosygin, his colleagues and I—in an Ilushin 18. Kosygin invited me to sit with him in his special cabin and asked some very searching questions. They were anxious to know if Nehru's policy would be continued as we were later anxious to know if Khruschev's policies would be continued after the latter's fall. But, there was a difference. Nehru's position in India, as the architect of her internal policy of socialism, secularism and democracy and the foreign policy of non-alignment and peaceful co-existence, was unique. Khruschev was part of a team though he gave his own emphasis to certain things. Nehru's successor might also shift the emphasis in India's policy away from the Soviet Union. This is what the Soviets were concerned about and wanted to find out—especially in view of their deteriorating relations with China. I was too grief-stricken to give any detailed answers to the searching and subtle questions. I told him briefly

that Nehru's policy had had the backing of Gandhi and enjoyed
the support of the Indian people. No matter who succeeded
Nehru, there could be no basic change in our policy. However,
it was important that they assure India of there being no change
in Soviet policy either.

Kosygin then asked me about various political parties, their
strength, influence and following, etc. I told him, again briefly,
that ours was a multi-party system, which stood together whenever there was an external threat. He asked if there was likely to
be a change in our stance towards China or our relations with
America. I told him that any change was unlikely in the foreseeable future, but much would depend on the state of the Indo-
Soviet relations. Hence their added importance. I think he got
my point.

We landed at Palam early next morning. Visa and other
formalities were waived. I drove straight to Teen Murti House
(Nehru's official residence) while Kosygin and party went to
the Soviet embassy. I went up to pay my last respects to the
mortal remains of the great man who had inspired us all through
our student days and later. His body lay in State. Nehru's face
looked pale and calm—almost as I had seen him two months
earlier. One missed the sparkle in his eyes and the charming smile
on his lips. He seemed to be in deep thought with "many more
promises to keep and miles to go before I sleep"—a quotation
from Robert Frost which he kept by his bedside. I went up to
Indira Gandhi and uttered a few consoling words. Mrs Pandit,
Rajiv Gandhi, Krishna Hutheesing, and other members of the
household were all there. Sheikh Abdullah who had cut short his
visit to Pakistan had tears in his eyes. D.P. Dhar, G.M. Sadiq,
Ghulam Mohammad Bakshi, P.N. Haksar, G. Parthasarathy,
Mir Qasim H.C. Sarin, Bijji Kaul, R.K. Nehru, Rajan Nehru
and Padmaja Naidu were also present. Delegations came from
various countries to lay wreaths on the cortege. Central ministers
including Morarji Desai, T.T. Krishnamachari and Gulzari Lal
Nanda were vying and jostling with each other to take their
"proper" place. Lal Bahadur Shastri, as modest as ever, remained
in the background. I went upstairs to the balcony to watch the
last remains of Nehru being taken away on a ceremonial gun
carriage from the house he had occupied for 17 years as the

Prime Minister of India. Mournful music broken by shouts of "Jawaharlal *Amar Hai*" (Nehru is immortal) with crowds weeping and wailing moved one to tears.

Next morning I met Nanda, Shastri and other leaders, to brief them about Kosygin who was going to call on them. When Kosygin called on Shastri the latter was in tears and chocked with emotion. He could not speak for a few seconds, then thanked Kosygin, his government and people for their sympathy and assured them of continuing Nehru's policies.

Nanda was more composed and talked about many things. I had warned Kosygin not to talk about Kashmir on this occasion as it would raise unnecessary doubts in the Indian mind. But, on the advice of his embassy, Kosygin mentioned it to Nanda and asked his views about "greater autonomy" for Kashmir. I had forewarned Nanda. He let Kosygin have it—right and proper. Kosygin beat a hasty retreat and said it was not his own view but he was merely mentioning what others had told him. This was almost as crude an attempt by some Soviet advisers as that of Duncan Sandys and Dean Rusk to pressurise Nehru on Kashmir at the time of the Sino-Indian conflict in December 1962. It met the same fate; the difference however was that while the Soviets knew how and when to retreat gracefully, the Anglo-Americans persisted till 1965.

Shastri like Nehru encouraged me to stay on in Moscow and told me to write directly to him if necessary. I did not, however, have to take advantage of this as I knew his Principal Secretary, L.K. Jha, well. We had joined government service in the same year. Though our approaches differed on some issues, we respected each other's point of view and often exchanged ideas.

I met Indira Gandhi before leaving back for Moscow with Kosygin. At Shastri's suggestion, I pleaded with her to join his cabinet which would ensure continuity of Nehru's policies not only in appearance but in reality. This was important to maintain India's image at home and links abroad. A few weeks later, she joined the cabinet as Minister for Information and Broadcasting.

On my return to Moscow many Nehru memorial meetings were held. I was asked to address the main one in the Hall of Columns which is reserved for memorials to the greatest leaders of the Soviet Union and the socialist countries. Kosygin presided. I was impressed by the dignity, solemnity and representative character of the meeting and the rich and warm tributes paid to Nehru by the Soviet leaders.

The void left by Nehru's passing away from the scene was there, but its poignancy was to some extent lessened because of Shastri succeeding him. I did not notice any significant departure from Nehru's policy. There were attempts by some to create a shift in the emphasis but Shastri did not fall for them. There was also a similar attempt in the USSR, especially towards a rapproachment with Pakistan. This did not, however, produce any significant change towards India for a few months until President Ayub Khan visited the USSR in April 1965.

In the meanwhile some delegations—mainly Parliamentary and cultural—exchanged visits between the USSR and Pakistan. The Pakistanis told the Soviets that their friendship with China did not stand in the way of developing friendly relations with the USSR and that their membership of SEATO and CENTO was only nominal and they would not support any move against the Soviet Union. They pleaded that the supply of Soviet tanks to India was a threat to Pakistan without mentioning the Patton tanks they had received from the USA. Some Soviet leaders were impressed by Pakistani pleas and told me so on their return. Their main aim was to keep their options open and try to wean Pakistan away from China, they said. I warned them, in the most frank and friendly manner, that we knew Pakistani leaders better than they. If the Soviet Union fell for their propaganda, they would not only weaken India's friendship, but might even drive her into the western camp. It was for them to consider what they valued more—the friendship of non-aligned and democratic India or the doubtful promises of the unstable and shaky military dictatorship of Pakistan which had military alliances with the West and was also close to China.

President Ayub Khan came to Moscow in April 1965. He was a man of great charm who produced good first impressions and said the right things in the right manner to the right people at the right time. He won the sympathy of some sections of the Soviet leadership—in the Party, government and armed forces. He pretended to be a dove and got some minor concessions in the way of civil aircraft, helicopters and some transport trucks. What he got was not so important, but that he had succeeded in making a dent on the Soviet mind, in spite of his double alliance with China and the West.

There were two schools of thought in India—one that wanted to go over to the West and the other that wanted to neutralize Pakistani efforts with the USSR. I went to India for consultations and persuaded Shastri to pay a visit to the Soviet Union in response to their invitation. He saw my point and, with the support and advice of others, accepted my recommendation.

The visit of Shastri and his wife to the USSR in May 1965, was memorable for more than one reason. The Soviet leadership was impressed by Shastri's modesty and gentleness and his genuine conviction and faith in Nehru's basic policies. Shastri was also impressed by the friendship of the Soviet leaders and their convictions born out of common interests to strengthen and not weaken ties with India. Some people had tried to poison Shastri's mind against the Soviet Union. I was keen for him to see things for himself and draw his own conclusions, just as it was necessary for the Soviet leaders to meet this new man of India and make their own assessment.

This strategy worked and we were able to set the Indo-Soviet friendship again on a firm footing. The Soviets soon discovered that Pakistan's main aim was to weaken India and grab our territory in Kutch and Kashmir. They were at first a little disappointed that we did not "beat the hell" out of the Pakistanis. Malinowsky told me frankly that in a short war quick success was what counted. I told him we did not wish to destroy Pakistan or grab its territory, also we had to keep adequate forces along the Chinese border. We could not, therefore, score a quick victory. The western powers, especially the USA and the UK, were playing their usual games. We would beat back the Pakistanis in a few days. As a military man, he did not quite appreciate my point of view. He said: What you need is a strong, well equipped and more mobile army and not a large, heavy footed one. You need more effective fighter interceptors and bombers and more modern artillery and weapons. I took him at his word and asked, "Why don't you help us to get all these?" He threw up his hands and said: "That is your job Mr

Ambassador. You must talk to our political leadership at the highest level. They alone can decide, not I."

I met Zakharov, Chief of Army; Gorshkov, Chief of Navy and Vershinn, Chief of Air Force. They were friendly, sympathetic and understanding, and more or less, repeated what Malinowsky had said, though not as bluntly. Rikhi Jaipal and O.P. Malhotra, my two chief aides, met the others and we got going. Shastri's visit was of considerable help in putting across our needs to the Soviet political leadership at the highest level. We could have got even more if the Government of India had pursued the matter more seriously. As usual, we tarried and hesitated and lost some excellent bargains and opportunities.

A full-fledged Indo-Pak war broke out in September 1965. It had been simmering since April in the Rann of Kutch. The war lasted barely two weeks. We had an edge over Pakistan but it was not a complete victory. Appeals from the West, suggestions from the USSR and pressure of opinion in the Afro-Asian world, plus our own assessment that further conflict would only drain our resources since we did not covet any Pakistani territory, resulted in our agreement to a cease-fire on 20 September, 1965.

The statement of British Prime Minister Harold Wilson, attributing and insinuating aggressive intent on our part produced a strong reaction in India. Americans were licking the Pakistani wounds and the failure of their Patton tanks in the hands of Pakistani soldiers. The Soviet leaders considered this a golden opportunity to wean Pakistan away from the West and bring about a rapproachment between India and Pakistan through their good offices. Kosygin called me and made an official proposal to invite the two Asian countries on the Soviet Asian soil to meet and talk among themselves. The Soviets would be there to give any help we needed. It was an offer of "good offices" and not "mediation."

Some top Soviet leaders privately assured me that it was not a shift in the Soviet policy against India, but an attempt to wean Pakistan away from the western and Chinese influence. If India and Pakistan could get together and solve their problems with the help of the Soviets, it would have a sobering effect on China. Such an agreement arrived at on Soviet soil would have the backing of the Soviet Union. Their own prestige was at stake

and they would do everyting to help. Even if there was no agreement, the attempt was worth it. It would break the strangelhold
of the West on Pakistan and serve as a warning to China not to
fish in troubled waters. But, there was no reason why the
conference would not succeed, given goodwill and sincerity on
both sides. They did not want India to make any concessions to
Pakistan in Kashmir or elsewhere. It had not been a decisive war
though India had an edge over Pakistan. Another Indo-Pak
conflict would not serve the interests of either country but ruin
the economy of both. The Soviet Union was taking a risk in
offering her good offices, but the risk was worth taking in the
larger interests of peace and her own security in the region.

I was impressed with these arguments. I believe they were
simultaneously sounding Pakistan but her reaction had not yet
come. I asked if this would mean any reduction in or stoppage
of their military supplies to India or increase in the quality and
quantity of such supplies to Pakistan. They assured me that
there was no such intention. India was a bigger country, her
needs were greater, she was not a member of a military alliance
and had to be prepared to defend her territory against the
Chinese threat. I asked if the Soviet Union would guarantee any
agreement that was reached between India and Pakistan. They
said they would witness it, endorse it, and guarantee it if the two
sides wanted that.

All this was verbal and nothing in writing was passed on by
either side. Each was trying to probe the other. It was at a high
political level and I was able to check and cross-check from
different members of the Politbureau that it had their full
backing.

Of course the Soviet leaders had their own interest in this. It
would be a feather in their cap and steal the thunder from the
West and China. It would create a friendly area in the soft,
southern underbelly of the USSR. It would strengthen their
claim to be an Asian country, and give them a say in Asian
affairs. It would also relieve them of the constant problem of
having to take sides betwen India and Pakistan and might
encourage the two to talk directly with each other. If they did
not succeed in direct talks the Soviet Union could always be
there to help. It would decrease the western, especially American,
influence in Pakistan and also isolate China.

All this might happen if the conference succeeded. What if it failed? The failure could be blamed on India and Pakistan. It would show that the Soviet Union was a genuine friend of both, and had staked its reputation to bring them together. It was unlikely that both would turn to the West—Pakistan might but India was unlikely to. In any case, Pakistan was already aligned with the West and it would be no loss. As for India, she might become "neutral" or "equidistant," but she could not depend on the West which, in the past, had let her down vis-a-vis Pakistan and was unlikely to take her side now or in the foreseeable future. If India wanted to take help from the West against China, no harm would be done thereby. It might even relieve the Soviet Union of some worries. Such perhaps were some of the un-expressed calculations in the Soviet mind.

There was a risk for the Soviet Union, but it was a calculated risk, with the odds in their favour. What was there in it for India? Why should India agree to it? This was the question being debated in the Indian Cabinet after I sent them the Soviet proposal. It was being debated in the Pakistan Cabinet too. The Soviets were waiting anxiously and eagerly for a response from both.

India's first reaction was somewhat negative and Pakistan's "acceptance" was hedged-in with "ifs" and "buts." The Soviets seemed to have drawn a blank in the first round. But, they persisted. I was a little surprised at their hectic diplomacy and told them that if Pakistan was going to put conditions, we were not going to accept them. It was not as if they were victors and we the vanquished. The Soviets said that India was bigger, had less reason to be afraid and could afford to be "generous" and "magnanimous" in victory etc. I said plainly to them that this would not do. If they could get an unconditional acceptance from Pakistan, I would recommend my government to do the same.

I had not yet conveyed our initial reaction to the Soviet side because I wanted to find out Pakistan's response. I urged my government to reconsider the matter and gave my reasons for and against. On balance, I felt it was a risk worth taking. If we accepted and Pakistan did not, they would be put in the wrong, and vice-versa. If we accepted without any preconditions, their conditional acceptance would still put them in the wrong. If we rejected the invitation outright and they accepted conditionally, they might have an edge over us. And if both put conditions we would only "equate" ourselves with Pakistan and thereby show our weakness rather than strength. An outright rebuff by both to the Soviet offer would only give a handle to China and the West to fish in troubled waters, as they had done in the past.

Apart from all this, there was the important consideration that the Soviet prestige was involved. We had not refused similar offers from western countries in the past. The British proposal for arbitration on Kutch, for instance, was accepted by us, though it proved to be ultimately to our disadvantage. We had previously accepted the ceasefire agreement in Kashmir in 1949, mainly on Anglo-American "appeals." This was the first instance in history where the Soviet Union had offered its good offices to two non-communist Asian countries to meet on the Soviet-Asian soil. It would shift the focus from America and Europe to Asia. Asian problems would not require to be solved in Europe and America. It might encourage direct negotiations between India and Pakistan without third party intervention, in due course.

In any case, it was not the Soviet Union's intention, or in their own interest, to take the side of Pakistan against India. They would try to be neutral at Tashkent, and might put some pressure on Pakistan if she became unreasonable. It was in the Soviet interest to maintain its friendly relations with non-aligned India. She would not risk it for the doubtful advantage of friendship with a western aligned Pakistan. Their hope was to try to wean Pakistan away from the Western and Chinese influence. This was their hope. If the conference was held it would raise their prestige in Asia. If it was a succes it would stabilize peace on the sub-continent and not make it a battleground for Sino-Soviet and Soviet-American rivalries. India had nothing to lose and might gain something. Soviet friendship for India was important, especially in view of the Chinese threat and the pro-Pakistani stance of the West.

These and other considerations must have weighed with the Government of India and they finally conveyed their principled agreement for the holding of the Tashkent conference. Pakistan realized she could not hedge any more and also agreed ultimately to come without any preconditions. The West was somewhat surprised but did not object to their ally Pakistan meeting India on the Soviet soil. They perhaps thought the conference would fail and strain the friendly relations between India and the USSR and turn India and Pakistan more towards them.

It was against this background that the Tashkent Conference was held from 4 to 10 January 1966.

My principal colleagues and I established ourselves in the Intourist Hotel at Tashkent, a few days in advance. So did the Pakistan embassy and the Soviet officials nearby. Rikhi Jaipal, B.S. Das, J.S. Teja and N.P. Jain were our embassy team. They all had their contacts with the Soviet heirarchy and the press and each looked after his own flock. Our team from Delhi was quite formidable. Besides Prime Minister Shastri and his personal staff, there were Defence Minister Y.B. Chavan, Foreign Minister Swaran Singh, Foreign Secretary C.S. Jha, Principal Secretary to Prime Minister L.K. Jha, Home Secretary L.P. Singh and General Kumaramangalam.

The Pakistani Delegation included President Ayub Khan, Foreign Minister Bhutto, Minister of Information and Broadcasting plus their secretaries and the embassy team from Moscow. The Soviet team was headed by Kosygin and included Foreign Minister Gromyko, Defence Minister Malinowsky, Marshal Sakalov and others. The Soviet, Western, Indian and Pakistani press was fully represented with a sprinkling of other Asians and East-Europeans. Every hotel of Tashkent was full.

The Indian and Pakistani delegations stayed in a large compound in separate villas. There was a "neutral" villa in between where the heads of the two delegations and their aides could meet each other or the Soviet delegation when necessary.

The weather was beautiful, cool, sunny and pleasant. It was plus 20 degrees C in Tashkent as against minus 20 degrees C in Moscow. The place had an Asian look and atmosphere. The Soviets could not have chosen a better place. The Soviet press struck a positive and optimistic note from the start, while the Western press pointed out only the difficulties and predicted failure. It was a tough going for a whole week. Everyone worked hard, but none harder than Kosygin and Gromyko. They would sound each delegation first thing every morning and last thing every night. They carried the views and suggestions of one to the other, subtly, gently and faithfully, and tried to bring the two viewpoints closer. They were patient, persevering, polite and never gave the impression of pressurizing either delegation. Only once I heard Gromyko getting tough with Bhutto on the telephone from our villa. This was when Bhutto tried his best to make Ayub Khan go back on his commitment in his own hand-writing "not to have recourse to force." Gromyko told Bhutto in my hearing on the phone, "I am sorry but you are not telling the truth. You are going back on your President's word." Bhutto had to give in but sulked and tried to create other difficulties.

Negotiations went on, mainly behind the scenes, through the good offices of the Soviet delegation. When they were stuck with both delegations on some crucial point, they suggested a direct meeting between Prime Minister Shastri and President Ayub. It was their meeting in the neutral villa which solved the first main hurdle about not having recourse to force. The Pakistanis would not agree to a "No War Pact" but did agree not to use force. This was on the fourth day, i.e. 7 January 1966. On 8 January, a real crisis developed regarding withdrawal from the new ceasefire line to the old ceasefire line in Jammu and Kashmir. The Pakistanis insisted on keeping Chhamb which they had taken and yet wanted the Haji Pir area back which we had occupied. Shastri was firm as a rock and would not give up Haji Pir unless they gave up Chhamb. It seemed as if the conference would break up on this issue. Kosygin first tried to persuade Ayub Khan. When he failed, he came to Shastri and pleaded for our giving up Haji Pir. Shastri was firm and told him, "You will have to look for another Prime Minister of India to agree to this. I will not. I cannot." Kosygin shifted his ground and said that this was not his idea, he was only conveying to us what Ayub Khan had told him. He would try his best to persuade him to give up Chhamb in exchange for Haji Pir. Shastri said he would agree to it only in the larger interest of peace provided Ayub did not go back on his solemn assurance to renounce the use of force.

It was the afternoon of 8th January. That evening there was a press conference in Hotel Tashkent. About 300 journalists were present. C.S. Jha and I used to brief them. When a western correspondent asked, "Is it true that the talks are on the verge of breakdown?", I replied, "The nearer you get to the summit of a mountain, the stiffer the climb." This was a true reflection of the state of negotiations. Neither Pakistan nor India could afford to break the conference. Pakistan was being deliberately difficult in order to pressurize India. But, Shastri was a tough negotiator.

He stood very firm on not giving up Haji Pir unless Pakistan gave up Chhamb. He did this after consulting the Foreign and Defence Ministers and General Kumaramangalam. He not only consulted all of us in the delegation but even took a poll in the Indian press corps about it.

He sounded the Indian press corps next morning as to what their reaction would be to an exchange of Haji Pir for Chhamb. With one exception, they all said if Pakistan was willing to renounce the use of force, the exchange would be a good compromise.

This was the way a democratic leader conducted his negotiations. He had come to his own conclusion but wanted to take his team along with him and give them a feeling of full participation. We never felt we were being dictated to or dominated. We looked upon him as one of us whom we loved, admired and respected.

That afternoon Ayub Khan came to Shastri's villa, had lunch with him and agreed to Shastri's proposal, over-ruling Bhutto. That was a day of rejoicing in all the three camps, but not for Bhutto. However, we could not be certain until all other points had been thrashed out and finalized. Bhutto was quite capable of creating last minute difficulties. On 10 January, in the morning the final draft of the Tashkent declaration was exchanged and the signing ceremony took place that afternoon, much to the surprise of the western press.

The signing ceremony was a solemn affair. Kosygin did not try to dominate the scene or claim credit for the agreement. He let Ayub Khan and Shastri take the leading roles and gave them all the credit. Kosygin was only a "witness" to the signing of the document. Ayub and Shastri shook hands warmly and it appeared as if a new chapter in Indo-Pak relations was going to begin. Ayub Khan suggested that Shastri visit Pakistan on his way back which the latter politely declined as he had an appointment in Kabul the next morning.

There was a reception and a banquet that evening by the Soviet Government. About an hour before that Shastri had an important meeting with Kosygin. I was also there. They exchanged ideas about China, Pakistan, India, the USSR, etc. Kosygin asked Shastri what we wanted in the way of cooperation and assistance in various fields. Shastri was too proud and modest to ask for anything. He merely said, "Our ambassador will be seeing you from time to time. We rely on your friendship and appreciate your efforts to make this conference a success. But for you it would have been much more difficult." This was true and Shastri meant it.

Kosygin, in his turn, offered his congratulations and thanks to Shastri for his "wisdom, statesmanship and spirit of conciliation" without which it would have been impossible to reach agreement with Pakistan. He expressed the hope that India and Pakistan would begin to talk directly and resolve their problems bilaterally.

This was indeed a moment to remember. Two Asian neighbours (India and Pakistan), two people with a common racial, cultural and historical background, divided by a foreign imperialist power before it quit the subcontinent, trying to rid themselves of the legacy of imperialism. Their problems were similar, they spoke the same languages (Punjabi, Bengali, Urdu), ate the same food, wore the same clothes, heard the same music and yet had become hostile to each other because of the machinations of foreign powers. Two bloody wars had ruined their economies, an arms race was draining their resources. How long could they go on like this? Here was an opportunity for both to make a fresh start and open a new chapter in their post-independence relations. Tashkent was only the first step, the beginning. Would the Tashkent spirit survive or would it also meet the same fate as the Panch Sheel?

I came back with Shastri from the reception at about 10 pm dropped him at his villa and then went with L.K. Jha to meet some pressmen. We returned about midnight and went to sleep. At about 1.30 a.m., L.K. telephoned me from his room in the hotel that he had just received a message from the villa that Shastri had suffered a severe heart attack. I rushed to the villa and found Shastri's body in the lap of Dr Chug, his personal physician, who was crying. I telephoned Gromyko and informed him of the tragedy. In the meanwhile a team of Soviet doctors had arrived and soon followed Kosygin, Gromyko, Molinowsky and others. Our own delegation members came in tears. Then came Ayub Khan and his delegation. A team of Soviet doctors and Dr Chug examined the body of Shastri and wrote a unanimous report attributing his death to a massive heart attack. They injected medicines to preserve the body for the flight to Delhi.

I have cried only thrice for any public leader—the first was at Gandhi's assassination, the second at Nehru's death and the third at Shastri's. Each was different from the other and yet all three had their own greatness. Gandhi was in a class by himself. Nehru was the maker of modern India. Shastri would have been the builder of post-Nehru India if he had lived. Modest, gentle, soft-spoken and shy but, firm like a rock when it came to principles, or national interests, he was a man of peace, practical and realistic in his approach to problems. He had a sweet way of smiling when he was pleased with something. He never shouted or lost his temper. He had gentler and more effective ways of showing his disagreement or disapproval. He would either keep a stony silence or knit his forehead in a frown which conveyed more than words could.

Shastri believed in both Gandhi's and Nehru's ideas and wanted to combine the two in building a new India. He was, perhaps, the only Indian leader in the post-Nehru era who could have done this. His sudden and untimely death was an irreparable loss to India. He sacrificed his life to save peace. But for him, Tashkent would not have been a success. It needed courage and conviction for an Indian Prime Minister at that time to take risks to save peace and prevent war. Another man in his place might have got cold feet and refused to sign the agreement. But Shastri was a man of courage. He was convinced that the Tashkent agreement was the best possible in the stalemate that followed the Indo-Pak conflict of 1965, and the only way to save peace and prevent war. Alas, India was not lucky enough to have the leadership of this "great little man" after Tashkent.

The scene in Tashkent was tragic. It gave a silent, solemn and moving demonstration of the love and friendship of the Soviet people for India and this great leader. The Soviet leaders insisted on joining as pall-bearers and even Ayub Khan lent his shoulder. The people of Tashkent, old and young, men and women, boys and girls—turned out a million strong, lining up both sides of the road, twenty deep, from the villa to the airport. More than half the population of Tashkent had turned out within a few hours to pay their last respects to this great Indian.

Shastri's name will go down in history as a man of peace. He gave his life to improve relations between India and Pakistan, to prevent the resumption of war between them, to usher in an era of negotiation and conciliation, rather than confrontation and conflict. But, peace and friendship are a two-way street. Will India and Pakistan learn to live as good neighbours after the Tashkent and Simla Agreements? There is no alternative except the ruination of both. Tashkent was the first step. Simla the second. Let us hope that the third will be a step towards ensuring real, durable and lasting peace and cooperation between the two.

We owe it to Gandhi, Nehru and Shastri and to the ardent desire and common interests of over 700 million people of India and Pakistan to work for this goal and achieve it in our life time. Let not future generations in India and Pakistan blame us for not having tried. Shastri, like Gandhi and Nehru, will always symbolize for us the spirit of sacrifice and peace, the spirit of Tashkent, and the dire necessity of living in peace and friendship with our neighbours.

19 The Emergence of Indira Gandhi

We left Tashkent on the morning of 11 January 1966, with the last remains of Shastri and reached Palam three hours later. There was a huge concourse of solemn, sad and mournful people, at the airport. Those who had voiced their resentment on hearing the news of the Tashkent Agreement had sunk their differences in this moment of sorrow. I remember the words of Atal Bihari Vajpayee, the leader of the Jana Sangh Party at the memorial meeting in Ramlila Grounds the next day. He said in beautiful Hindi—"*Bhārat Mātā Ki Gode Khāli Hai, Par Bhārat Mātā Ki Kokh Khāli Nahin*"—"Mother India's lap is empty, but not her womb." This simple and simultaneous tribute to Shastri and to Mother India symbolized in a few words the sorrow of the Indian people as well as their hope and confidence for the future.

The immediate scene was not so hopeful. The scramble for power had already started. Various calculations, permutations and combinations were being made. Should age and seniority govern the succession to Shastri or the more democratic method of secret ballot? The democratic process prevailed. Indira Gandhi was elected leader of the Congress Parliamentary Party, defeating her rival, Morarji Desai, by over 150 votes. Morarji took his defeat with good grace and Indira made a friendly gesture by naming him Deputy Prime Minister. It seemed as if the ruling party would still hold together and follow in the footsteps of their great, departed leaders.

However, this was not so easy. The Congress Party had held together too long. It was not a political party really, but a conglomeration of many ideologies—rightist, centrist and leftist. There were various groups and factions inside it, each hoping to control the "young" Prime Minister and guide her to their own way of thinking. Indira Gandhi proved more than a match for the older and more senior party leaders. She had been President of the Party in 1959, had toured with her father extensively, knew practically all the leading figures in various states. Being Nehru's daughter gave her an aura that no other leader had. She tried to stand on her own right and merit, but she seemed to lack confidence in the first year or two. She accepted advice from certain colleagues and advisers to devalue the Indian rupee by 57 per cent at one stroke. Economically it may perhaps have been justified to some extent, but politically it was a blunder with the 1967 elections in the offing.

I was still in Moscow when Indira Gandhi was returning from her first trip to the USA as Prime Minister. I met her at the airport and ventured to express my grave apprehensions about the proposed move. I had received a hint to this effect from one of her colleagues who had visited Moscow a few days earlier. Mrs Gandhi looked at me as if to say "What do you know of economics?" She said she had been advised by financial experts and leading economists in India and abroad that it was necessary to devalue the rupee in India's national interest. She was not an economist herself, she said, but if it was in the country's interest, she would even sacrifice the party's interest for it. That was a commendable stand to take provided it really was in the country's interest. The extent of devaluation was steep. Few steps had been taken to follow up this drastic reduction in the exchange rate of the Indian rupee, to increase trade, conserve foreign exchange and stabilize internal prices. It proved to be an economic failure and political disaster in the 1967 general elections when the ruling party for the first time, lost its big majority at the centre and in some states.

Signs of instability began to appear on India's horizon. The ruling party had to depend on the support of some leftist parties and elements to avoid defeat in Parliament. This widened the gulf between the right and left wings of the Congress party, between the elders and seniors on one side, and the junior and younger elements on the other. Indira Gandhi was looked upon by the latter as their leader and created a "left of centre" image for herself. She antagonized some of the older elements who had sided with her in the hope of keeping her under control. This estrangement was partly ideological and partly due to difference in age and temperament. Differences increased and led to the "split" of the Congress Party in 1969. Mrs Gandhi gave the split an ideological tone by confronting the senior leaders with her "Twelve Points" at Bangalore. The crisis deepened when she sponsored V.V. Giri as the presidential candidate against Sanjeeva Reddy who was the older group's nominee. The elders' group was nicknamed the "syndicate" and this name somehow stuck. They had opposed Mrs Gandhi's first proposal to nominate Jagjivan Ram, the senior-most Harijan leader and member of Parliament and government. Giri stood as an independent, but with Mrs Gandhi's support, and won by a narrow margin.

Giri's election was a victory for Mrs Gandhi. It was also the defeat of the "syndicate." Indira Gandhi, when driven to the wall, can show courage and guts. She had staked her political career and reputation on Giri's election. It was a gamble but luck favoured her. The result of the election heartened the younger and more "progressive" elements in the party and the country. They expected Indira Gandhi to take a bolder leftist line on the country's social, economic and political problems, as well as in foreign policy matters.

Indira had proved herself a shrewd politician, outwitting the older leaders in the "syndicate." Would she be able to fulfil the hopes and expectations she had aroused, especially among the younger and more progressive elements? This was to be her chance and test. She had lost the support of the older Congressmen, who formed the Congress (O). It was a conservative group and allied itself with other conservative parties in Parliament. The ruling party's strength was thus further reduced. It had to seek the support of the more leftist parties like the CPI, regional parties like the DMK and minorities, like the Harijans and the Muslims.

Mrs Gandhi was in a tight corner—but sometimes she is at her best in a crisis. In normal times she is apt to be hesitant and indecisive, vaccillating and wavering. In a crisis she seems suddenly to take courage and strike at the right moment and right place. Her main weakness was that she did not prevent crisis situations developing through timely action and well thought out programmes. Sometimes she gave the impression of itching to create a crisis in order to test the strength or weakness of her opponents. She left her options open; if she found them too strong she was willing to compromise, and if she found them weak, she had no compunction in destroying them. When she is challenged her strong will and determination and her courage and conviction come to the fore, which lie dormant in normal times.

Mrs Gandhi tried to introduce measures which would create a psychological effect and produce a more progressive image of her party and government, internally and externally, and put her opponents in the wrong. Bank nationalization, abolition of princes' privileges and similar measures were symbolic of the "new look" in the Congress party. They exposed the "syndicate" and other conservative parties that opposed them and strengthened the more socialist and progressive elements throughout the country. These were not very radical measures, but they gave a new direction to government's policies and thinking.

However, the Congress party, even with its "new look" was not in a position to introduce any major reforms. It could not muster a two thirds' majority in Parliament for any fundamental changes in the constitution. It lacked the organizational strength and political will even to implement fully the reforms already passed like the agrarian law, the law against untouchability, etc. It depended for support on the rich farmers in the rural areas and the big traders and industrialists in urban areas. Bureaucratism and corruption were hampering progress in every field. Casteism, regionalism, factions within factions and, groups within groups, were eating at the vital organs of the party, at every level, especially at the top and middle levels. Contact at the grass roots was neglected. The party was getting too smug and complacent, swollen headed and flabby in the middle. Mrs Gandhi alone could not carry the whole of India on her shoulders, but her colleagues and party members left everything to her. She was described as "the only man in the cabinet."

Mrs Gandhi by herself was a pragmatist, slightly left of centre, shrewd, aloof and distrustful. She kept her cards close to her chest and did not completely trust anyone else, like all politicians. She was capable of taking bold and courageous decisions but she lacked the will to see them followed through and implemented. She seemed also to lack her father's vision and warmth to attract and keep dedicated and honest people around her for long. She was, perhaps, a victim of circumstances. A lone child and lonely, she had to depend on her own inner resources and talents when her father was in prison and her mother sick or no more. As long as her father was alive, she kept close to him, but after his passing away, she was literally alone. At one time she thought of giving up politics and taking to social and educational work. Politics was in her blood and circumstances drove her into the political arena.

Indira Gandhi had watched her father at close quarters. She had seen how he was let down by some of his colleagues and the administration, how his progressive and farsighted policies were sabotaged and not implemented. But, Nehru was an idealist and a philoospher. He looked at things in the wider world perspective and against the background of history and historical forces. Indira Gandhi was no visionary. She was practical, pragmatic and down to earth. She was always cold, aloof and distrustful of others. She had courage and determination and a strong will. For a time her qualities stood her and the country in good stead. We needed a leader who was strong and determined, could stand up to foreign pulls ahd pressures and resist domestic threats. Indira Gandhi could fulfil the role and did for some time.

I came back to Delhi in June 1966 as Secretary in the Ministry of External Affairs, after spending over three-and-a-half-years in the Soviet Union. I watched Indira Gandhi during her talks with foreign dignitaries abroad. During her visit to Cairo, Yugoslavia and Moscow in 1966, she conducted herself with great ability, dignity and determination. She impressed Presidents Nasser, Tito and the new Soviet leadership as a progressive leader of courage and conviction and the national leader in India who could steer the country to the goal of socialism. They looked upon her not only as Nehru's daughter but a leader in her own right and listened to her with respect and attention. That a frail woman, not yet 47-years-old, should be elected as the leader of the largest party in a country the size of India, was no mean achievement. They went all out to befriend her and she made the right and correct responses. She was not a leader you could take for granted.

Soviet leaders were trying to befriend Pakistan again and were thinking seriously of giving some military supplies to her. Mrs Gandhi told them in no uncertain terms what its repercussions on Indo-Soviet relations would be. What she did not want to say herself, she left to others.

There was a banquet in St. George's Hall in the Kremlin for Mrs Gandhi. I was sitting between Polyansky and Mazurov. Brezhnev and Kosygin flanked Mrs Gandhi. Most members of the Politbureau were present. I said to both Polyansky and Mazurov, in a deliberately loud voice, that if the Soviet Union gave military hardware to Pakistan they would not only fail to wean her away from China or the USA, but might lose the friendship of India. It was a strong, blunt and provocative statement, and meant to be so. The other Soviet leaders heard it, as I had wanted them to. There was silence for a few seconds. Brezhnev and Kosygin tried to reassure Mrs Gandhi that they had no intention to encourage an arms race on the sub-continent. They realized the difference between peaceloving, non-aligned, democratic India and Pakistan militarily aligned to the West. They would continue to supply our economic and military requirements according to our agreements and not send any weapons to Pakistan.

We had gained respite for some time. But, nothing in international relations is permanent. With rapidly changing conditions in various parts of the world, international relations also undergo change. We had to be wide awake and watchful of changes and shifts in other countries.

Mrs Gandhi did not believe in putting all the eggs in one basket. She tried to improve relations with the USA but drew almost a blank. Nixon had a prejudice against India and in favour of Pakistan. He felt he was treated rather coldly during his unofficial visit to India in 1968 and made much fuss of in Pakistan. His global strategy was different from that of Kennedy. He propounded his "Asian Doctrine" which meant, in effect, reducing the Soviet influence in Asia, cutting India to size, helping America's client states and exploiting Sino-Soviet differences by befriending China and antagonizing the Soviet Union.

Mrs Gandhi, or for that matter, any Prime Minister of India, could not accept this thesis. Nixon's Presidential halt in India in 1969 enroute from Guam proved a fiasco. There was no meeting ground between Nixon and Indira and the two drifted apart.

In the non-aligned world, Mrs Gandhi made a deep impression, especially at the 1969 Summit Conference in Lusaka. India was looked up to by most non-aligned countries to give a lead and find solutions to complicated problems inter-se and vis-a-vis the developed world. K.B. Lall was elected as Chairman of the Economic Drafting Committee and on me fell the burden of Chairmanship of the Political Drafting Committee. We succeeded in getting almost unanimous approval for the two draft declarations—political and economic. I was faced with a difficult situation when most of the Muslim countries insisted on changing the Cairo Declaration's resolution on Cyprus. I was able to presuade the Drafting Committee to agree to refer the question to the Heads of State and government, who were meeting in less than half-an-hour. I telephoned President Kaunda and informed him of the situation, so that he may be forewarned.

When the question came up before the meeting, Kenneth Kaunda handled it with superb skill. He appealed to reason, emotion, non-aligned solidarity, etc., and got the resolution through almost unanimously with only two members speaking against it. Later 14 more noted their dissent. I had first met Kaunda in my house in London in 1961 when he was still leading his country's struggle for independence. He had then struck me as closer to Gandhi's and Nehru's ideas than many Indian leaders. Although he came from the warlike Massawa tribe, he was a man of peace and a believer in non-violence. At Lusaka I found in him an able leader, an ideal administrator a man of the people and a skilful negotiator.

Another African leader who impressed me at the preparatory meeting in Dar-es-Salaam and then at Lusaka, was Julius Nyrere of Tanzania. I had met him also in London in 1961 when he was leading his people to independence. He had since grown from a school master to a great leader of the African people. Less emotional than Kaunda, Nyerere was more practical and down to earth and able to carry various groups in his own country and in Africa along with him.

Jomo Kenyatta, President of Kenya, was a different man altogether. Mrs Gandhi visited Nairobi on our way back from Lusaka. We met "the tiger," as he was called, in his country-house, outside Nairobi. He still had the tiger's flashing eyes but he had settled down to a quiet, comfortable life. Though still regarded with respect and fear by his colleagues, he did not interefere in the day-to-day affairs which he left to younger colleagues. He was getting old, but did not look his age.

Africa is the "coming continent." It is resurgent and seething with not only an urge for racial equality, but a movement for economic and social independence. Whether it will achieve its goals peacefully or through violence, is not certain, but that it will achieve them in the forseeable future is-evident. Various powers are trying to extend their influence in different countries of Africa, but they are unlikely to succeed for long. African nationalism is not going to be the stooge of another country or ideology. It will find its own "African" solutions to African problems.

Mrs Gandhi took a keen interest in foreign affairs and had personal contacts with important heads of government or state. There was no obsession of Pakistan and China so as to neglect the medium and small countries in Asia, Africa and Latin America. She visited Singapore, Malaysia, Australia and New Zealand in 1968 and was bold enough to suggest an international convention or agreement to ensure respect for the sovereignty, integrity and neutrality or non-alignment of countries in this region, especially Vietnam, Laos and Cambodia. She also visited several countries in Latin America and the Carribean and was the first Indian Prime Minister to do so and also visited neighbouring countries like Nepal, Bhutan, Burma, Sri Lanka to develop close ties with their leaders. In 1970 Mrs Gandhi addressed the Silver Jubilee Session of the UN General Assembly and met leaders of various countries. She improved the image of India abroad and put India on the world map again after Nehru's death.

A country's foreign policy can be successful only to the extent that her internal policies are, as the foreign policy is a reflection of internal policy and internal conditions. Mrs Gandhi's success in internal affairs was limited. The food situation was far from satisfactory. Agrarian reforms existed only on paper and were not implemented. The green revolution had increased agricultural production but benefited mainly the rich farmer who could afford the necessary inputs. The poor farmer remained poor. Landless agricultural labour was under-employed and lived

below the poverty line. Educated unemployment was increasing
and thousands of Indian medical doctors, engineers and teachers
sought employment abroad. Students were discontented because
their education was not employment-oriented. Industrial production did increase but the profits went mainly to large industrial houses and big business. On the credit side, however, must
be mentioned the strengthening of the public sector and improvement in the treatment of Harijans, Muslims and other minorities.
There was also greater harmony between the centre and the
states and between the north and the south. Indira Gandhi
adopted a wise linguistic policy and did not try to impose Hindi
on non-Hindi speaking areas. The tribal people got a better deal
and the problem of Nagaland was tackled firmly and with imagination. She emerged as the most outstanding national leader,
acceptable to all regions of the country.

Mrs Gandhi was able to successfully tackle the Kashmir
problem and win Sheikh Abdullah's trust and confidence. The
Sheikh was an outstanding leader in his own right and a firm
believer in India's policy of secularism, socialism and democracy.
He had made great sacrifices to remove the shackles of feudal
rule in Kashmir from 1931 onwards. It is a pity that Nehru
could not utilize Abdullah's influence and talents in the wider
perspective of India, let alone Kashmir.

I had known and admired the Sheikh from my student days
in Kashmir and tried to bring about an understanding between
him and Mrs Gandhi in 1967 when he was living under house
detention in Delhi. I had three meetings with him alone lasting
about 12 hours and tried my best to appeal to his patriotism, the
unity of India, peace on the sub-continent, and pointed to the
lack of leadership among Indian Muslims, the growing evils
of communalism, casteism and regionalism, etc. He agreed with
all this but insisted that the wrongs done since his arrest in
1953 must first be undone. He was bitter at times but for a
man who had been imprisoned for a total of 20 years, he was
large-hearted.

G. Parthasarthy conducted negotiations with the Sheikh and
Afzal Beg with patience and perseverance for a long time. He
was entrusted with this delicate task because of his rapport with
the Kashmir leaders, since the days of his father who had been
Prime Minister in the state. He would not give up until an under-

standing was reached and deserves credit for bringing the two sides close. Syed Mir Qasim, who was the Congress Chief Minister in Jammu and Kashmir, played a vital role in offering to step aside and let the Sheikh form a government. Mrs Gandhi herself played the most crucial role by removing the Sheikh's suspicions and assuring him of her understanding and support. More than anyone else, the Sheikh himself deserves credit for the understanding arrived at. The rest was a matter of details. The principles had been agreed to. G.P. again came into the picture and settled most of the details with Afzal Beg. L.K. Jha (Governor, J & K) in the concluding stages and P.N. Dhar, Secretary to the Prime Minister, played a helpful, constructive and catalytic role.

All these developments made Pakistan's Military ruler, Yahya Khan, suspicious. Bhutto played his usual game, trying to win power for himself. While he did not succeed with Ayub Khan at Tashkent, he was able to mislead and beguile the simple-minded Yahya Khan. He advised Yahya not to follow up the result of the elections held in April 1970, in East Pakistan by allowing Sheikh Mujibur Rahman to become the Prime Minister of the whole of Pakistan, as the leader of the majority party. Bhutto had ambitions of becoming the undisputed ruler of the whole of Pakistan, if possible; if not, then at least of West Pakistan, no matter at what cost. The military leadership of Pakistan fell into Bhutto's trap and started an unprecedented campaign of atrocities, suppression of Bengalis, oppression of intellectuals and minorities with such ruthlessness and cruelty as had not been seen since Hitler's days.

The Bengali population of East Pakistan, who outnumbered the West Pakistanis, had suffered as second class citizens since the creation of Pakistan in 1947. They were treated as a colony of West Pakistan, to provide raw materials and foreign exchange for the development of the western wing. What was worse, they were treated with contempt and their language and culture criticized. The Bengalis had been seething with anger and discontent for over twenty years. They now had an opportunity of establishing themselves as equals with West Pakistanis. Mujib's party had won all but one seat in the elections held in April 1970. According to the law, constitution and convention he should have been called by Yahya Khan to form the Government of Pakistan as its Prime Minister. But, this did not suit Bhutto. There was no love lost between Bhutto and Mujib. They did not trust each other.

Mujib then demanded autonomy for East Pakistan under his six-point formula. Negotiations were held in Dacca between the two sides. When agreement seemed almost in sight, Bhutto put a spanner in the works and persuaded Yahya Khan not to agree.

On the night of 25 March 1971, started an unprecedented massacre of Bengalis by the West Pakistan armed forces. Bhutto was watching this from his suite on the eleventh floor of Hotel Intercontinental in Dacca. He slipped away the next day by air to Lahore, having won his first round by getting Mujib imprisoned and out of the way. May be he could still be the Prime Minister of the whole of Pakistan, if the Bengalis cowed down and yielded to brute force. That was not to be and so started the war of liberation in Bangladesh.

The struggle of the East Pakistanis for autonomy developed into a struggle for liberation and the emergence of an independent Bangladesh. This was mainly due to the stubborn and shortsighted attitude of Pakistan's military rulers and the strong reaction of the East Bengalis against the reign of terror launched by the West Pakistani military forces in the eastern wing. There was natural sympathy for the Bangladesh struggle in the adjoining West Bengal and the rest of India. After Mujib's arrest and confinement in a lonely cell in a West Pakistan jail, his elected colleagues fled Dacca, and sought refuge in India. There was a huge exodus of people from East Pakistan into the neighbouring states of India. Hindus, Muslims, Christians and Buddhists came in thousands every day—some with maimed limbs which had been chopped off by West Pakistani soldiers, some with shots fired in their backs when they tried to flee, women with harrowing tales of rape, children still crying out of fear. I saw them at the border post at Bangaon, treking into India in a continuous stream, as late as June and September 1971.

I also met Tajuddin and his colleagues in Calcutta who had formed an emigre government and hoisted the flag of independent Bangladesh in the areas bordering India. They wanted immediate recognition. There was widespread sympathy for them in all Indian circles. My colleague, S.K. Banerji, and I pleaded with Mrs Gandhi on my return to Delhi. She pointed out that unless Bangladeshis established effective control in some areas and proved to the world through their own struggle that the people were with them, recognition by India would only create the impression that India was trying to divide Pakistan by setting up a puppet regime in Bangladesh. She said, "When the time comes, we will do it."

Meanwhile, hundreds of thousands of refugees from Bangladesh had entered India. The Pakistani Government tried to fan communal flames in India by destroying hindu temples in East Pakistan, driving out non-Muslims and forcibly converting Harijans who formed the bulk of the non-Muslim population. The large influx of refugees upset the economy of India, strained its communications, health and housing, created law and order problems. But, the people of India stood by their persecuted neighbours and shared their salt and bread with them. It was a sign of maturity of the Indian people that they did not fall a prey to Pakistan's efforts to rouse communal passions. There was not a single communal riot or fracas between Hindus and Muslims in India throughout the struggle for liberation in Bangladesh.

Having failed to provoke India into communal frenzy, the shortsighted Pakistani rulers in Bangladesh started border raids and incidents in the neighbouring Indian states. Having failed to suppress the brave Bengalis of the eastern wing to submit to terror and brutal force, they tried to divert world attention and sympathy for Bangladesh by provoking a war with India.

Mrs Gandhi's government had given moral, political and material support to the Bangladesh guerillas, but our armed forces refrained from crossing the border in spite of provocations from Pakistan. Mrs Gandhi still believed that if Sheikh Mujibur Rahman was released, a fair settlement between him and Yahya Khan might be possible. She undertook a two-week tour to the USA, via the UK, France, Belgium, Austria and West Germany, in the last week of September 1971 to persuade the western leaders to put some pressure on Yahya Khan to release Mujib and come to terms with him. Swaran Singh, P.N. Haksar and I accompanied her on this trip. Her meeting with Nixon was a non-starter. Nixon would not even say whether Mujib was still alive, let alone get him released. He would not even agree to persuade Yahya Khan to open a dialogue with the already elected leaders of the eastern wing of Pakistan. He wanted to give at least two years' time to Yahya for some kind of a settlement. He expected the Bangladeshis to wait patiently till then and India to go on accepting hundreds of thousands of refugees. He was either misinformed or he deliberately ignored the realities. May be he felt sore with India for having entered into a treaty of Peace, Friendship and Cooperation with the Soviet Union and wanted "another Vietnam" on India's doorstep. It is also possible he thought that Pakistan was still capable of forcing its eastern wing to surrender to brute force and make them settle down in a couple of years. It is also likely that his hatred for the USSR and his newborn love for China encouraged him to adopt a pro-Pakistan, anti-Bangladesh and anti-India line.

Mrs Gandhi was firm with Nixon. She warned him that the situation was explosive and could not be defused unless Mujib was released and a dialogue started with the already elected leaders of East Pakistan. She told him in no uncertain terms that India would be forced to retalitate if Pakistan continued its provocations across our border.

Mrs Gandhi addressed the National Press Club in Washington D.C., met leading members of the Senate and House and others. The US press at that time was like a breath of fresh air against Nixon's suffocating policy. Nixon had tasted blood in Vietnam and was not going to give in to logic or humanitarian considerations in Bangladesh. So, he continued supplying weapons to Yahya Khan, quietly and surreptitiously, even against the ban imposed after the 1965 Indo-Pak war. Nixon's tilt towards Pakistan and against India was not only political and economic (he had stopped aid to India already), but also military.

Mrs Gandhi visited London, met Heath and others there and convinced them. They seemed powerless against Nixon's obstinacy. It was the same in France and Belgium. Vienna and Bonn were more sympathetic but could hardly do anything apart from influencing opinion in western Europe, eastern Europe and the Soviet Union were fully in agreement with Indias's attitudes; so was most of the non-aligned and developing world. Only China and the USA were with Pakistan.

Mrs Gandhi's diplomacy had made a dent on world public opinion and on the thinking of most governments. The Islamic world was divided but could not afford to take an openly anti-Bangladesh attitude (Bangladesh had more Muslims than the western wing of Pakistan). Mrs Gandhi did not want to give the struggle in Bangladesh a religious colour and left most of the Muslim world to its own devices, except a few friendly non-aligned countries like Egypt.

Events in Bangladesh were moving fast. The influx of refugees into India was increasing. Harrowing eye-witness accounts of atrocities by Pakistani soldiers were pouring in every day. But, there was also a heartening change in the situation. The freedom fighters were gaining ground and making it impossible for the Pakistani forces to function at night anywhere. Even during the day they were confined mostly to the cantonments near a few big towns and cities.

Pakistan was getting desperate. Whether on their own, or in consultation with their US and Chinese allies, the military leaders of Pakistan violated India's air space in the east several times. India tried to localize these incidents by not going into East or West Pakistan. We shot down a few Pakistani planes on our own territory in West Bengal. Having failed to provoke India into war in the east, the Pakistani rulers launched an unprovoked attack on nine Indian airfields in the west and north including Kashmir. This was at 6 pm on 3 December 1971.

I had just returned to my office from a meeting in Parliament House presided by the President. All India Radio asked me if they should put it on the news. The Prime Minister was in Calcutta, so was the Defence Minister. I consulted Sam Manekshaw, Chief of Army Staff, and with his agreement gave the OK to AIR. They put it on their evening news at 6.30 pm on 3 December 1971.

Fortunately, we had some previous inkling about the possibility of such a "blitzkreig" attack by Pakistan. Yahya Khan, in one of his drunken moments, exactly ten days earlier, had boasted to an American newsman that he would himself be leading the war against India in ten days. We had tracked two Pakistani agents who were in contact with Pakistan and received back messages from them which we intercepted. Ashwani Kumar, who held the dual charge of Inspector General of Police, Punjab, and Inspector General of Border Security Force, had passed on the vital information about Pakistan's "D" day to us a couple of days earlier. The Indian Air Force was alerted and had cleared the airfields of all our planes. All the Pakistanis could hit was one small observer plane in their 'blitzkreig'.

Mrs Gandhi rushed back from Calcutta when she heard the news. She came straight from the airport to her house and immediately thereafter to her office in South Block. The three Chiefs of Air, Navy and Army (who had already met her at the house) were there, so were the members of the Political Affairs Committee (Foreign, Home and Defence Ministers). Haksar, I

Defence Secretary (K.B. Lall), Home Secretary (Govind Narain) and Cabinet Secretary (Swaminathan) were also there. It was 10 pm on 3 December 1971. Mrs Gandhi was calm, cool and confident. After consulting her colleagues, she approved the strategy proposed by the Defence Chiefs, and directed the rest of us to keep in close touch and prepare the country and the world for what was coming.

Pakistan formally declared war on India on the morning of 4 December, though they had already started it the previous evening. Our people rose as one nation to meet the threat. Our soldiers, sailors and airmen proved more than a match for the Pakistanis. Our side was fighting a war which had been thrust on us while Pakistan was fighting a war to continue its Hitlerite atoricities on its eastern wing. Pakistani forces in the east collapsed like a house of cards within one week. We did not have any designs on the Pakistani territory and did not take this opportunity of recovering some areas in Pakistan occupied Kashmir (POK) because that would have meant prolonging the war and considerable hardship and sacrifice for the people of both countries. India had nothing against the people of Pakistan. We sympathized with them for suffering a misguided and adventurous military dictatorship.

India recognized Bangladesh and its independent government on 6 December 1971—two days after Pakistan had declared war on us and when the freedom fighters had driven the Pakistanis to take shelter in a few towns. Mrs Gandhi had kept her word and redeemed her pledge. The Pak Commander wanted to surrender but Yahya Khan would not agree as he still hoped to receive help from the USA and/or China.

Mrs Gandhi declared a unilateral ceasefire on 17 December 1971. The Pakistani forces in Bangladesh surrendered to the Joint Command of India and Bangladesh. Over 90,000 Pakistani soldiers were taken prisoners. The whole world hailed her wisdom and statesmanship in declaring a unilateral ceasefire. The people of India called her "Durga" and "Shakti"—the two goddesses representing power and strength. Even Jana Sangh leaders like Atal Bihari Vajpayee, joined in paying tribute to her. She rose to power through patience and perseverance. Some called her even greater than her father, Nehru. She had shown more courage and determination, taken greater risks and succeeded in inflicting a decisive defeat on Pakistan for the first time since independence. She had defied threats by the US Seventh Fleet in the Bay of Bengal, ignored China's noises, helped Bangladesh to win its freedom and raised India's prestige and stature in the world.

How was she able to achieve all this? A frail woman, aloof and lonely, quiet and shy, how was she able to rise to such heights? Was it her own wisdom and statesmanship? Was it the collective wisdom of her colleagues? Did luck and circumstances favour her? Was her success due, in part at least, to the Indo-Soviet Treaty? We shall try to examine these and connected factors in the next chapter.

21 Indo-Bangladesh Treaty and Simla Agreement-1972

Bangladesh was a sovereign independent country, recognized as such by many, but not yet by Pakistan and her friends and allies. It was going ahead under the leadership of Sheikh Mujibur Rahman, or Bangabandhu, as he was popularly known. He was in his mid-fifties, smoked a pipe and spoke in simple but chaste Bengali which even I could understand with my elementary knowledge of Sanskrit. He was a great orator and his voice could bring tears in the eyes of his listeners. He was highly strung and emotional and at the same time realistic. I met him in London on my way back from the UNO in early December 1971, just after he had been released by Bhutto and was convalescing. He warned me against Bhutto's lack of principles when I related his antics in the Security Council. He said he would like to visit India on his way back and personally thank Indira Gandhi, the government and people of India for their moral, material and political support in the liberation of Bangladesh.

He came in a plane provided by the British Government and halted at Palam on his way to Dacca on 10 January 1972. There was a huge crowd waiting to welcome him. His speech at the airport made a deep impression on his listeners. Mrs Gandhi welcomed him in simple but warm language. He was full of gratitude and praised India highly. He did not forget to thank other powers and nations who had shown sympathy for the struggle of Bangladesh.

His reception at Dacca by a million strong crowd broke all previous records. The people were naturally excited, as if their father had come back alive from the assassin's gallows. He towered head and shoulders above his colleagues and was the undisputed leader of Bangladesh.

Bengalis are very sensitive. We had to bend over backwards not to give any impression of pressure, influence or taking advantage of our friendship. Subimal Dutt, born in East Bengal (now Bangladesh) had retired from the post of Secretary to the President. He was a former Foreign Secretary. At Mrs Gandhi's suggestion, Haksar and I were able to persuade him to go as our first Ambassador to Bangladesh. He did a first class job there and no one could have done better. He understood the Bangladeshis, spoke their language and got on well with the leaders and the people.

Mujib visited Calcutta in March 1972 and invited Mrs Gandhi to visit Dacca. She went there in May 1972. The reception she got at Dacca was something to be seen to be believed. India had already withdrawn her forces from Bangladesh two weeks before the agreed date. We were short of foodgrains ourselves but agreed to give more than a million tons to Bangladesh. We also extended our cooperation in building rail, road and air communications. I suggested to Mrs Gandhi that we should try to cement our friendship with Bangladesh in a solemn treaty. This was the time to do it, before other powers came in and tried to fish in troubled waters. She was sceptical at first but when I told her that Dutt also favoured it, she asked me to sound Mujib informally and get his reaction.

The next day we were going on a steamer down the river. Mujib and his officials were there and so were Mrs Gandhi, Swaran Singh, Dutt, Haksar, I and K.P.S. Menon (Jr) who was our Joint Secretary dealing with Bangladesh, and is now High Commissioner there.

I first sounded the Foreign Secretary of Bangladesh, but he expressed his misgivings, as such a treaty might annoy Peking. I said it would not be aimed against Peking or any other country and as two sovereign, independent neighbours we had every right to cement our ties in a solemn treaty. He did not commit himself. After a while Mujib called me and asked what I was discussing with his Foreign Secretary. I broached the subject and was pleasantly surprised to find him not only positively responsive but even enthusiastic about it. He said he had suggested it to Mrs Gandhi in Calcutta in March, but she had not given him a "yes" or "no." He asked me to clear it with her first so that he could then talk to her. I told Mrs Gandhi about it. She called the Foreign Minister, our Ambassador and Haksar and sought their views. They were all for it. Later Mujib settled it in principle with Mrs Gandhi. I was directed to sit with the Bangladesh Foreign Secretary and present a draft the same evening. This was done during our return journey on the boat. Each delegation kept a copy and it was agreed to discuss and finalize it the same evening.

A few changes were made at the instance of Mujib. He wanted to mention "nationalism" as one of the principles and Mrs Gandhi agreed. He wanted a text in Bengali also. Dutt sat till midnight to write the Bengali text and get the Bangladeshis' OK to it. The texts were given to the press for printing around midnight and were ready by 8 am. The signing ceremony was at 9 am.

If the Bangabandhu had been a little more careful about his security and lived, Indo-Bangladesh relations might have become a model between two sovereign, independent friendly neighbours. But, rifts developed in Bangladesh's armed forces. Fissures developed in the political leadership itself and between them and the armed forces. Some foreign powers and their agents played the usual role. Bangabandhu, his family and his leading colleagues were murdered in cold blood.

India could have intervened and perhaps saved the situation temporarily. But Mrs Gandhi rightly decided not to do so. The Bangladeshis themselves must solve their internal problems. Any intervention by India would have antagonized the proud and sensitive Bangladeshis. What happened in Bangladesh after that is another story and need not be repeated here. However, there is no doubt that Bangladesh and India will have to work in close cooperation and friendship to resolve their differences and work out joint solutions to their common problems, without interference from outside powers. One thing appears certain. Having gained independence from Pakistan through blood and tears, sacrifice and suffering, the Bangladeshis will not become part of Pakistan again, willingly or by force. The one possibility is that Bangladesh, India and Pakistan may, one day, become an area of peace, cooperation and friendship. Their problems are similar, their economies are, by and large, complementary, and not competitive. They have everything to gain and nothing to lose by agreeing to solve their problems bilaterally or trilaterally without outside interference, on a footing of sovereign equality.

India tried to bring this about slowly and steadily. The Simla

Agreement of 1972 was a step in this direction and both India and Pakistan have recently reaffirmed it. It was not easy to bring this about. A lot of hard work and mutual discussion preceded it. Pakistan, as Bhutto argued, was a defeated country. Any concession by her would smack of dictation by the victor, India. India must, therefore, be generous and give Pakistan time to recover its lost confidence and everything would be all right then. These were the usual Bhutto tactics. We had not forgotten his antics in the Security Council in December, 1971, nor his obstructionist attempts at Tashkent.

He wanted India not only to vacate all West Pakistan territory occupied during the war, but also the immediate return of 90,000 Pakistani prisoners of war. He was reluctant to agree to give up the use of force (as at Tashkent) or to accept the actual line of control in Jammu and Kashmir, which gave back to India about 400 sq. miles more of her own territory than the old ceasefire line. He also wanted to bring in the UN machinery under Article 33 of the Charter—of arbitration, mediation, etc. to settle bilateral disputes. And what is more, he did not want to mention Kashmir at all. He also wanted immediate restoration of diplomatic relations with India but would not recognize Bangladesh.

The Indian delegation stood firm on the actual line of control, with the exception of Chhamb which was exchanged for "Chiken's Neck" on military advice. We also stood firm on the issue of prisoners of war who had surrendered to the joint command of India and Bangladesh and could not be returned without agreement of the latter. We maintained that if Pakistan would recognize Bangladesh and settle the matter with them, we would go along, but without the agreement of Bangladesh, we could not. Bhutto said that he would recognize Bangladesh within two weeks of his return. We said we would welcome such a move and then consider the matter in consulation with Bangladesh.

On the question of peaceful and bilateral solution of bilateral problems also we stood firm, as this was really the essence of the proposed agreement and would pave a new and better way of settling bilateral differences bilaterally and peacefully without outside intervention. Our experience had shown that outside intervention only complicated issues and did not facilitate their solution.

With Mrs Gandhi's permission I reminded President Bhutto

that at Tashkent, when he was Foreign Minister of Pakistan, he had said that Kashmir was the basic cause of all our differences. I asked why he was now hesitant even to make any mention of it. He put on his diplomatic smile and said he remembered Tashkent and admitted what I said but added that he did not represent a defeated country at Tashkent as he did at Simla. The people of Pakistan would think he had given-in to pressure if he accepted any mention of Kashmir now. *"Insha Allah*, in due course, we shall settle it finally, bilaterally and peacefully without prejudice to the recognized position of either side." It was a clever way of keeping the question alive and his options open to raise it at the UN again should circumstances favour him. We insisted that some mention was necessary, may be in terms as indicated above by him. He would not agree and suggested that the two official delegations discuss the matter further.

Bhutto had with him three of his Ministerial colleagues, apart from Secretary General Aziz Ahmad and his two aides, his D.I.B. and Special Assistant Raza Ali, and a host of Pakistani pressmen. He wanted to show to his team that he was being tough and wanted to give them a chance. He knew they would not succeed in getting better terms than he could, but he did not want to give in till the last. He sent his stooges to various members of our delegation, ministerial and official, to plead with us, but we were firm and unanimous in our stand. Haksar and I prepared a final draft which we cleared with Swaran Singh, Chavan, Jagjivan Ram and Fakhuruddin Ali Ahmad—the four colleagues Mrs Gandhi had brought with her to Simla. Mrs Gandhi then discussed it with her colleagues and cleared it. We were asked to take it to Bhutto who said, after studying it, we would be informed after lunch. At 3 pm our officials' delegation met the Pak officials' delegation. Aziz Ahmad played his usual role and rejected our draft outright, calling it deliberately "worse than before." We did not prolong the argument for we knew Aziz Ahmad could dare not say "yes" and only his boss Bhutto could. We, asked some of Bhutto's stooges to tell him to settle the matter with Mrs Gandhi. He got the message and agreed to our final draft within half-an-hour of his meeting Mrs Gandhi, the same evening, i.e. 2 August 1972. The Agreement was signed the same night. Bhutto took the credit for getting our agreement to vacate the Pak terrritories we had occupied. He could not afford to go back empty handed. Half-a-loaf was better than none. He agreed to our draft hoping perhaps that he would be able to put pressure on Bangladesh through his Islamic and other friends to agree to the return of 90,000 prisoners. As for the other provision regarding Kashmir and the bilateral approach, he would wait and see if he could get out of them, if necessary, by going to the UN again.

As soon as he returned to Pakistan, he was the same old Bhutto, fulminating with anger against India and swearing to have his prisoners back. He did not breathe a word about recognizing Bangladesh. We decided to go step by step, and re-establish diplomatic relations only when the situation had been normalized. We insisted on the Simla spirit of peaceful and bilateral settlement of bilateral questions without outside intervention. The whole world, except China, applauded the Simla Agreement and the Simla spirit. It was a step forward from Tashkent and a step towards peace and cooperation on the sub-continent. Given goodwill on both sides, it could usher in a new era of conciliation and end the old one of confrontation.

There were no secret clauses or understandings, aide memories or any secret documents exchanged between the two Heads of Government or the two delegations. It was an open agreement openly arrived at. It proved India's bonafides and vindicated Mrs Gandhi's pronouncements before, during and after the war, that we had no designs on Pakistan's territory. It was the only example in recent history where the victor returned enemy territory, occupied by it, to the defeated country within about eight months of the end of war.

There was quite a lot of fraternization between the Indian and the Pakistani journalists, but alas, not among the officials. We tried our best but they were perhaps afraid. They did, however, attend a reception I gave for Aziz Ahmad and his colleagues at the Cecil Hotel. The Ministers on both sides met each other freely.

D.P. Dhar, who was the leader of our Officials' team, talked better Urdu than Aziz Ahmad, who stuck to English. Unfortunately, D.P. suffered a heart attack in his hotel suite on the third night and could not take further part in the discussions as he had to be hospitalized. P.N. Haskar took his place and conducted the discussions ably and with a subtle sense of humour that made even the glum Aziz Ahmad smile and laugh sometimes. I felt unwell on the last evening and, not wanting to follow D.P. into hospital, motored down to Chandigarh after the final successful meeting between Bhutto and Mrs Gandhi, I received and saw off the Pak delegation the next morning on their return journey.

I had participated in several negotiations with foreign countries before. The Simla negotiations in 1972 were, perhaps, the most challenging and difficult and, therefore, their success was even more satisfying. It showed that team work is most important. Members of the same delegation must not speak with different voices, but may divide their tasks for informal discussions. Sometimes it is more difficult to carry one's own colleagues than those of the opposite side. Mutual discussion and complete trust in each other is most important in a delegation. There should be no rivalry or jealousy between various members. Judged by these criteria, both the official as well as the ministerial side of our delegation was ideal, unlike Pakistan's which was more of a one-man show.

Some extreme rightist parties thought we should not have agreed to return the territories we had conquered in the war. That would have been easy enough but it would have sown the seeds of further trouble in the future. A defeated country should never be humiliated, otherwise it will rise again like Nazi Germany did. Some said we should have agreed to hand over the prisoners of war. That, would have been breach of faith with Bangladesh. Some objected that we should not have given up Chhamb, but our military experts felt, after three bloody conflicts, that it would always be a weak and indefensible pocket.

The reference to a "final settlement in Jammu and Kashmir" and the clause relating to bilateral settlement of bilateral differences without outside intervention gave hope of ushering in an era of friendship between India and Pakistan. The Delhi Agreement of August 1973, between the three countries of the sub-continent was a happy solution to the problem of Pak prisoners of war. It was an extension of the bilateral spirit of the Simla Agreement to a trilateral, sub-continental level. Therein lies hope for the future of the sub-continent. If we can convert it into an area of peace, friendship and cooperation, the voice of the 800 million people of the sub-continent will be respected by the rest of the world. If eastern and western Europe, the countries of the Arab World, Africa and Latin America can join together, there is no reason why the countries of Asia cannot make a start at a sub-regional level. ASAEN is there, but not very effective yet. It India, Pakistan and Bangladesh would get together on the basis of sovereign equality and partnership, they could extend their area of peace and cooperation to cover the whole of South Asia. It could then play its natural role of becoming a bridge of peace and understanding between South-East and South-West Asia and be able to stand up to great power military rivalry in this region.

The Simla Agreement of 1972 and the Delhi Agreement of August 1973, have to be looked at in this wider perspective and not judged by narrow chauvinistic and temporary gains or losses. They contain the seeds of sub-continental peace and progress which can be extended to the east, west, north and south of us.

D.P. Dhar was sent as our Ambassador to the USSR in January 1969. He was asked to sound the Soviet leaders about further extending cooperation with us in various fields. It was in our common interest to stem Chinese expansion and American penetration in our region. He developed a personal rapport with the Soviet leaders through his suave manners and sense of humour. He had the full support and backing of Mrs Gandhi. Negotiations on a draft Indo-Soviet Treaty went on for about two years. Indian leadership was at first hesitant to go as far as entering into a Treaty of Friendship and Peace with the USSR. Mrs Gandhi was inclined towards it, but not sure of the attitude of her colleagues. I had taken over as Foreign Secretary in June 1968. She sent me to Moscow to sound the Soviet leaders. I exchanged drafts with them of the proposed treaty, without commitment on either side. D.P. followed up matters.

We had studied various treaties on the subject, like the Afghan-Soviet Treaty, the Soviet-Finnish Treaty, the Soviet-Egyptian Treaty and others. Our draft was different from them in several respects. It did not amount to a defence pact. There was no obligation on either side to send its troops to the other, nor was there any commitment to allow use of one's territory to the other. It expressed respect for India's policy of non-alignment as "an important factor in the maintainence of universal peace and international security and in the lessening of international tensions." The only commitment was that "should either party be subjected to an attack or threat thereof the two shall enter into immediate consultations to remove such threat and to ensure peace." This was the sovereign right of any country and non-alignment did not mean we would not enter into consultations with others. There was a commitment not to "enter into or participate in any military alliance directed against the other party and to prevent the use of its territory for any act which might inflict military damage to the other party." This was also not against our policy of non-alignment, but it did secure us against the possibility of any help by the USSR to an eventual aggressor or threat of aggression against India. The question of India giving such help against the USSR did not arise as India was already non-aligned.

The draft was more or less finalized by the end of 1970 but the question was what was the most opportune time to sign it. Mrs Gandhi was still not sure of the reaction of her colleagues and of Parliament.

Meanwhile, the struggle for liberation in Bangladesh started. Pakistan became more and more bellicose against India. D.P. and I felt this was the right moment. We consulted Haksar. He said it was upto the Prime Minister. We went to her and she again wondered whether her colleagues would react favourably. She decided to put it before the PAC (Political Affairs Committee). They were in full agreement. It was decided to inform the Soviet Government to send a representative to sign the Treaty in Delhi. They may have been a little surprised but they did not hesitate. Gromyko came and the Treaty was signed by him and Swaran Singh on 9 August 1971, after it had been approved by the cabinet.

The support in Parliament and the country was almost unanimous. With very few exceptions the Treaty was hailed by everyone. The timing of it was most appropriate. India was not alone in helping Bangladesh. The Treaty served as a warning to China and America to keep their hands off the sub-continent. Although China made some noises, she did not physically intervene. America was more audacious and sent its Seventh Fleet into the Bay of Bengal hoping to frighten India and Bangladesh. It had the opposite effect. The Seventh Fleet would not dare to land in Bangladesh because they knew Soviet submarines were following them. India had already sunk the "Ghazi" given by the USA to Pakistan. Also, public opinion in America and practically the whole world was against Nixon's adventurist policy.

To whom can one give credit for the victory in Bangladesh and the defeat of Pakistan in December 1971? First and foremost to the brave freedom fighters and people of Bangladesh who lost almost three million people in their struggle. Next, to the people of India who stood by their oppressed brethern in Bangladesh at great cost to themselves. Last but not the least, to the soldiers, sailors and airmen of India who fought with courage and valour to defend the motherland.

Indira Gandhi deserves credit for her wise leadership and calm confidence, which inspired us all to work together as one team day and night—the Chiefs of the armed forces, Cabinet Secretary Swaminathan, Principal Secretary to Prime Minister Haksar, Defence and Home Secretaries, K.B. Lall and Govind Narain and last but not the least, D.P. Dhar who acted as a link between us all. We met twice almost every day either in the Cabinet Secretary's room or my room which was more central.

Swaran Singh was Foreign Minister at the time. I have not found another Foreign Minister so balanced, steady with strong common sense and pleasant to work with. I accompanied him to the UN when the Indo-Pak war was six days old. The UN General Assembly had already passed a resolution with 104 votes asking for an immediate ceasefire and withdrawal of troops. The Security Council was seized of the matter when we arrived in New York on 9 December 1971. Swaran Singh, G. Parthasarathy, Samar Sen (our Permanent Representative at the UN) and I met over a hundred heads of delegations. Most of them, including some friends of Pakistan, told us they hoped that this war would end immediately. They admitted privately that Pakistan was in the wrong. They said the sooner we won, the better for India and Pakistan. They realized that the tide had turned against Pakistan and felt embarrassed at having voted for the UN General Assembly resolution earlier.

In the Security Council, however, America and China were working hard to pressurize India. The Soviet Union and Yugoslavia were fully with us. France and the UK were trying to play the honest broker.

India and Pakistan were invited to speak in the Security Council meeting. Bhutto, dressed in his Sunday best, with a maroon silk tie and a matching handkerchief, was fulminating and literally forthing at the mouth. He ended his vituperative and melodramatic speech by telling Swaran Siugh, "Sardar *Saheb*, I warn you, you will not be able to take East Pakistan."

Swaran Singh did not even look up to acknowledge Bhutto's

"warning." He replied gently, calmly but in measured tones, "Mr Bhutto, Bangladesh is neither yours nor ours to take. *Sonar Bangla* (Golden Bangladesh) belongs to Bangladeshis and to no one else."

There were verbal duels between the Chinese and the Soviet delegates, and also between the American and the Soviet delegates. When Bhutto found that the Soviet Union would even use its veto, should the Security Council pass a resolution against India and realized that Pakistan was fast losing the war, he tore up the Security Council documents in the face of the President of the Council and walked out of the hall, literally boiling with rage. He is a good actor but this was no play-acting. It was the deliberate act of a desperate man.

Swaran Singh impressed everyone with his gentle diplomacy, calm and dignified manner and a quiet, confident tone. He is a first rate negotiator and can tire out the patience of even the Chinese. Perhaps, if we start negotiations with China in the near future he would be an ideal negotiator on behalf of India.

Mrs Gandhi's sense of timing, her shrewd and correct assessment, her leadership during the whole crisis, showed her at her best. She was, to some extent, lucky in that Pakistan precipitated the war. It was the wrong war against the wrong country, for an unjust cause and fought at the wrong time. It could not be denied, even by her political opponents, that she showed statesmanship, wisdom and leadership in a difficult situation. She was patient, persevering, calm and confident throughout and never flapped or took a wrong step during the whole crisis. Her unilateral declaration of ceasefire was an act of the highest statesmanship. It raised India's prestige abroad and removed doubts and suspicions among our neighbours. Would Indira Gandhi maintain these high standards in future years? Would she utilize the unique opportunity she had of leading India to play her natural role in setting an example of how a developing country could combine economic growth with social justice, non-alignment with peace and cooperation, through the democratic process?

With a decisive victory against Pakistan, the success of her policy towards Bangladesh, a comfortable two thirds' majority in Parliament and in most of the states, Mrs Gandhi had a unique opportunity of using her position and power to bring about the urgently needed social and economic reforms in the country and strengthen our foreign policy. We did not face an immediate external threat though, our army, navy and air force did need some modern weapons and replenishment. For a while, it seemed Indira Gandhi was going to fulfil the high expectations she had aroused and the promises she had made, even better than her father had been able to do. She got the bank nationalization and the abolition of princes' privileges bills passed without much difficulty. Ceilings on urban and rural property were also fixed. The public sector was strengthened and production of steel placed under one coordinating agency SAIL (Steel Authority of India Ltd). She brought in some progressive and younger elements into her government at the Centre. But administration in most of the States was at a low ebb.

There was discontent among students and workers, prices of daily necessities of life were rising rapidly, shortage of food grains due to failure of two successive crops and a sense of frustration among most opposition parties and leaders produced a grave law and order situation and encouraged black marketeers and hoarders to make hay. The Allahabad High Court verdict on Raj Narain's election petition against Indira Gandhi and the result of the Gujrat elections on 12 June 1975, heartened the opposition and the ruling party felt concerned and insecure.

I was in India on a short visit in May-June 1975 and heard the news about the proclamation of internal emergency broadcast by AIR on the morning of 26 June. It came as a shock to many people. The immediate reaction was mixed. The common man and woman thought it might give them some relief from the forces of disruption and disorder, stabilize the prices of essential commodities, and control black-marketing and smuggling. The majority of the masses in the rural areas were already living below the subsistence level. The intellectuals and the press resented censorship and government controls. The administration thought they would have more powers and a freer hand to implement government's polices and programmes. The armed forces were kept aloof and did not get involved.

I left for the USA on 29 June. The reaction to the Emergency in the US media was sharp and critical. The US administration observed a discreet silence. We had to answer many questions on the basis of the meagre information we had from official sources and the censored press. In an article on the centre page of New York Times I wrote that the problems of India would be solved by the people of India, in India, and not by anyone else, or anywhere else. I also said publicly that by its very nature the emergency could only be temporary and elections would be held in a matter of months rather than years. This was my personal conviction and belief, but not shared by many.

The first six months of the emergency seemed to have brought about some improvement in the economic situation, stabilized prices and halted smuggling, black marketing and disorder. On the debit side, the ruling party became over-confident and lost touch with the people. The administration became authoritarian and the police sometimes exceeded their authority. The censored press could not report about this and the people, by and large, were unaware. A shocking example of abuse of authority was the ruthless and brutal manner in which the sterilization programme was carried out in some of the northern states. It caused a revulsion in the minds of most people and was mainly responsible for the total defeat of the ruling party in the northern states in the March 1977 Parliamentary elections.

I visited India again in December 1975. Some people who believed in Nehru's policies and ideals, as well as others who wished Mrs Gandhi well, advised her to scrap the emergency at the end of December 1975, and hold elections in early 1976. She seemed to be personally inclined to agree, but many Congress members of Parliament and Chief Ministers of states advised her against it. They had a vested interest in continuing in power. However, Mrs Gandhi had the courage to hold elections in March 1977, much against the advice of some who wanted the emergency to continue. She was not in agreement with them and asserted her will. May be she thought, as most people including the opposition did, that she still would come back with a clear, if not a two-thirds majority, in Parliament. Whatever her calculations or mis-calculations, she deserves credit for taking a political risk and keeping her promise to ascertain the people's will.

Is Mrs. Gandhi's and her Party's fall from power permanent

or only temporary? Who can say? Nothing is permanent in politics.

Polarization of politics is possible but not likely in the immediate future. What is more probable is the growth of regional pulls and parties, with casteism cutting across ideological and regional lines. Meanwhile, there is danger of the social and economic gulf widening between urban and rural populations, between different sections both in urban and rural areas, based on class, caste, political power and influence.

It is not a classical Marxian or capitalist situation, but a peculiarly Indian phenomenon. It is capable of throwing up all kinds of forces, good and bad, social and anti-social, progressive and obscurantist. In such a mixed and confusing situation, no one can predict with any degree of precision or certainty what is going to happen in the near future. Who comes to power is not so important. What is important is that the country must get emotionally integrated, the centre and states must cooperate and not go against each other, casteism, untouchability and exploitation of certain classes by others must be removed, not only on paper but in reality, that economic production and productivity must increase with due regard to a minimum need-based wage for agricultural and industrial labour. Last but not the least, the intelligentsia, the youth and the masses must be enthused and given a feeling of participation and a say in the building up of the country, adequate opportunities for employment and a reasonable standard of living.

Whichever party, and whoever its leader, that can chalk out and implement a minimum common programme within a short time-frame deserves to be in power. Party labels are not so important, personalities even less. What counts is the people and people's interests and not those of a few privileged persons or sections. This change is bound to come and will come sooner than later, one hopes, peacefully and democratically.

What effect recent changes in Government are having or will have on India's foreign policy and external relations in the political, economic and defence fields remains to be seen. But certain trends are already visible. These will be dealt with in the last chapter. Meanwhile, let us have a look at Nixon's America to which I was accredited from June 1973 onwards.

23 Nixon's America

I was to retire at the end of 1972 and took four months' earned leave—something I had never done. In fact almost four years of my accumulated leave had lapsed. Looking back I think it is a mistake not to take the leave one has earned. Even politicians, ministers, journalists and others would feel better and work more efficiently if they took Sundays off and went away from their scene of activity for a month every year. No one is indispensable and the sooner we learn to let others carry on the job, the better. It is perhaps a mistake to continue to live where one has worked. It makes one feel nostalgic. One misses the attention one received and the chair one occupied before. I had, therefore, decided to live away from the dust and din of Delhi diplomacy and lead a quiet and peaceful life in the mountains. My son and I bought a small five acre barren plot of land in the inner regions of the Himalayas. I planted some fruit trees and built a little cottage to live in after retirement. Perhaps, here I could do some reading and a little writing besides planting fruit trees, growing flowers and vegetables.

But, that was not to be yet. I was sent for and asked if I would go as India's Ambassador to the USA. My first reaction was negative. P.N. Haksar and Swaran Singh told me that the Prime Minister wanted me to go and I should not say no. I saw the Prime Minister. She said she wanted to send someone who could stand up to the Nixon administration and cultivate the American people, especially intellectuals, youth and others. I said I was hardly suited to this job, because I had, in some Americans' eyes, a reputation of being pro-Soviet. I suggested a few names of eminent Indians who would go down better with the Nixon administration. She said she did not want those people and my experience of China, Russia, the UK South-East and South-West Asia, and my four-year stint as Foreign Secretary would enable me to see things in proper perspective. She did not care what some Americans thought of me. She knew I was pro-India and not pro or anti any other country. I asked if I would have her full confidence and support. She smiled and said otherwise she would not have asked me. I said I would think it over for a couple of days and then give her the answer.

I consulted a few close friends and they advised me to accept the offer. I had high regard for Haksar and valued his opinion. He is a man of high integrity and great ability, honest, patriotic and dedicated. I told him that I would go as long as he stayed on his post for it would be difficult to get on with someone else with whom I had not worked so closely. I had known Haksar since my student days, but got to know him better when he joined the foreign services. We had worked together and closely, as a team when I was Foreign Secretary and he Secretary and then principal Secretary to the Prime Minister. We had very close views on most matters and often consulted each other. We had come closer during the negotiations of the Indo-Soviet Treaty, the Indo-Bangladesh Treaty and the Simla Agreement. Why did Haksar want me to go to America while he himself stayed on in India? I asked him. He thought for a while, as is his habit (even when he does not need to think and knows the answer, he wants to give the impression that he is attaching importance to the other person and not giving a casual reply). After a while he said he understood and respected my hesitation, but as long as he was at his post, I need not hesitate to go to the USA. He himself had wanted to quit for some time, but was staying on as the Prime Minister needed him. So why should I refuse? That clinched the argument. I told Mrs Gandhi of my decision and also that if I found or she felt that I was not the right person she should call or let me come back.

So, off I went to America where I had served almost 25 years earlier. Truman was the President then and now it was Nixon. Americans were getting involved in Korea then, while now they were deeply entangled in Vietnam. At that time America was the only nuclear power but now the USSR matched her and the UK, France and China had also exploded atomic bombs.

India at that time was emerging as a non-aligned, peaceful, democratic country. Now she was perhaps the most important non-aligned democratic and developing country. But our internal problems were worse, if anything. Did we want the US aid, even if it was resumed? Was it possible for Nixon's America to respect India's policy of non-alignment and undo the tilt against her? Could India have an equation with Nixon's America?

These were some of the many questions in my mind when I flew to the USA in May 1973. In diplomacy there are no constants except national interests and basic principles of national policy. In a rapidly changing world situation, no country, big, medium or small, can afford to keep a rigid line. One has to try to develop contacts and increase areas of understanding with other countries and governments. It is an Ambassdor's duty to project his country and interpret his government's policies faithfully to the people and government of the country he is accredited to, and vice versa. He should try to improve relations between the two, to the extent possible, keeping in view his country's national interests and basic policies.

I went to America with an open mind and determined to do my best. As Foreign Secretary I had met the senior men in the State Department like Secretary of State, William Rogers, his Under Secretary, Sisco, and Nixon's National Security Adviser Henry Kissinger. I had also met Nixon when he visited India in 1968 as a non-official and later when he halted enroute from Guam as President in 1969. I had also met him when Mrs Gandhi visited the USA in 1971.

But these meetings had been brief and formal. We had talked and disagreed about many things, such as Vietnam, China, Russia. I was then Foreign Secretary and could talk to them with authority. Would I be able to do the same now as Ambassador? They knew I had the full confidence of my government and Prime Minister. I decided I would not change my style, but perhaps soften it a little. I would now have more time to study the American scene at close quarters.

I had to wait for about four weeks to present my Letters of Credence to Nixon. This was not unusual, for Johnson had introduced a new system of "collecting" half a dozen Ambassadors and receiving their credentials on the same day, one after another. He was a busy Texan and had little time for formal ceremonies. Nixon continued this practice. I did not mind, for it gave me time to get a feel of the scene in Washington D.C. and collect my impressions and thoughts.

When I presented credentials at the White House, Nixon was

dressed in a deep blue lounge suit, and I in my closed-collar black suit. He was all smiles and when we posed for press photographers, he put his arm round me and told them, "We are old friends. He comes from a great country." I found these remarks a little artificial, considering our strained relations at that time, but kept my mind open. When I talked to him for about 10 minutes, after presenting my credentials, no one else was present. I told him frankly that unless he was prepared to get PL 480 funds out of the way, Indo-US relations were not likely to improve. He promised he would issue instructions immediately and see that this question was settled amicably. I handed him a letter from Mrs Gandhi which mentioned, among other things, that I had her full confidence etc. We exchanged the usual pleasentries and then I drove back to my Embassy where I had called my senior colleagues—Eric Gonsalves (Minister Political and then Ambassador to Japan) and others.

I had always followed the practice of holding regular meetings with senior and junior officers and the whole staff when I was Ambassador elsewhere and Foreign Secretary in Delhi. I found this most useful and I believe it kept the embassy family together and gave each member a sense of participation. I decided on developing close contacts with the White House, State Department, Defence, Commerce, the Treasury and other departments of the US government, as well as the media, industry, universities and last but not least, fellow Indians in the USA. I was able to visit 44 of the 50 states in the USA, including Hawai and Puerto Rico, but could not visit Alaska for want of time. I addressed about 100 colleges and universities, a dozen chambers of commerce and prestigious clubs like the Commonwealth (i.e. California Commonwealth and not the British) Club in San Francisco, the Executive Club in Chicago, Asia Society, New York, Foreign Relations Committees and World Affairs Councils. I had to hold press conferences and appear on TV wherever I went. The National Press Club in Washington was good enough to invite me to address them and it was considered an honour for my country. I also met the publishers, editors and diplomatic correspondents of national, regional and local newspapers, wherever I went. The local Indian Association and Indian Students' Association invariably invited me to speak to them.

I have mentioned these details to give an idea of the kind of programme an Ambassador of India has to keep in the USA. I used to tour 10 to 15 days every month, mostly by air. Meetings with various sections of the American people gave me an insight into their thinking and feelings. At times I wondered whether the USA really was one country. The deeply religious Bible belt in the south, the Boston Brahmins and the WASPS (White Anglo-Saxon Protestants) in the east, the hardy, sturdy pioneering types in the north and mid-west, and the more liberal unconventional and easy going people in the west, plus the special ethnic States like Puerto Rico and Hawai—all made up the great United States of America. It was more a continent than a country, not unlike India, though almost three times its size and one third its population.

What held them together as one nation? Communications, a standard pattern of living (TV, radio, automobiles, gas stations, drug stores, mechanized agriculture, well equipped libraries and beautiful campuses etc.), a President elected by direct vote of the people, one common language (American English) spoken by all (though there were also Spanish and French speaking areas), a standardized free market economy (with some state control and regulation in basic and heavy industry)? All these were there but there was something else, more important, that held them together in spite of racial, regional and other differences. It was perhaps the spirit of innovation and research, the spirit of 1776, the American War of Independence, the will and determination not to bow to any other power. The USA has vast natural resources, advanced science and technology, hardworking and intelligent people who have opportunity to rise to the highest. This is what keeps them busy and going.

I also noticed social and racial tension, a high unemployment and crime rate, and poverty in the midst of plenty. The blacks, the Mexican wet-backs, the Red (American) Indians, were discriminated against socially and economically, though it was not the official government policy—almost like untouchability in India. People had a high standard of living. Almost every family owned at least one, if not two, automobiles, TV and radio sets, and had a house or apartment to live in. There was a rat-race to get to the next higher social rung, tough competition and extreme nervous tension.

Money was the new god, it seemed, and ruled everywhere. You could get away with many things if you had money. It could buy influence and power. Corruption was rampant in many places, high and low. People did not seem to bother too much about it, as long as prices were reasonable, wages were decent and they had the main creature comforts. They would tolerate many things but when it came to the President of the USA, they expected him to be super-human, incapable of commiting any wrong. The least flaw or human weakness in him shocked and rocked the whole nation. They saw in their President something like the British still do in their monarch—perhaps it was a hangover from the old days.

The Watergate crisis gripped the whole nation and almost upset the political structure of the country. I arrived in the USA when it was just boiling and Sam Ervin's Senate Committee was holding its daily televized enquiry. I used to watch it on the TV for two to four hours every day. It revealed a shocking state of affairs. It exposed the weakness and vulnerability of the American system. It also vindicated America's faith in democracy which, I believe, emerged clearner and stronger out of this crisis—at least for some time to come.

Most people were shocked by the revelations of Watergate, but they did not wish to see their President humiliated or the Presidency weakened. They heaved a sigh of relief when Ford pardoned Nixon. A few raised their eyebrows, some insinuated that there had been a deal between Nixon and his vice-President, before Nixon resigned. It may have cost Ford a few thousand votes in his Presidential election in 1976, but not more.

By and large the people were happy to leave Nixon and Watergate behind them and get on with their life and work. This is a peculiar trait in American character. They can be cruel and even vindictive when someone in authority lets them down, but having kicked him out, they can be generous and forgiving. They are too busy to remember bad dreams for long and try to forget them and get on with their jobs as soon as possible.

The Nixon administration, unlike the American people, had long memories, was, vindictive and spiteful, callous and cruel, conceited and domineering, tough physically as well as mentally, insensitive to other nations' feelings and pride. How else can one explain Nixon's policy towards Vietnam and Bangladesh?

Some people think it was Henry Kissinger's and not Nixon's policy. I do not think so. I remember once suggesting to Kissinger to persuade Nixon to give the slogan "Vietnamising the peace" rather than "Vietnamising the war," which he had announced with great fan-fare. Kissinger said it was a good idea and he would put it to his President. When I met him next he said Nixon would not bite it. Not that Kissinger was an unwilling instrument. As a professional, he lent his talents and skill to whatever Nixon finally decided, including the Christmas carpet bombing of North Vietnam.

As Ambassador of India, I was naturally concerned about Indo-American relations, and tried my best to repair them. I used to meet Henry Kissinger often when he was the National Security Adviser to Nixon. When he became Secretary of State I maintained my contact with him. He was a frequent guest at my dinner parties, much to the surprise and envy of many Ambassadors. But it was no special favour to me personally. He wanted to give the impression that America was undoing its anti-India tilt and the two countries and governments were getting closer. This would give him an aura of respectibility in Asia and Africa, which he needed badly after his role in Vietnam and Bangladesh. It would also increase his bargaining power with China, the USSR and even smaller countries, like Pakistan, Iran and the non-aligned and developing world, where India was respected. It was a calculated move.

Henry Kissinger had achieved only part of his ambition. He wanted to go down in history as a great Secretary of State. May be one day he might even rise to the Presidency, if the law against foreign-born naturalized Americans could be amended. I recall Mike Mansfield, the Senate majority leader, toasting him as the "greatest Secretary of State we have had" at one of my dinner parties. Congressman Bingham and others seriously proposed that the law may be amended to enable Henry Kissinger to stand for the Presidentship one day.

Kissinger was the only one among Nixon's top aides who managed to come out almost unscathed through Watergate. Kissinger was shrewd and clever. He was also a learned scholar, with a sense of history, ready wit and humour, indefatigable energy and unsatiable appetite—not only for food and drink, but also for intellectual pursuits. He had strong common-sense, was amoral and considered almost any means justified to achieve his aims and objectives. He was interesting, fascinating, scintillating, but also dangerous, if taken literally at his word. He was a past-master at coining new phrases, and chose his words carefully, so that he could keep his options open and give his own interpretation to them, that suited his strategy in a particular situation. Such was the man I was dealing with. One could not be too careful with him.

I had several informal as well as formal talks with him. The former were held over a simple lunch, *téte-a-téte*, either in his office or at my house. He sometimes had his Special Assistant Rodman with him and I my number two, Venkateshwaran, a shrewd and able officer. Our talks were wide-ranging from China to Cuba, Malaysia to the Middle-East, Africa to Argentina, eastern and western Europe, Japan, the Gulf and of course, South and South-East Asia. He assured me several times that the tilt against India was over, America had no quarrel with India's policy of non-alignment or friendship with the Soviet Union. India was the "pre-eminent power" in South Asia and had to play her due role in the region and, as a leading non-aligned country in the world. There was no clash of national interests between India and the USA. America did not wish to weaken India. A strong, stable, non-aligned and peaceful India would add to the stability and peace of the region. It would stem the tide of Chinese expansionism. America did not want to create a sphere of influence in our region, but she did not want it to become a sphere of Soviet or Chinese influence either, etc., etc.

This was all sweet talk, but I was not convinced that it was Nixon's policy. Nixon had a definite slant towards Pakistan and against India. Apart from his global policy of anti-Sovietism, it had also something to do with his personal dislike for Mrs Gandhi and his liking for the military rulers including Bhutto in Pakistan. He had not forgotten that in 1968 he had been treated to an Indian vegetarian non-alcholic lunch by Morarji Desai, then Deputy Prime Minister, while he had been given a right royal banquet in Pakistan, with all the fanfare due only to a head of government or state. He had said as much to some of his fellow travellers in the plane on his way back from India. He had also not forgotten Mrs Gandhi's cold, culculated indifference to his Seventh Fleet and her straight talk regarding Bangladesh in 1971. How then could Kissinger talk like this?

I told Kissinger that no one would believe me in India if I even mentioned his "new" American policy as he had propounded it to me. I suggested he visit India and make public statements, as well as give official assurances to this effect to my government. He welcomed the idea. He was invited and visited India in October 1974.

Kissinger is a man of high intelligence, a convincing conversationalist, philosophical and professorial in his public speeches, propounding great ideas and doctrines, citing historical parallels and trying to make new history. I told him that was all very fine but India had learnt by bitter experience to judge by deeds and not only words. He asked me what was it that would impress India. I replied we did not care much for the US aid. We would not ask for it. Since the US had suspended it unilaterally, it was for them to resume it or not. He said, "Fair enough. I don't agree with the bureaucrats in the State Department and the Treasury who want India to make a formal request for aid. I shall see what can be done." I said the most important thing was not to give arms to Pakistan which had now half of its previous borders to defend and only one front to face. He said others would give arms to Pakistan, like China, if the US did not, and it would only increase China's influence there. I replied we were talking about Indo-US relations and how to improve them and not about China-Pak relations. If the US was interested in retaining her influence in Pakistan, she could give more economic aid to her. An arms race on the sub-continent was not in the interest of either India or Pakistan. We did not ask for any arms from the USA, so why should Pakistan get any? She had other sources of supply as we had. We would deal separately with these other sources. But any attempt by the USA to "equate" India and Pakistan for defence requirements, to balance one against the other, or to try to tilt the balance, would not do. The old 'parity complex' between India and Pakistan had to be given up. India faced a threat from China. She was prepared to enter into a non-aggression or no-war pact with Pakistan. Usually it was the smaller country that wanted a no-war pact with a bigger neighbour. Here was India, the bigger of the two, asking for one. It was because we had no territorial ambitions or designs against Pakistan. We had vacated over 5,000 sq. miles of her territory which we had occupied in 1971, and wanted peace and friendship with her. This was the only way of preventing Soviet or Chinese or even American influence increasing in the area.

Kissinger listened patiently and replied that the USA had no intention of giving arms to Pakistan "for the time being." I had a suspicion that Nixon had not forgotten the Seventh Fleet's empty threat in the Bay of Bengal and the defeat of his military ally in 1971. He wanted to keep his options open. I told Kissinger that if he was going to play politics in India, it would not sell. He had better make up his mind what he could say and what assurances he could give and implement. Making tall promises and going back on them later would be worse than making no promises. He said he would think it over.

I warned him that Mrs Gandhi was not a person easily taken in. He said, "Don't I know? Even Nixon said the "lady is tough.""

I told Kissinger that like the American people, the Indians were open-hearted, sincere and simple. But, unlike the Americans, they had thousands of years of history behind them —some glorious, some not so glorious, and some bad. We had much in common in our way of government, freedom of the press and fundamental rights, etc. America was a rich and powerful country while India was neither. India did not want to imitate the USA, but if the vast natural and human resources of India could have the advanced technology of the USA on reasonable terms, she could become economically prosperous in a decade. Why could we not set up an Indo-US Joint Commission to explore areas of cooperation in various fields like economics, science, culture etc.? Kissinger welcomed the suggestion. He naturally wanted his visit to India to be a success, another feather in his cap.

Some people in India thought I was becoming pro-American. This, however, did not inhibit me. I had been called pro-China when I negotiated the Panch Sheel Agreement in 1954, and pro-Soviet when I was Ambassador in the USSR. It is a pity that some people in India cannot think of Indians being pro-India but must dub them as pro this or anti that country. It reminds me of the Dulles thesis "those who are not with us are against us." If you are not anti-communist then you must be a communist; equally if you are not anti-USA then you must be anti-USSR.

Kissinger came to India with his newly wedded wife Nancy.

She is quite the opposite of her husband—tall, modest, even a little shy, soft-spoken, a chain-smoker, but a careful eater. He is the talkative, assertive academic who has taken to diplomacy like a duck to water, fond of eating, drinking (wine only) and was quite a "swinger" before his marriage to Nancy. They made a good couple and complemented each other. We fixed several programmes for her during the day when her husband was busy in his talks. She wanted to visit Kashmir and her husband almost agreed, but then changed his mind; instead they spent a day in Bangladesh which was a good idea.

Mrs Gandhi cold-shouldered Kissinger's visit on the day of his arrival when she went out of Delhi to keep a previous engagement. Kissinger mentioned this to me in confidence, but took it in his stride. However, she made up for it by giving him an extra hour and lunch on the last day of his stay.

Apart from this little damper, his visit created a good impression, because of the great public speeches he made and the right things he said to the right people at the right time. He had kept his word about his public speeches and private assurances. But would he also implement his promises?

The Indo-US Joint Commission was set up and an agreement signed by Kissinger and Chavan who was Foreign Minister. The PL-480 settlement was also made, thanks to the indefatigable efforts of Daniel Patrick Moynihan, the US Ambassador to India. The rest remained to be seen.

Meanwhile the international situation became tense in the Middle-East. Kissinger was engaged in his "shuttle diplomacy." He had made a name for himself in bringing about the first disengagement agreement. I suggested to him that this was the time to bring in the Soviets and go to Geneva for a Mid-East conference. He agreed in principle but said he did not like Gromyko chasing him in every country. I said he should welcome it because Soviet involvement in any Mid-East settlement along with the USA, would make it all the more enduring and credible. He did not reply because he had other ideas in mind. He wanted to convert the Arab World into an American sphere of influence and cut down the Soviet influence which had been growing there since 1956.

I told him that pouring sophisticated weapons and large-scale arms into the Gulf countries might create more Vietnams there.

ndia felt concerned because these arms might again find their way to Pakistan. Would it not be better to have an agreement for peace, cooperation and non-aggression in this region—to start with, between Iran, Pakistan, Afghanistan, India and Bangladesh. He thought for a moment and then said, "It is a good idea, but it would sound better if it came from the Shanshah of Iran." I said I was not speaking for my government but I thought they would welcome it. He replied that the Shanshah was visiting Washington, D.C., in the near future and he would put it to him as his own idea. He probably did but nothing came of it because Pakistan would not agree. It needs to be pursued further in the interests of peace, security and stability in the region and to prevent an arms race.

We talked about the Indian Ocean. I pointed out that Brezhnev had agreed in the joint communique issued at the end of his visit to India in 1974 to the idea of a conference of all interested states on an equal footing. Why was America dragging her feet and not making a similar response? He did not perhaps like the Soviet Union taking a lead over the USA in this matter or had other ideas. He merely said he would think it over but did nothing about it.

I began to wonder whether Kissinger was really serious about improving Indo-US relations. He was so much involved with crisis situations that he had little time for normalizing relations elsewhere. I had sent him a message on his marriage to Nancy expressing the hope that this would be "the beginning of not getting exclusively involved with crises and devoting more time to normal situations." That was Kissinger's trouble. He loved the limelight, to be the trouble shooter in trouble spots, to put out fires and start new ones to be able to put them out by himself. He kept everything under his own control and the State Department practically became a one-man show. He was even his own PRO and would brief the Press "off the record", knowing fully well they would make use of what he said. Sometimes he deliberately leaked things to some of his press favourites to fly a new kite in the diplomatic sky. He loved meeting heads of state and government, film stars and powerful and influential men in the US Congress. He was not very popular with his opposite numbers in western Europe. He was really a European who had by a quirk of fate become an American. He knew and understood Europe better than most of his predecessors. He knew where and when to hit hardest. This did not please the Europeans and some, like the French Foreign Minister Jobert, openly retaliated.

As a German and disciple of Matternich and Bismark (both of whom he admired) he thought he knew how to deal with the Russians by alternately playing soft and acting tough. He believed in playing the power game in politics, and trying to exploit differences among others to gain more power and influence for America. This was the old 19th century European game. He gave it new names, shrouded it in mysterious and high sounding phrases. When I posed the question to him, he replied, "I agree with you in principle that there should be peaceful and cooperative co-existence between different political and social systems and ideologies, but before this can happen there must be a "systemic" change in the configuration of world forces and ideologies." This game of words and phrases could be and was played by others, like Peking, which had more than one Kissinger. Perhaps that is one reason why Kissinger made a bee-line for China, as soon as he could, surreptitiously from Nathiagali in Pakistan, through Yahya Khan's good offices. He liked intellectual bouts with equals. He seriously thought that America could exploit Sino-Soviet differences to its advantage. The Chinese also thought they could play on the anti-Sovietism of Nixon and turn it to their own advantage.

Both Kissinger and Nixon failed to understand the new resurgent Asia, Nixon even less than Kissinger. They bent over backwards to please China in many ways. Nixon even tried to eat corn flakes with chopsticks during this visit to China in 1972 to impress the Chinese. The Chinese are not taken in by such gimmicks, but they also played the game, only with greater skill. Liaison Missions of America and China were established in Peking and Washington respectively. China had much more to gain from this than the USA. The Sino-US flirtation continues but without any diplomatic marriage in sight yet. However, the Chinese were able to influence the US policy in Asia and towards the USSR while America hardly made any dent on China's policy. China did not change her basic stand on Taiwan (Formosa) while the US hardened its stand on a few "expendable" areas like India.

The difficulty with the US policy makers is that they cannot plan for a long term policy in spite of a plethora of planning experts and paraphernalia. The US President has a tenure of four years—about a year is spent in post-election "settling down" and more than a year in preparation for the next election. *Ad hoc* decisions are taken on each crisis as it occurs and there is little consistency, except perhaps in matters which are of major concern to them. Their priorities are different from those of the USSR, China or India. However, the US policy makers understand military power and economic strength, but not the more enduring things that sustain older civilizations. Kissinger was no exception. He was essentially a European, a German, thrown up by circumstances to a position of power and influence in America. He has no "feel" for Asia and perhaps "thinks" that orientals only believe in face-saving formulas. This is an old myth which is perhaps more applicable to modern American policy and "shuttle" diplomacy.

We had a taste of it in early 1975. Henry Kissinger sent a message to me through Ingersol (who was Acting-Secretary of State during his absence in the Middle-East) on 19 February 1975, that the US was going to lift the ban on the supply of arms to India and Pakistan on 24 February. I sent word back immediately that this was a breach of the understanding he had given to me and my government that they would not take a final decision until they had had full discussion with us. I suggested that a final decision he postponed until Kissinger had discussed it with Chavan who was scheduled to visit Washington in March for the second meeting of the Indo-US Joint Commission. Ingersol expressed his ignorance about any such understanding (not surprising because Kissinger did not always confide in his colleagues), but promised to send the message. He did and pat came Kissinger's reply that he regreted the decision was final and could not be postponed. This was conveyed to me on 22 February 1975, and the US announcement was going to be made on 24 February. Kissinger was keen to do this because he had given a secret promise to Bhutto during his visit to Washington a fortnight earlier (5 February 74). I considered it a breach of faith and told my government that I proposed to issue a statement and they should do the same. They agreed, I drafted a statement in consultation with Eric Gonsalves, Shiva Ramakrishnan and others, telephoned it to the Foreign Secretary in Delhi and got the OK. I called a press conference at the Chancery immediately after the announcement was made by the State Department and made the following statement:

"We have noted with deep regret and disappointment the decision to lift the US arms embargo announced by the State Department today and have already lodged a strong protest against it. We do not accept or agree that the lifting of the arms embargo will not lead to an arms race or hinder the process of normalization under the Simla Agreement; our opinion is based on our experience of the past two decades when three bloody conflicts took place in the sub-continent in which American arms were used against India, in spite of American assurances to the contrary.

"Our differences with Pakistan are temporary and can and will be solved bilaterally and peacefully if there is no outside intervention. This was the solemn agreement signed in Simla and we are determined to carry the Simla process forward, in spite of the impediments that may be placed in its way by the lifting of the embargo.

"The trouble in the past has been that outside powers, especially some of the great powers and, in particular, the USA, have taken a partisan attitude on the problems of the sub-continent and thus encouraged tension and conflict, even perhaps without intending to do so. The arms embargo imposed in 1965 was a wise decision in the light of past experience. The one time exception in 1970 was neither one time nor an exception. The lifting of the arms embargo further reduces the credibility of the US assurances which have proved inoperative in the past. It shows that the US administration's policy towards the sub-continent is based on the concept of power, balance of power, of creating influence through supply of arms, a policy that has failed in the sub-continent and some other adjoining areas.

"We hope that any attempts to involve the sub-continent in great power military alliances and rivalries will not be encouraged. We are non-aligned and hope to create in the sub-continent an area of peace, friendship and cooperation on the basis of the sovereign equality of nations instead of an area of tension and conflict as it has been in the past.

"There is no conflict of basic interests between the people of India and Pakistan. Our common enemies are poverty, shortage

of food, illiteracy, disease, etc. What we both need is to moder-
nize our agriculture, health, social services, etc. and not an arms
race which neither of us can afford.

"India is as much interested, if not more, than any other
power, in the integrity, stability, security and progress of a
friendly Pakistan. This is why India returned over 5,000 sq.
miles of Pakistani territory under the Simla Agreement and over
90,000 prisoners of war under the Delhi Agreement.

"It is regrettable that the US Government should have felt it
necessary to change its policy of an arms embargo which had
helped relax tension and the process of normalization. It is all
the more regretable because of the adverse effect it will have on
Indo-American relations. India attaches importance to its friendship with the USA, but friendship is a two-way street."

Foreign Minister Chavan also made a statement though not in
the same language. His statement was aimed mainly for India
and ours for America. We had deliberately chosen words which
would bring home to the American people the strength of
India's feelings in terms they understood like "credibility,"
"inoperative," etc., which had become current coin during the
Watergate proceedings. It was meant to have an effect on
Kissinger and it did. He called a press conference the same afternoon. A question was "planted" with an American news agency
reporter, "What is your reaction to the sharp statement by the
Indian Ambassador?" He tried to drive a wedge between Chavan
and me by calling Chavan's statement "realistic" and mine
"unacceptable." On being asked whether he would ask for my
recall, he replied in the negative.

I was asked the same evening on Channel 26 of PBS as to
what my reaction to Kissinger's statement was. I said that while
part of my statement was unacceptable to him, part of his was
unacceptable to my government. There was some press comment
on this public exchange between Kissinger and me. One columnist in Washington D.C. wrote a column headed "Tikki Kaul
the wrong guy to pick on." Another in Chicago entitled his
column "Nicking Dr K. in the credibility gap" and said, "Kaul,
in his statement, had struck a nerve which Chavan had missed.
He knew Kissinger well enough to be aware that he is especially
sensitive to one American problem—the credibility of the US
assurances."

My Government and Foreign Minister supported my statement in Parliament and the controversy died down as quickly as
it had arisen. But the US administration's credibility had a sharp
decline in Indian eyes. Chavan postponed his visit as I had
forewarned Kissinger. I believe that Kissinger felt a little
"guilty" perhaps, about the timing and manner of his statement.
The public quarrel was patched up privately and we began to
meet again, though not as frequently as before. Kissinger had
the courtesy to tell me at my farewell meeting in the summer of
1976, "We respect you for the courage and conviction with which
you have defended the interests of your country." I should like
to thank my colleagues in the embassy and in our Foreign Office
who stood by me and spoke with one voice.

I came home for consultations in May 1975, and asked Mrs
Gandhi to let me come back as I had done two years and there
was not much more I could do. She would not agree and asked
me to stay a "little longer." The emergency in India was proclaimed on 26 June 1975, and I left for the USA on 29 June.
The rest of my tenure in the USA was mainly engaged in meeting
leading senators and congressmen, the media representatives,
professors, students and fellow Indians. I met President Ford,
Vice-President Rockefeller, Kissinger and others too, but it was
not with the same enthusiasm as before. Perhaps a more malle-
able and ductile person was needed as Indian Ambassador to the
USA. I wrote accordingly to Mrs Gandhi, several times, but
each time she asked me to stay on a "little longer." The "little
longer" became more than a year, until at last I handed over
charge in September 1976, to Kewal Singh who had earlier
succeeded me in London, Moscow and as Foreign Secretary.

Administrations and administrators come and go, but the people remain. A country endures because of the stamina and character of its people. I utilized my continued stay in the USA to get to know the American people. One could talk freely and frankly to them without the fear of being misunderstood, even if they did not agree with one. The American people, like us Indians, are open-hearted and frank, say what they feel and appreciate the same in others. I found them good listeners if you had something new or interesting to say, otherwise impatient and easily bored. The question-answer period was the most interesting and stimulating. The youth and the students, in particular, impressed me as much more internationally minded than the older generation. They had been through Vietnam and had seen how dirty a war could be.

I met most of the leading senators and Congressmen and found them, with a few exceptions, much more friendly and open than the US administration. Senators Hubert Humphrey, Mike Mansfield, William Fullbright, Gaylord Nelson, Charles Mathias, Hollings, William Saxbe, Tom Eagleton, Sherman Cooper, Frank Church, Edward Kennedy, Jacob Javitts and Cranston are a few names that I recall as being friendly, understanding and helpful to India. Among the Congressmen I regarded Zablowsky, Lee Hamilton, Frelighuysen, Bingham, Whalen, Fraser, some of the many friends of India. A lone Congressman from Maryland was the incorrigible critic.

President Ford was quite a contrast to Nixon. He was pleasant and always willing to listen, open to conviction and not dogmatic or aggressive. He spoke with sincerity and frankness, and was affable and polite. Perhaps he lacked strength in his office as President because he came to it through the backdoor, unexpectedly, when Nixon had to resign. In spite of the pardon he granted to Nixon, he lost only by a narrow margin to Carter in November 1976. I would not be surprised if he came back to fight another Presidential election and, may be successfully, now that Watergate is over and done with. But of this one can be certain that Nixon has died a political death and cannot again be resurrected. Kissinger is capable of coming to power again but he can never be the President. People admire his intellect but do not trust him. He would, however, make an excellent President of a prestigeous University or the head of a research organization.

Elliot Richardson who resigned during Watergate, struck me as an honest, sincere intellectual who has the making of a President, John Simon, Treasury Secretary, is a man with a keen sense of humour. He once told me during the Watergate crisis, "The ship of state leaks only at the top." Robert McNamara, President of the World Bank, is a delightful contrast to the McNamara who was Defence Secretary. Arthur Burns, who was Chairman of the Federal Reserve, was an honest, outspoken, fearless and independent economist. His wife is a poet and a very pleasant person. Sleisinger, Defence Secretary, impressed me as a tough, businesslike, and honest man. Commerce Secretary Dent, was pleasant but not very helpful or effective.

Governors of states, unlike in India, are elected and not nominated. They are, therefore much more powerful and influential. Governorship is sometimes considered a stepping stone to the Presidency. Governors Carter of Georgia and Brown of California, were two contenders for Democratic nomination to the Presidency in 1976. They are both outstanding and unusual in their different ways.

Nelson Rockefeller was Governor of New York and then Vice-President and a contender for the Republican nomination to the Presidency in 1976. Carter, as Governor in the southern state of Georgia, was popular among blacks—no mean achievement. I called on him when he was Governor and presented him with a packet of Indian tea. He of course gave me a packet of peanuts. He is deeply religious, coming as he does from the Bible belt. He is also practical and pragmatic. After the dirt that was washed in Watergate, he came like a breath of fresh air to Washington, D.C. But, whether he will be able to bring about any healthy changes in Nixon's domestic and foreign policies remains to be seen. The domestic atmosphere does seem a little cleaner but foreign policy has not shown much of the Carter touch yet. The two men who seem to be colouring and shaping Carter's foreign policy are Secretary of State Cyrus Vance, and Zbignew Brzezinsky, the former perhaps slightly less hawkish than the latter. Carter's extension of human rights and freedoms to the international arena has not made much of a dent, because it seemed politically motivated against the USSR, rather than a universal doctrine applicable to the USA itself and her allies.

Mayors of big cities are also important in their own parishes. Mayor Daly of Chicago was an institution in himself and ran this important city for twenty-six years. He was largely responsible for swinging the Democratic Convention in favour of Carter. Mayors of New York City are also powerful and wield considerable influence. Jews are influential in New York City and in the media, trade and commerce and helped Carter to win against Ford in 1976. Another important factor is the Black vote in the USA. They number about 20 million in a population of 230 million and were an important factor in tilting the scales in favour of Carter.

Among the many black Mayors three impressed me the most —Bradley of Los Angeles, Jackson of Atlanta (Georgia) and Walter Washington in the district of Columbia (Washington D.C.). The most outstanding black American in recent years was the late Martin Luther King (Jr). I made a pilgrimage to the Centre for Social Change established in his memory at Atlanta, Georgia, and presented some books on India to it. Mrs Coretta King, the parents of her husband and Miss Lilian Carter graced the occasion.

On the TV Network, PBS invited me quite often while ABC. GBS and NBC occasionally. I appeared on "Face the Nation," "Today" live, coast to coast programmes. The Press Observers' Club, the National Press Club, the Democratic and Republican Women's Clubs, Church groups, Law Societies, Chambers of Commerce, were also our hosts at many functions. I addressed a Publishers' and Editors' meet on the West Coast at Sao Palto and another in the mid-West near St. Louis (Missourie). Both provided a delightful change from the hackneyed Washington and New York scene. Those present included most leading publishers and editors of the region. They looked at things differently from the political pundits of the Capital or the Boston Brahmins of the East.

The Bicentennial of American Independence was celebrated in 1976. India sent a troupe of folk dancers and handicraft workers who attracted the largest crowds in various cities of the USA. But what was appreciated more than anything else was a volume on "India-USA-1776-1976" written by M.V. Kamath, US correspondent of the Times of India and published by the Embassy. An editorial in the nation-wide WTOP radio channel praised it highly while all circles welcomed it. It could and should have a second edition.

There are a number of Indian Yogis and Swamis with large American followings. Among them may be mentioned Swami Rama in Chicago; Swami Satchitananda, founder of Integral Yoga Institute in Connecticut; Swami Vishnu of the Shivananda Divine Ashram with headquarters in Val Morin (Canada) and branches in California, upstate New York, Florida and Paradise Island (Bahamas). Yogi Bhajan, a tall Sikh has converted about 200,000 American youngmen and women, weaned them away from drugs, and given them a separate dress, religion, identity and self-respect. His headquarters are in Santa Fe (New Mexico) and Los Angeles, with about 200 branches all over the country. There are many transcendental meditation centres with head-quarters at the University of Iowa. They charge a regular fee from their students and run courses of study and training of teachers in TM. We also came across the Hare Krishna groups but did not get mixed up with Bal Yogeshwar's followers as he had become a controversial figure. I also visited two Yogashrams run by Americans—the Prem Ashram in Bedford (Virginia) and the Divine Light Ashram at Cleveland. Both are doing good work in their own way.

Functions at the Christian, Buddhist, Hindu and Islamic Societies attracted many Americans. The Gandhi Institute in Washington D.C. which we helped set up, is doing excellent work.

We cultivated the fairly large number of Indian Associations and Indian Students' Associations throughout the United States. The AIA (Association of Indians in America) with its head-quarters at New York covers the Eastern half of the USA. The ILA (India League of America) with headquarters in Chicago covers the north and north-west. The west coast has its own organizations while the south is not so active except in Dallas and Houston (Texas). We met a number of Indians who are eminent in their respective fields like Professors George Sudershan, Raja Rao, Harish Chandra, Patel, Haridas Mazumdar and others.

They gave us help and cooperation in studying the problems of India in the fields of medicine, physics, education and social sciences, engineering and various forms of technology, research and development. They came in good numbers to our annual meeting in the embassy and made some valuable suggestions which were forwarded to the Government of India. Contacts between them and various institutions in India were thus built up. Their counterparts in India exchanged programmes and visits as consultants or visiting professors. There is vast scope for developing such contacts with people of Indian origin, not only in the USA but in other countries also where there is a sizeable Indian population. Some of them have made notable contributions to the country of their adoption and most are eager to do something for the land of their birth.

Indians in America are, by and large, patriotic, prosperous and eager to maintain cultural links with India. We also found the Americans generally, and the youth in particular, keen to know more about India's culture in general and music, dance and yoga in particular. Some yogis and swamis have done good pioneering work, but no one can excel Ravi Shankar, Ali Akbar Khan and Alla Rakha who are almost household names in young America. The Government of India would do well to encourage them and other non-official organizations in India and the USA to project India's culture there. Visits by Lata Mangeshkar, Mukesh, Asha Bhonsle, Hema Malini, Sunil Dutt, Asha Parekh, Raj Kapoor and others were greatly appreciated. Such visits should be more frequent.

Zubin Mehta the world renowned conductor is in a class by himself and a human dynamo. He is perhaps the youngest conductor of the New York Philhormonic Orchestra—the highest honour any conductor can aspire for. He is proud of his Indian heritage and has retained his Indian Passport. His wife, Nancy, is of great help to him.

The Indian students in America are facing some serious problems and are probably going to have even greater difficulties in future. They number about 15,000 at present. Most of them came to the USA on student visas when they were required to finance themselves only for a year during which they could qualify for scholarships, stipends and various odd jobs on the campus. They could also seek work outside the campus during vacations and thus meet their expenses. After taking a degree, they could undergo practical training for one to three years on a paid job. And having stayed in the USA for 5 years, they could qualify for permanent immigrant status or the "green card" as it is called, though it is blue in colour. Since 1974, however, the US immigration laws have been tightened and are enforced even more harshly than they were intended. Jobs, except on the campus, are not allowed. Three years' financial guarantees are required. Many students who had come before 1974 have had to give up their studies in the middle and have naturally turned bitter. They cannot get jobs in the USA or back home in India where the problem of educated unemployment is assuming serious proportions.

The Government of India must give serious and urgent consideration to this problem. They should take it up with the US Government and also discourage Indians going to the USA in large numbers just in search of a career. It is not an easy problem to solve but it can and has to be tackled with imagination and speed. We raised some voluntary subscriptions from well off Indians in big cities and set up local committees to help deserving and indigent Indian students. This can, however, be only a temporary measure and a more permanent solution has to be worked out. The seminar on "Indians Overseas" held in November 1977, at the India International Centre in Delhi and inaugurated by Foreign Minister Vajpayee, has made some suggestions which deserve urgent consideration by the Government of India.

The other Indians, who came before 1970, are doing well. They are mainly in the various professions, like teaching, engineering, medicine and in import-export trade etc. Most of them are American citizens at present. The older Indian immigrants, like the Sikhs and Punjabi agriculturists in California are US citizens and fairly prosperous. They are the offspring of the organisers of the Ghadar Party which launched the movement for the independence of India in the USA against heavy odds. We were able to construct a hall and a small building as a memorial to the martyrs of the Ghadar Party at 5, Wood Street in San Francisco. The Indian community contributed generously and the Government of India also gave help. Dr G.B. Lal, the oldest surviving Ghadar Party leader, the then Indian Consul-General in San Francisco, Romesh Arora (now High Commissioner in Fiji), deserve credit for bringing all the Indians together to achieve this. The Government of India should seriously consider creating a Ghadar Memorial Foundation or Trust for the benefit of the younger generation of Indians in this area.

The total number of persons of Indian origin in the USA is anywhere between 200,000 to 300,000 at present. Considering their relatively small number they have contributed proportionately more to the USA in various fields, like medicine, mathematics, physical sciences, agriculture, and trade, than perhaps any other minority. They have certainly given as much, if not more, to the USA than they have got from her. Their numbers are likely to grow in the future and they could become an even more important minority if they were united and well organized. At present there are numerous regional, religious and linguistic societies among them. What is needed is one organization for all Indians in the USA, with branches all over, without disturbing the smaller societies. The AIA and the ILA could play a mutually catalytic role and set an example to others by merging in one body all Indians in the USA. This should be left to them and such a move should start from within rather than from outside. India can however, certainly help, both through official and non-official channels, to strengthen their cultural links with India, as other minorities are helped in the USA by their mother countries.

There are three important minorities in the USA, apart from the Puerto Ricans, Chinese, Japanese, Jewish and other racial groups. The first is the Black community. It is becoming conscious and proud of its black complexion. They do not like to be called "negroes" and are rediscovering their roots in Black Africa. "Black is beautiful" is the new slogan. The "Afro" hair styles are becoming popular among them. These are straws in the wind but they do indicate a resurgent spirit which can no longer be placated by mere palliatives or crumbs of bread thrown from the affluent American table. Desegregation, integration in schools and school buses, protests against discrimination in hotels, clubs, employment, etc. are growing. The unemployment rate among blacks in America is above 20 per cent as against the national average of about 7 per cent. The blacks have made a mark in the field of sports, music, theatre and literature. Given the opportunity, there is no reason why they cannot make good in other fields also. If they do not get the opportunity peacefully, they will wrest it by violence. The high crime rate among the black youth in the USA is a symptom and warning which has to be taken note of. If we do not tackle our problem of the Harijans and the landless speedily, we may face a similar situation.

The other important, but neglected, community is that of the American Indians or Red Indians. They are scattered in various states in the south, south-west and north. They have been "preserved" like museum pieces in their "reservations" but are now coming out and fighting for their rights, with the support of film actors like Marlon Brando and others. They number about one million and comprise about 20 main tribes. They are developing a common consciousness as the original inhabitants of America, but they are so widely scattered in several small pockets that the move for unity is not easy.

We visited New Mexico where they are fairly well organized, and met some of their leaders in various "reservations"—most of them appointed by the US Government. They are given the high-sounding title of "Lt. Governor," but have little power and less funds. The Red Indians are being lured by big automobiles and TV and liquor shops run by Whites in their settlements. Some of them with whom we talked showed awareness of their problems. When asked "Would you like to become one united state within the USA or like to continue in different settlements?," they answered, almost unanimously, they would prefer the former. Some said they would like to have an "independent" state of their own while a few said they were too scattered about to form one state. It is difficult to foresee their future—whether they will get integrated with the whites and thus lose their identity, remain separate in scattered groups or unite. At present, they do not exercise any significant influence on American politics or economy, but they have the potential to acquire both. Our own hill and scheduled tribes present a similar, though not identical, problem which must be tackled with imagination and speed.

The third large minority community is that of the Mexicans. They number about ten millions and are mostly farm hands and unskilled workers. Large numbers of them cross the border rivers at night to find jobs in the USA. Hence their nick name "wet backs." They are having a hard time with the US immigration authorities. Some local unions also resent their influx. But, as a Mexican Ambassador in the USA told me, their numbers are likely to increase as the US is short of farm hands and unskilled labour. They will form an increasingly important minority in the USA in the coming years and exercise their influence in both politics and the economy. Fortunately we do not face this problem in India, except for periodic influx of refugees from some neighbouring countries.

There are other ethnic minorities or racial and religious communities like the Catholics, Mormons, Seventh Day Adventists, etc. There are the Scandinivans in Minisota and Wisconsin, the Yugoslavs and Poles in Milwaukee, the Arabs (Lebanese mostly) and the Jews in big cities, the New Englanders and WASPS in the east and north-east, the descendants of old planters in the south and those of the original pioneers in the mid-west and west. Puerto Ricans in New York are a growing and important minority.

This, in brief, is a spectrum of the multi-racial society of the USA. It is a fascinating scene, not unlike that in India, rich in its diversity. The USA is a young country and therefore more dynamic and less tied to tradition—good and bad—than an ancient country like India.

America could be an important factor in helping and cooperating with the less developed countries of the Third World. Will the US administration do so, without trying at the same time to influence and interfere in the internal affairs of these countries. The US priorities are not yet such as would inspire hope. World leadership came to America after World War II, when the world was divided into two hostile military blocs and the cold war was at its coldest. Non-aligned countries like India kept out of these blocs, but some developing countries were sucked in. There is an increasing trend among the developing countries away from military alliances and towards non-alignment. Most of them still depend on the developed countries for economic assistance and military hardware. There is danger of a new form of economic influence and military domination—so called "neo-colonialism" —gaining strength. The developing countries of the Third World will have to increase cooperation *inter se* and fight this trend, to make their newly won independence real and meaningful.

The developed world is not playing the game. Terms of trade, transfer of technology and economic cooperation are such that the rich countries are getting richer and the poor poorer. The gulf between them is widening. This can produce serious situations and pose a threat to world peace.

It is time a country like the USA gave a lead in this matter, by removing the unfair and unequal restrictions, tarrif, quota and other barriers in their trade with the developing countries, under the general scheme of preferences. But the USA is dragging her feet and ganging up with other developed countries to resist this. It is a short-sighted policy and cannot stand the test of time.

The energy crisis is an example of what can happen. The USA with less than 6 per cent of the world's population is consuming more than 35 per cent of the world's energy. She may be able to afford this luxury for some time, but even the common man in affluent America felt the pinch of the raise in the price of oil by the OPEC. The worst sufferers, however, were the developing oil importing countries like India.

The time has come when there is an urgent need to consider some way of pooling together the resources of the world, harnessing and using them in a manner that is fair and equitable to all countries, especially to the poor two-thirds of humanity living in the Third World. We must treat global problems in a global manner so that the largest number of the most needy countries are not left to live below the poverty line any more. To achieve this, the developing countries will have to work hard, cooperate *inter se*, improve the living conditions of the poor in the society, become as self-reliant as possible, and thus be able to stand up to the developed countries and not be at their mercy.

Wendel Wilkie gave the call for "One World," Washington, Lincoln and Jefferson were men of vision. Roosevelt tried in the Atlantic Charter to free the world from want and fear. But, we are still far from the goal of "One World" or the Four Freedoms. Developed countries like America and developing countries like India, could give a lead in this matter, but will they? A Mahatma Gandhi or a Jawaharlal Nehru in India could, a Roosevelt in

America could, but alas, the world has seen a steady deterioration in the quality of life and leadership in recent years. .

The America of 1977 is different from the America of 1947. So is India and so is the world. Different yes, but are they any better off than they were three decades ago? In some ways yes and in some no. The cold war is not so acute now, non-alignment in American eyes is not "immoral," but a valid and viable policy for newly independent and developing countries. There is now a "balance of terror" in the thermo-nuclear field which is preventing a direct conflict between the super-powers, but the nuclear weapon powers and their allies want to retain the monopoly of nuclear technology under their control. Wars by proxy are still raging in the developing world. The battle of ideologies and rivalry in creating military and ideological spheres of influence is in full swing. General disarmament and nuclear disarmament in particular, are not in sight. The economic gulf between the developing and developed countries is increasing.

The Middle-East is facing internecine conflict and violence. Peace is nowhere in sight. The Gulf countries are becoming the dumping ground for obsolete and not so obsolete American weapons and present possibilities of mutual conflict. Many countries in Africa are becoming the battle-ground for conflicting ideologies and interests of the big and super powers. The Carribean and Latin American countries are becoming pawns in the game of big power politics and facing internal upheavals. South and South-East Asia are not yet free from this scourge and are groping for some kind of regional and sub-regional cooperation. The Far-East and the Pacific area present a grim picture of the fallout from Sino-Soviet and Soviet-American rivalries and their triangular diplomacy. Only eastern and western Europe have taken some concrete steps towards detente but even there the spectre of war hangs like a heavy cloud. SALT II and MBRF (Mutual Balanced Reduction of Forces) are far from fruition.

The world situation today presents a picture of no peace and no war, but of acute tension in which diplomacy becomes more difficult but also more important.

Three decades of independence, of peace and war, of social and political unrest, of some economic progress but not much of social justice—this in brief is the record of India since Independence. Independent India, free from the shackles of foreign rule, represented hope—not only for India but for the freedom of the rest of the world still under the colonial rule. Gandhi was the symbol of this spirit of freedom and hope. Nehru tried to translate some of Gandhi's ideas and his own into reality. He laid the base for India's industrialization, launched many multi-purpose projects which helped in generating power, irrigation, industrial and agricultural development. He maintained high standards of government and politics. He did not succeed fully because his party became involved too much in the loaves and fishes of office and not enough in the welfare of the masses. Nehru strengthened the non-alignment movement and raised India's prestige in the world, as a force for peace and lessening of tensions.

After Nehru, Shastri tried to combine the best of Gandhi and Nehru. But, he lived too short a time to make any significant impact. The Tashkent Declaration is a monument to his spirit of sacrifice and love for peace.

During her eleven years' tenure as Prime Minister, Indira Gandhi did many good things but, partly due to her own make up and partly because of extraneous circumstances, was not able to utilize the opportunity she had of strengthening socialism and democracy. But she has a place of her own in India's history. In foreign affairs she strengthened India's position and stature in the world.

1977 was a turning point in India's post-independence history. Thirty years are, perhaps, not enough to overcome, in a peaceful and democratic way, the after effects of centuries of superstition and stagnation, imperialist domination and colonial rule in a vast and an ancient country. India is still, by and large, orthodox, conservative, tradition-bound and caste ridden. Yet, if we look at other countries that became independent at about the same time as India, we have perhaps, not done badly in comparison. But that is cold comfort. Forty per cent of our people still live below the poverty line. Harijans are still being ill-treated. The country is still not emotionally integrated. Regional, religious and caste rivalries and antagonisms still persist.

If we look at those countries which call themselves developed, they did not achieve much in the first 30 years of their independence. Some had the advantage of colonial empires to feed the "mother" country with cheap raw materials and labour, some had vast natural resources and a comparatively smaller population than India. Even the socialist countries which went through bloody revolutions were not able to achieve as much in the first 30 years as India has done, but there was less disparity in incomes, more employment, less exploitation of man by man, and more social justice with economic development, than there has been in India since independence.

We have vast natural and human resources, the third largest number of scientists and trained medical doctors, engineers and technicians in the world. But, we have not been able to harness them fully. Besides, we do not have the time to wait as others had. We have to make up for centuries of neglect and exploitation. We almost missed the industrial revolution and we cannot afford to miss the technological revolution. What is most important, we have yet to have a social revolution to reduce the gap between the rich and the poor, to raise the standard of living of the masses, and to give equality of opportunity to all.

It was to this India that I came back from the USA in November 1976. The Emergency was still on. It had produced a temporary sense of security and discipline. There was an apparent calm on the surface but people were seething with suppressed anger at the excesses committed by the authorities, especially in the northern states. Population control is necessary, but it had been introduced in an autocratic and arbitrary manner. You cannot emasculate a whole nation through compulsory sterilization. You cannot beautify a city through bulldozers alone. Some good things had been done, but in a bad way, through pressure, force, violence and terror. Because of censor-

ship of the press, people at large, inside and outside the country, were unaware of the excesses committed in the name of
Emergency.

Whether internal Emergency was justified or not when it was
proclaimed it was kept longer than necessary. The ruling party
had become smug and complacent, its organization flabby. It lost
touch with the people. The administration was authoritarian and
unresponsive to people's feelings, all opposition was ruthlessly
suppressed.

One could not realize the magnitude of the problem from outside. Even inside the country, there appeared to be a mixed
opinion about the benefits and evils of the Emergency. I decided
to tour some states in the north and south when I came back.

Wherever I went, especially in the Hindi-speaking belt, I
found a strange atmosphere. People did not talk freely. They
seemed to be afraid of something. It was a strange feeling which
I had not experienced in India before, not since independence.
It was suffocating and such a situation could not last. I exchanged my impressions, doubts, and feelings, with some friends and
found them of the same opinion—that elections must be held so
that people can have a chance to give their free verdict. We
heaved a sigh of relief when Mrs Gandhi announced on 18 January 1977, that elections to Parliament would be held in six weeks.

What happened in the elections is well known. The people
expressed their suppressed resentment at the excesses committed
during the Emergency in no uncertain terms. Elections saved
the country from the brink of disaster. There was enthusiasm
and rejoicing at the defeat of the Congress Party. The massive
vote was really a negative vote against the Congress and not a
positive vote for the Janata Party.

There were doubts in the minds of some whether the new
ruling "party" would be able to hold together. The Janata party
comprised many disparate elements and ideologies—even more
than the Congress party. Would they be able to formulate
coherent economic, social, political, defence and foreign policies
and implement the many promises they had made during the
elections?

Initial doubts disappeared for a while when Morarji Desai
was elected leader of the Janata Parliamentary Party and thus
became Prime Minister. His cabinet represented the cross section

of the constituent units which had joined hands against the ruling Congress. Some were bitter having suffered detention without trial for a year-and-a-half. Some were inexperienced and impatient to undo everything—good and bad—the previous government had done. Some started a tirade against the Nehru name and family and did not spare even Jawaharlal, the maker of modern India. Morarji tried to hold the balance, smoothed ruffled feelings and took a reasonable and conciliatory stand on most matters. This has so far kept the party at the centre together for a while in spite of internal conflicts and ideological, personal and temperamental differences.

Morarji of 1977 was a different man from the earlier Morarji. He had mellowed considerably. although he still had his fads. Prohibition is a matter of principle with him and he insisted on enforcing it within four years.

This reminds me of his visit to London in 1961 when I was the Acting High Commissioner. I invited him to stay at "Sun House" with me. He readily accepted. I asked him about his food habits and he said his staff fussed about it unnecessarily. He ate simple vegetarian food, took cow's milk, dried nuts and fresh fruit. I had no problem with this. But when I told him I had invited Edward Heath and Harlod Wilson to a quiet dinner with him at my house next day, he insisted that I do not serve any alcohol. I reluctantly agreed. But, he went a little further and suggested that I do not serve any meat either. To this I did not agree, for it would not be hospitable to force only vegetarian food on guests used to eating meat everyday. He did not insist but said "when Vijayalakshmi was High Commissioner she served only vegetarian food at meals given in my honour." I heard this in silence and did not reply or commit myself not to serve meat.

I telephoned Heath and Wilson to have their drinks before coming to dinner, but I thought it would be churlish to ask them to have their meat course also before coming. They came, having had their evening drink or two and teased me at the entrance by asking, "Are we going vegetarian too?" I said no and they appeared relieved. Morarji may not have liked my serving meat to my guests but he seemed to appreciate my not serving alcohol and not eating meat myself. I did this out of respect for him.

A few months later Chagla took over as High Commissioner when Morarji came again to London. Chagla gave a party for him where he served both meat and alcohol and Morarji did not say anything. I recall asking Shastri in May 1965, in Moscow whether I could serve alcohol at my lunch in his honour. He said I could do as I thought fit. I did serve alcohol but requested my colleagues not to drink out of respect for Shastri. Meat was served though Shastri was a vegetarian.

Coming back to the Indian scene it looks rather confused after-one-and-a-half year of Janata rule at the centre and one-year in half a dozen northern states. There is talk of giving the benefits of development to the rural poor, abolishing untouchability and introducing total prohibition in four years, ending unemployment in ten years and so on. But, the record so far does not seem to justify these pious hopes and brave pronouncements.

The rural and urban poor and the lower middle class are the worst sufferers. Inclusion of rich farming communities among "backward" classes and reservation of jobs, etc. for them is a dangerous move to exploit caste for political purposes. It can lead to caste and class conflict of a violent nature.

One significant development is that different parties are holding power in different states. May be this pluralism is a healthy sign, as well as a reflection of the different political trends in the country. The same political party cannot rule at the centre and all the states any more and, perhaps, just as well. Let there be healthy competition between various parties and states, let the people judge which is best for them in each state. But the unity of India at the centre must not be weakened. This is important for the integrity, stability, internal progress and external relations of India.

The situation presents both a challenge as well as an opportunity to the ruling and other parties to forge ahead in a spirit of cooperation, between the centre and the states, between the ruling and other parties and, what is more important, to enthuse the people, the masses, the intelligentsia, workers, peasants, youth and students.

A year-and-a-half is not long enough to judge a party's record. But, it is long enough to show the trends and direction, especially in foreign policy—in its political, economic and defence aspects—in a fast changing world. What are the new trends in the world today? A new configuration of forces and powers in the world is taking shape. China is trying to emerge as a super power. Japan has become a leading industrial power. The European Economic Community (EEC) is becoming more and more inward looking. Asia, Africa and Latin America are still groping for economic and political cooperation *inter se*. Strange combinations of power are emerging, based on narrow self-interest and not on ideology. The violent conflict between Vietnam and Cambodia and Chinese pressure tactics against Vietnam are examples of the new trends.

The world situation presents a picture of sunshine and shadow, of realistic optimism as well as cynical pessimism. War is not inevitable. Economic cooperation between the developed and developing countries is possible but not easy. Imperialism and colonialism in new forms are appearing and the old doctrines of gun-boat diplomacy and spheres of influence are not yet dead. Racial discrimination is still raging and has to be wiped out by concerted action. Disarmament is making slow progress and nuclear disarmament is nowhere in sight. The gulf between the rich and poor countries and between the rich and poor is widening, giving rise to social tensions.

The world is still run by different governments and not by one government of the world. The UNO reflects the realities and imperfections of its member countries and its Charter is still far from being fulfilled. But, there is one ray of hope in all these dark clouds—the younger generation in all countries, which wants peace and not war, love and not hate, racial equality and not discrimination, greater contact and cooperation rather than conflict and confrontation. It is this "other world" comprising the people in general and the youth in particular, and not the world of governments which are far behind world public opinion, that gives hope for the future.

There is a ray of hope in the development of a spirit of detente, born of a sheer sense of survival, between the USA and the USSR and their allies. The Helsinki Agreement is a milestone on this road. But, similar moves in Asia, Latin America and Africa are yet to come.

Sino-Indian differences are still looming large, though there has been no serious border incident since 1968. Indo-Pak differences are showing signs of a thaw. The basic differences of a disputed border between India and China, China and the USSR persist. The Kashmir question between Pakistan and India is still to be finally settled. Trade and transit through Pakistan to Afghanistan, Iran, etc., is still meeting with resistence from Pakistan.

The intricate problems between India, on the one hand, and China and Pakistan on the other, cannot be divorced from the play of great power politics. With Pakistan the chances are that relations might improve, slowly and steadily, unless outside powers or internal upheavals come in the way. With China it will take a long time to repair strained relations and the present euphoria seems unrealistic and too simplistic. India's relations with the Soviet Union and eastern Europe are steadily growing and will continue to grow, unless the votaries of the new good-dess of "genuine" non-alignment weaken the basic principles of India's foreign policy. With the USA there are bound to be ups and downs, because India features rather low in the US priorities, while the USA is high on our list. This unequal and imbalanced relationship cannot endure. But, as India grows stronger, more prosperous and united, the US policy makers will have to pay more attention to the Indo-US relations. With the UK and western Europe, India is coming to some kind of a balanced relationship based on the realities of the present situation. With the countries of Asia, generally, and with South-East Asia, South-West Asia and the Gulf countries in particular, India will have to make greater efforts to work out more enduring and closer cooperation. With Japan and Australasia, as with western Europe, India has to come to a mature and realistic relationship. India's relations with Africa have a great future—especially with East Africa which borders on the Indian Ocean. Latin America and the Carribean countries present interesting possibilities in the field of culture and commerce which have yet to be fully explored. The Commonwealth will probably continue as a sort of talking club, meeting periodically and issuing joint communiques. It could do much more in the field of scientific, economic, technical and cultural cooperation.

It is in the non-aligned world which cuts across regional, racial, geographical and geo-political barriers, that India can play an important global role. But, she will have to be more active and not merely go along with the main stream. Non-alignment must be made stronger and more effective, both inside and outside international forums, and take a stronger and not weaker line against racial discrimination, economic domination, political or military interference. It must bring about greater cooperation among the non-aligned *inter se* and between them and others. If and when alignment disappears then non-alignment will have achieved its own *nirvana*, in a military sense, but not till then. Even then the need to struggle against economic, political and ideological pulls and pressures will make non-alignment necessary.

There seems to be a growing trend to score debating points over the previous government by bending over backwards to give the impression of improving relations with the neighbouring countries. While high level contacts are a good thing, it is not wise to raise undue expectations either among our own people or others. This is, unfortunately, what is being attempted at present. It is an indication of a short-term policy of reaching "agreements" by making concessions all along the way. Such agreements cannot endure and may indeed give rise to serious differences later.

The Farrakha Agreement is one instance. India has given away part of her vital interests without getting anything concrete in return—not even an assurance, that bilateral problems will be settled bilaterally, without outside intervention or involvement. On the contrary, the concessions made by India seem to have encouraged Bangladesh to involve third countries in the development of the eastern rivers, flowing in India and Bangladesh. A firm, frank and friendly attitude would be more realistic in the long-term interests of the two countries.

Our relations with Nepal and the recent agreements entered into with them are another example. We have given in all along the way—especially in matters of trade and transit. This will only increase Nepal's appetite for making further demands which India cannot agree to. Why don't Nepal and Bangladesh adopt similar tactics in their dealings with China? Because China is firm while we are over-anxious to please. It is time the Government realized how far she can go without injuring India's national interests.

Even more serious is India's eagerness to make a show of imp ovement of relations with Pakistan, China and America, without any solid ground or concrete basis for it. Of course, we must try to improve relations with these countries, but this can not be done by mere wishful thinking on one side or the other. The desire must be mutual and based on a reciprocal under- standing of and respect for each other's vital interests.

A mere show of "genuine" non-alignment is not going to fool anyone. It is only a cover to hide a pro-western stand and is not even "neutrality." What does it really mean? That we are not more friendly with the USSR than with China or the USA? that we shall be neutral in their disputes and sit on the fence? that we shall give up our sovereign right to use nuclear technology, including underground nuclear explosions, even for peaceful purposes? that we shall give up our claim to territories illegally occupied by China and Pakistan? Let us not try to fool ourselves or delude others by diplomatic gimmickry.

We must be more realistic and mature in our appraisal of these and other problems. We must realise and make others realize that there are some fundamental differences between us and these countries and unless these are tackled successfully, there can be little improvement in our relations with them. These differences cannot be just brushed under the carpet or wished away by Mantram of "genuine non-alignment."

Take the USA, for instance. Where does India figure in its list of priorities? Somewhere at the bottom-after the NATO countries and Japan, Latin America and the Carribean, the Gulf and the Middle-East, Australia and the Pacific and well after China and the USSR. And where do we figure in the Soviet eyes? After Warsaw Pact countries and the socialist camp but fairly high in the rest of the world.

We must accept geographical, geo-political and regional reali- ties and base our own priorities accordingly. India is important not only in South and South-East Asia, but in the whole of Asia. India has not merely a sub-regional and regional role in interna- tional affairs but a global role in the non-aligned and developing world. We must not allow ourselves to be treated as a third rate power to be tempted by dangling carrots or threatened with big sticks. We must base our relations with other countries strictly on reciprocity and sovereign equality. We must not equate friends with foes, or weaken our basic principles to please this or that power.

Some situations affect us more directly and vitally than others. We cannot afford to adopt an equidistant posture of the so called "genuine" non-alignment. It would be a denial of the very basis of our foreign policy and a weakening of our position in the non-aligned world. Our policy of non-alignment has been tested by time and stood the test. Let us not denigrate it to a concept of "neutrality" or worse, by qualifying it as "genuine" non-alignment. Dynamic, positive yes—but "genuine" only raises doubts in our own mind and that of others that perhaps we have not been "genuine" in the past. This cheap gimmickery will not wash or sell but only lower our prestige and influence in the non-aligned world and vis-a-vis others.

The temptation to run down anything the previous governments have done in order to gain cheap and temporary advantages, must be resisted—especially in the field of foreign affairs, where one has to deal with sovereign, independent countries. India's foreign policy is based on the principles and ideals of our long struggle for independence and was formulated in the hard and difficult times of the cold war and the fast changing world situation after World War II. It cannot and should not be treated lightly, as if it were a slogan to catch votes in an internal election.

Similarly great care needs to be exercised in dealing with our defence and foreign-economic policies. Unfortunately even there a tendency is creeping to rush for temporary advantages at the cost of our long-term interests. We must examine carefully who are our potential enemies and who are our dependable friends—on the basis of compatability and mutuality of national and strategic interests. Of course we must not be entirely dependent on others or put all our eggs in one basket. Diversification in patterns of trade and economic cooperation and in defence production and procurement may be necessary, but it should not be done in a manner that will make us lose trusted friends and give us only temporary and dubious advantages. Above all we must try to be as self-reliant as possible and not neglect or hamper the development of our own resources and skills, research and technology by relying too much on foreign resources even in fields where we have the potential know-how.

India is a big country with vast resources and we must conduct ourselves in a manner befitting our dignity and position, our potential and real importance. Foundations laid by Gandhi and built upon by Nehru must not be weakened. Future generations will not forgive us if we do so.

India's role in the world under Gandhi's inspiration and Nehru's leadership was remarkable. India has still a long way to go to make her full contribution in national as well as international affairs. But, no one can stop India's march towards her goals of democracy and socialism at home and peaceful co-existence and non-alignment abroad—neither domestic obscurantists nor foreign agents. The India of Gandhi and Nehru and of Tagore's dreams is enduring and immortal.

Epilogue

Political forecasts are not easy to make, especially when the situation is as fluid as it is in India. Casteism, regionalism, communalism and linguistic chauvinism are more powerful today because they have entered the body politic. Economic, social and political ideologies and idealism are at a discount. It is not a classical Marxian or capitalist situation, but a peculiarly Indian phenomenon. It is capable of throwing up all kinds of forces—good and bad, social and anti-social, progressive and obscurantist, revolutionary and counter-revolutionary. Polarisation of politics is possible but not likely in the immediate future. What is more probable is the growth of regional pulls and parties, with casteism cutting across ideological and regional lines. Meanwhile there is the danger of the social and economic gulf widening between and within urban and rural areas, based on class, caste, political influence and economic power.

The "leftists" are divided, not knowing how to come together and are criticizing each other for their past mistakes instead of joining hands in the present and for the future. The "centrists" have no coherent ideology and indulge in slogans, flirtations with other parties, and mutual bickerings. The "rightists" are present in large numbers in all parties, except among the communists, though even the communists as well as the two Congresses and the Janata Party—all have their own leftists, centrists and rightists.

It is a strange spectacle where various political parties and leaders are divided among themselves and against others mainly because of personal ambitions and temperamental differences, caste or regional considerations, rather than on ideological grounds. The centre is getting weaker and the states more vocal and powerful. Regional parties seem to be gaining strength at the cost of national parties. States like Uttar Pradesh, Bihar, Madhya Pradesh and Maharashtra are finding it more and more difficult to administer their far-flung areas efficiently. Why can they not be sub-divided into smaller states?

The administration is demoralised and reluctant to implement the government's policies unless it is given clear orders and directives in writing. Some ministers at the centre and in the states, are inexperienced and instead of inspiring and setting a good example to the bureaucracy, are only making it the scape-goat for their own failures. The bureaucracy is afraid to take the initiative and reluctant to shoulder responsibility.

The result is neglect of the real and urgent problems—poverty, unemployment, insecurity, exploitation of the weaker sections, increasing unrest, crime and disorder. The people are becoming cynical, disheartened and no longer believe the tall promies made by various political parties. Corruption has become insti-tutionalised, black-marketing an established phenomenon, smug-gling and hoarding are not being dealt with effectively, the rich are making hay while the poor continue to remain poor.

How long will this last, how long can we go on like this? We cannot have a Gandhi or Nehru every ten years. Morarji may be able to keep the ship going for a time if he uses his determi-nation and will for the right causes and does not give in to in-ternal or external pressures. He emerged as the "Man of the Year" in 1977 and is now the Man of the Hour. The weeks and months ahead are important.

I do not wish to paint a disproportionately depressing picture of the Indian scene today. There are positive as well as negative trends. Fortunately, external threats, in a military sense, are not imminent, though in a political and economic sense they are as great, if not greater, than in the past. But, India has come of age and will unite against any external threat. We have staunch and reliable friends in the world and must not weaken our relations with them for the doubtful "friendship" of others. What is most important is the need to become self-reliant.

What are the new trends in India's internal policies and what is their impact on external relations?

There seems to be a slight shift from socialism and self-reli-ance to strengthening the private sector and bringing in some multi-nationals in a big way. The public sector is being tolerated but no longer controls the commanding heights in the economy. It is running at a loss because of a calculated and cold indifference from the government. Science and technology, research and development in the country, are receiving less attention and there is a growing trend to depend more and more on foreign resources. In the vital field of nuclear technology, we have given up our sovereign right to use underground nuclear explosions even for peaceful purposes. It is not going to deter the nuclear weapon powers and will only delay our own nuclear development.

There is a trend to drift away from Nehru's far-sighted industrial policy and the planning process has been "rolled" into *ad hocism*. Even in the defence field there seems to be a growing trend to collaborate more and more with some countries which have let us down in the past and less and less with those who are more dependable and have stood by us in times of need. The same trend is visible, even more clearly, in the political field— away from a dynamic independent foreign policy based on non-alignment, to a diluted "genuine" non-alignment which is but another name for "neutrality" between and "equidistance" from the great powers.

The problems India is facing are stupendous in magnitude. But, so are our natural and human resources, our talents and skills. What is lacking is political leadership and political will among our leaders.

1977 was a turning point and 1979 is a crucial year for India. The India of 1979 will be a live and kicking democracy, alert and on the march. No one can stop it. Some may try to side-track the people for a while but they will not succeed for long. It is only those parties and leaders who are alive and responsive to the hopes and expectations of the people that have a chance of survival. But, the people will survive, the country will survive. This is the lesson of our past history, of recent developments and our hope for the future.

Index